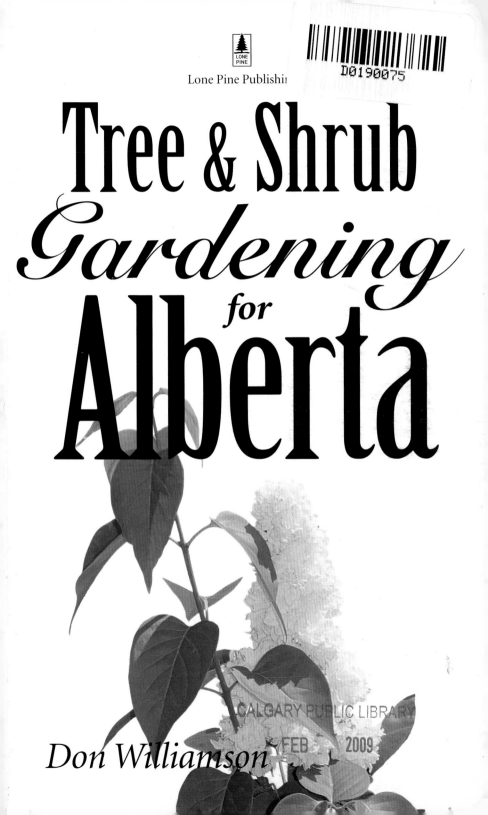

Lone Pine Publishing

Tree & Shrub
Gardening
for
Alberta

Don Williamson

The Publisher: Lone Pine Publishing
10145–81 Avenue
Edmonton, AB T6E 1W9
Canada
Website: www.lonepinepublishing.com

Library and Archives Canada Cataloguing in Publication

Williamson, Don, 1962-
    Tree & shrub gardening of Alberta / Don Williamson.

    Includes bibliographical references and index.
    ISBN 978-1-55105-634-0

    1. Ornamental trees--Alberta. 2. Ornamental shrubs--Alberta. I. Title. II. Title: Tree and shrub gardening of Alberta.

SB435.6.C32A57 2009   635.9'77097123   C2008-907458-0

Editorial Director: Nancy Foulds
Editorial: Wendy Pirk, Nicholle Carriere, Sheila Quinlan
Production Manager: Gene Longson
Book Design and Layout: Shannon Ladouceur, Megan Fischer
Cover Design: Gerry Dotto

Photos: Every effort has been made to correctly identify photographers whose works are in this book. If we have erred, please let us know. All photos are by Tamara Eder, Tim Matheson and Laura Peters, except: AAFC 80a, 81b, 94, 159b; AAFC-Mordon 165b; Sandra Bit 218a; Frank Burman 36, 41; Brendan Casement 267b; Janet Davis 26b, 88, 95a&b; Dean Didur 140a; Don Doucette 18a, 114b, 143a, 179, 193a, 302; Derek Fell 96, 97; Erika Flatt 26a, 28b, 83b, 101c, 210a, 301b, 304, 307b; Anne Gordon 244; Lynne Harrison 157, 175a; Instock 270, 271; Linda Kershaw 100; Dawn Loewen 13a, 46, 113b, 126b, 129b; Heather Markham 233a&b, 251c; Steve Nikkila 163b, 263; Kim O'Leary 58a&c; Alison Penko 14b&c, 20c, 24, 27a, 63b, 91a, 93a, 110a, 116, 124, 132b, 133b, 138, 141b, 149a, 153a, 154b, 186b, 187a, 203, 204, 225a, 237a, 239, 243b, 250, 265a, 274, 276, 277b, 278, 279b, 280b, 287, 288, 289b, 291c, 295a, 296b, 299a,c&d, 305a; Robert Ritchie 22b, 70, 72, 74, 89a&b, 106, 107a, 115b, 122, 123, 173a, 174a, 199b, 252, 254, 255a&c, 256, 260; Ian Sheldon 35, 39, 40, 49, 52, 53, 55, 61, 63a; Mark Turner 99, 117a, 209a&b; Don Williamson 92b, 245; Carol Woo 66b; Tim Wood 60b, 62a, 85a, 103a, 107b, 119a, 125, 133a, 137, 141a, 143b, 147a&b, 148b, 155a, 158, 159a, 205, 229a, 249b&c, 253, 269, 280a, 281b&c, 291b, 293a, 295b, 298, 299b, 303b, 304a, 305b, 306.

We acknowledge the financial support of the Government of Canada through the Book Publishing Industry Development Program (BPIDP) for our publishing activities.

PC: 16

CONTENTS

ACKNOWLEDGEMENTS

Greetings and blessings! I am grateful for the opportunity to bring my knowledge of trees and shrubs to my home province, and I first thank Shane Kennedy and all the staff at Lone Pine Publishing for making this a reality. I thank editor Wendy Pirk for making some wonderful improvements and for helping keep me on track. I thank our excellent production department, whose tireless efforts help turn out such great books. And I thank Nancy Foulds for her patience over the years. I have truly had fun working with all of you.

Lone Pine books are always a team effort, and this book is no different. A number of knowledgeable gardeners and horticulturalists have seen the text of this book, making comments and suggestions so that you have the most up-to-date knowledge available, and I am grateful. I thank fellow gardeners and writers Alison Beck and Laura Peters for their wonderful contributions, writing, photographs and research. I thank my sweetheart Darlene Morton, my personal pruning supervisor, for keeping me motivated and for providing some great tips that I have included in the book. I thank Olds College for providing me with a great, well-rounded education in horticulture.

I gratefully acknowledge the many people who provided photographs for this project, and the gardeners who allowed them to photograph their private gardens.

I thank the Creator, who made the trees and shrubs, the earth and the sun, and all of us to enjoy it!

THE TREES & SHRUBS AT A GLANCE

A PICTORIAL GUIDE IN ALPHABETICAL ORDER, BY COMMON NAME

Barberry
p. 82

Bearberry
p. 86

Beauty Bush
p. 88

Ash
p. 78

Birch
p. 90

Bittersweet
p. 94

Bog Rosemary
p. 100

Boxwood
p. 102

Black Locust
p. 96

Blueberry
p. 98

Buffaloberry
p. 104

Bush Honeysuckle
p. 106

Caragana
p. 108

Cedar
p. 112

Cherry
p. 116

Cotoneaster
p. 124

Chokeberry
p. 122

Crabapple
p. 128

Currant
p. 134

Daphne
p. 136

Douglas-Fir
p. 144

Dogwood
p. 138

Elderberry
p. 146

Elm
p. 150

Euonymus
p. 152

False Cypress
p. 156

False Spirea
p. 158

Fir
p. 160

Forsythia
p. 164

Genista
p. 166

Ginko
p. 168

Hazelnut
p. 172

Hawthorn
p. 170

Hemlock
p. 176

Holly
p. 178

Honeysuckle
p. 180

Kiwi
p. 198

Horsechestnut
p. 184

Hydrangea
p. 188

Juniper
p. 192

Larch
p. 200

Lilac
p. 202

Linden
p. 208

Maackia
p. 212

Maple
p. 214

Mock Orange
p. 222

Mountain Ash
p. 224

Ninebark
p. 228

Oak
p. 230

Pine
p. 234

Poplar and Aspen
p. 240

Potentilla
p. 246

Rhododendron
p. 250

Roses
p. 254

Russian Cypress
p. 262

Russian Olive
p. 264

Salt Bush
p. 266

Saskatoon
p. 268

Sea Buckthorn
p. 270

Smokebush
p. 272

Snowberry
p. 274

Spirea
p. 276

Spruce
p. 282

Sumac
p. 288

Summersweet Clethra
p. 292

Viburnum
p. 294

Virginia Crepper
p. 300

Weigela
p. 302

Willow
p. 306

Yew
p. 312

Yucca
p. 314

INTRODUCTION

T hose of us fortunate enough to live in Alberta hardly need reminding of the importance of trees and shrubs to the landscape. From the majestic wilderness areas to the attractive yards and parks in our cities and suburbs, trees and shrubs add a beauty and value to our land and our lives that many of us perhaps take for granted.

Trees and shrubs are woody perennials that live for three or more years. They normally maintain a permanent, year-round live structure above ground, but in cold climates some shrubs die back to the ground each winter. The root system, protected by the soil over winter, sends up new shoots in spring; shrubs that form flowers on new wood will bloom that same year. Such plants act like herbaceous perennials, but because they are woody in their native climates, they are still classified as shrubs.

In general, a tree is defined as a woody plant that has a single trunk and grows over 4.5 m (15') tall, whereas a shrub is multi-stemmed and no taller than 4.5 m (15'). These definitions are not absolute because some tall trees are multi-stemmed, and some short shrubs have single trunks. Even the height definitions are open to interpretation. For example, some maple cultivars may be multi-stemmed

and grow to only about 3 m (10') tall, but they are still usually referred to as trees. Furthermore, a given species may grow as a tree in favourable conditions but be reduced to a shrub on harsher sites. It is always best to judge the suitability of a tree or shrub for your garden by its expected mature size.

Some vines are also included in this guide. Like trees and shrubs, these plants maintain living woody stems above ground over winter. They generally require a supporting structure to climb upon, but many can also be grown as trailing groundcovers. Again, the definition is not absolute. With proper pruning, some vines can be trained to form free-standing shrubs, and, conversely, some shrubs can be trained to grow up and over walls and other structures.

Woody plants are characterized by leaf type—whether deciduous or evergreen and needled or broad-leaved. Deciduous plants lose all their leaves each fall or winter. They can have needles, like larch, or broad leaves, like maple and dogwood. Evergreen trees and shrubs do not lose their leaves in winter. They can also be needled or broad-leaved, like pine and rhododendron, respectively. Semi-evergreen plants are generally evergreens that in cold climates lose some or all of their leaves—for example, some types of viburnum.

The climate of Alberta is conducive to growing a wider variety of trees and shrubs than most people realize. Cold winters bring the dormancy that woody plants need to renew their growth cycle. Summers are warm enough to stimulate strong growth, a woody plant's primary defence against disease and insect attack.

Woody plants prefer gradual cooling to send them into dormancy. When cold air brings far-below-freezing temperatures within hours of warm "Indian summer" conditions in mid-fall, woody plants can be harmed.

Once winter arrives, woody plants can be stressed—and young ones even killed—if snow is scarce and the freeze line extends too far into the root zone. Winter winds can also test the mettle of woody plants. Some plants are susceptible to too much sun in winter; one side of the plant may be warmed enough to start the sap flowing, only to have nighttime temperatures freeze it again. Injurious cracks in the bark (sunscald) can then develop.

A burlap wall can provide woody plants with a measure of winter protection. Before the ground freezes, pound in wooden stakes on the

Ohio Buckeye
'Crimson King' maple

plant's south side. Choose stakes that are taller than the plant (think about the winter sun angle). Use two stakes for a flat screen or three if you want a mild "V" shape. Staple burlap to the stakes; the screen should be 10–15 cm (4–6") away from branch tips.

Although much of Alberta receives enough natural moisture to allow many woody plants to survive, the timing of that moisture can be questionable. Supplemental watering during summer and fall is nearly always needed for young woody plants and for all evergreens, even when the amount of rainfall is average. Fall is an important time to continue watering evergreens, which continue to transpire throughout winter, losing moisture to the atmosphere at a time when their frozen roots are unable to replace it.

Hardiness zones listed for a plant will help you decide what to place in the landscape as well as where to place it, but don't be put off because a catalogue or book says a plant is hardy only to a certain zone. Local topography in the yard creates microclimates— small areas that may be more or less favorable for growing different plants. Buildings, hills, low spots, drainage patterns and prevailing winds all influence your garden and its microclimates (see Getting Started, p. 24, for more information on assessing conditions in your garden and growing out-of-zone plants). Pick the right spot in your garden for that tender shrub, and you just may be surprised at how well it does.

Colorado blue spruce

'Rose Glow' barberry

ENDLESS SUMMER hydrangea

Ponderosa pine

'Little Princess' spirea (below)

Alberta soils are influenced by various factors, some dating back to the glacial eras. Many soil types can be found in a small geographical area, so you must be familiar with the particular soil profile of your yard and garden. Two very influential factors are how recently your home was built and whether it has a basement. Contractors digging foundations often unearth dense clay subsoil, which then becomes the top layer of your garden soil. This nearly impermeable layer creates an inhospitable environment for many trees or shrubs you may want to plant. The ideal soil for many plants is loose, deep, well drained and slightly acidic.

No matter what challenges you face in your garden, you will discover a tree, shrub or vine that thrives in your space. A trip to a nearby park, arboretum, garden show, public garden, display garden or botanical garden, where trees are labelled and unusual specimens are grown, is invaluable for showing you trees, shrubs and vines that thrive in your area. Also, keep your eyes open when walking through your neighbourhood. You may see a tree or shrub that you hadn't noticed before or that you were told wouldn't grow in your area. What is actually growing is the best guide.

Many enthusiastic and creative people garden in Alberta. Individuals, growers, societies, schools and publications located throughout the province provide information, encouragement and fruitful debate for the novice or experienced gardener. Alberta

HARDINESS ZONES MAP

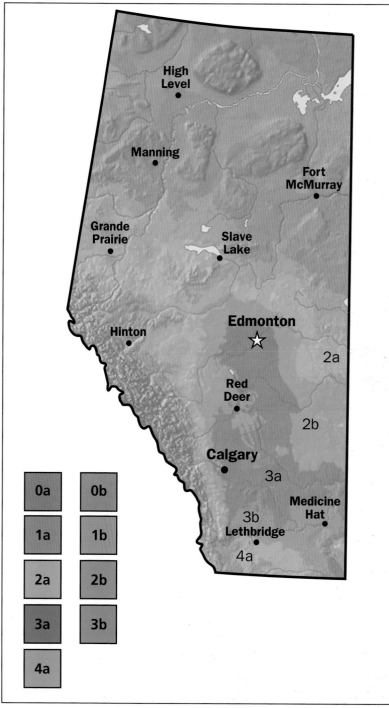

gardeners are passionate about their plants and will gladly share their knowledge and opinions about what is best for any little patch of ground.

Seek out these wonderful sources of inspiration and information. Open yourself to the possibilities—you'll be surprised by the diversity of woody plants that thrive here. Initially you may want to plant mostly tried and true, dependable varieties, but don't be afraid to try something different or new. Gardening with trees and shrubs is fun and can be a great adventure if you're willing to take up the challenge.

Virginia creeper

'Hansa' rose

'Chickadee' birch

Woody Plants in the Garden

Trees and shrubs create a framework around which to design a garden. These long-lasting features anchor the landscape; in a well-designed garden, they create interest year-round. In spring and summer, woody plants provide shade and beauty with their foliage and flowers. In fall, the leaves of many tree and shrub species change colour, and brightly coloured fruit attracts attention and birds. In winter, the true backbone of the garden is revealed; the sculpture-like branches of deciduous trees and shrubs are laid bare, perhaps dusted with snow or frost, and evergreens take precedence in keeping the garden colourful.

When carefully selected and placed, woody plants are a vital and vibrant element of any landscape, from the smallest city lot to the largest country acreage. They can provide privacy and hide unattractive views, but they can also frame an attractive view and draw attention to particular features or garden areas. Trees and shrubs soften the hard lines of such structures as buildings, fences, walls and driveways. Well-positioned woody plants create an attractive background against which other plants can shine. When used in groups, trees and shrubs can give spectacular flower or fall colour shows, and a truly exceptional species with year-round appeal will stand alone as a specimen plant in a prime location.

In addition, woody plants help moderate the climate in your home and garden. As windbreaks, they provide shelter from the winter cold, reducing heating costs

Birds and squirrels are frequent garden visitors.

Elms make great shade trees (below).

and protecting tender garden plants. A well-placed deciduous tree keeps the house cool and shaded in summer but allows much-appreciated warmth and light from the sun through in winter. Woody plants also prevent soil erosion, retain soil moisture, reduce noise and filter the air.

Attracting wildlife is an often-overlooked advantage of gardening. As cities expand, our living space encroaches on more and more wildlife habitat. By choosing plants that are beneficial to local wildlife, particularly native plants, we provide food and shelter to birds and other animals, thereby helping fulfill our obligation as stewards of the environment. We can bring nature closer to home. The only difficulty is that the local wildlife may so enjoy a garden that they consume it! It is possible, though, to find a balance and attract wildlife while protecting the garden from ruin.

When the time comes to select woody plants, think carefully about the various physical constraints of your garden and the purposes you want the plants to serve. First and foremost, consider the size of your garden in relation to the mature sizes of the plants in question. Very large plants are always a bad idea in a small garden. Remember, too, that trees and shrubs grow not only up, but also out. Within a few years, what started as a small plant may become a large, spreading tree. Spruces are often sold as very small trees, but many eventually grow too wide for a small garden. Always learn the mature width of the woody plants you select—and plant accordingly.

Another consideration that relates to size is placement. Don't plant trees and shrubs too close to buildings, walkways, entryways or driveways. A tree planted right next to a house may hit the overhang of the roof, and trying to fix the problem by pruning will often spoil the tree's natural appearance. Plants placed too close to paths, doors and driveways may eventually block access completely and give the property an unkempt appearance.

Consider, too, the various features (outstanding elements that attract you to the plants) of tree and shrub species. Many plants have more than one feature, thereby providing interest over a longer period. Decide which features (described below) are most important to you, and which will best enhance your garden. A carefully selected group of woody plants can add beauty to the garden all year. Whether you are looking for showy flowers, fall colour, fast growth, unusual bark or a beautiful fragrance, you can find trees or shrubs with features to suit your design. Consult the individual plant entries and the Quick Reference Chart at the back of the book (pp. 320–325).

Form is the general shape and growth habit of the plant. Trees come in a variety of shapes, from tall and columnar to wide and gracefully weeping. Similarly, shrubs may be rounded and bushy or low and ground hugging. Form can also vary as the year progresses and leaves develop and are lost. A unique winter habit can make a tree or shrub truly outstanding.

Swedish columnar aspen has a fastigiate form.

Dwarf Alberta spruce has a dwarf form.

White fir

'Blue Chip' juniper is a prostrate plant.

Cutleaf staghorn sumac (below)

You should be familiar with some growth form terminology when considering a purchase. A *shade tree* commonly refers to a large deciduous tree but can be any tree that provides shade. An *upright, fastigiate* or *columnar* plant has the main branches and stems pointing upward and is often quite narrow. *Dwarf* properly refers to any variety, cultivar or hybrid that is smaller than the species, but the term is sometimes mistakenly used to mean a small, slow-growing plant. The crucial statistic is the expected size at maturity. If a species grows to 30.5 m (100'), then a 9–15 m (30–50') variety would be a dwarf but might still be too big for your garden. *Prostrate* and *procumbent* plants are low growing, bearing branches and stems that spread horizontally across the ground. These forms are sometimes grafted onto upright stems to create lovely weeping plant forms.

Foliage is one of a plant's most enduring and important features. Leaves come in a variety of colours, shapes, sizes, textures and arrangements. You can find shades of green, blue, red, purple, yellow, white or silver. *Variegated* types have two or more colours combined on a single leaf. *Rugose* refers to leaves that are tightly wrinkled. The variety of shapes is even more astounding, from short, sharply pointed needles to broad, rounded leaves the size of dinner plates. Leaf margins can be smooth, like those of many rhododendrons, or so finely divided the foliage appears lacy or fern-like, as with some elderberry and sumac cultivars. Foliage often varies seasonally, progressing from tiny, pale green spring buds to the vibrant colours of fall. Evergreens provide welcome greenery even when winter is as its snowiest and coldest.

Growing plants with different leaf sizes, textures and colours creates contrast and makes your garden more interesting and appealing. An entire garden can be designed based on varied foliage. Whether it forms a neutral backdrop or stands out in sharp contrast with the plants around it, foliage is a vital consideration in any garden.

Flowers are so influential that their beauty may be enough reason to grow a tree or shrub that is dull the rest of the year, such as forsythia. Keep in mind that flowering generally lasts just a few weeks or occasionally a month; only a few woody plants flower for the entire summer. Grouping plants that flower at the same time results in different but equally striking effects than distributing them around the garden. To always have something in bloom, choose species with staggered flowering periods. An easy, effective way to create a season-long progression of blooms is to visit your garden centre regularly. People who shop for plants only in spring often have gardens dominated by spring bloomers.

Fruit comes in many forms, including winged maple samaras, dangling birch catkins, spiny horsechestnut capsules and the more obviously "fruity" saskatoon and crabapple pomes. Fruit can be a double-edged

Forsythia flowers announce spring's arrival.

Nanking cherry

Paper birch (below)

Mock orange has fragrant flowers.

Corkscrew hazelnut in flower

sword. It is often very attractive and provides interest in the garden in late summer and fall, when most plants are past their prime. When it drops, however, it can attract pests and create quite a mess and even a foul odour if allowed to rot on the ground. Choose the location of your fruiting tree carefully. If you know the fruit can be messy, don't plant near a patio or a sidewalk. Most fruit isn't terribly troublesome, but consider that some seasonal cleanup may be required.

Bark is one of the most overlooked features. Species with interesting bark will greatly enhance your landscape, particularly in winter. Bark can be furrowed, smooth, ridged, papery, scaly, exfoliating (peeling) or colourful. A few species valued for their bark are birch, cherry, corktree, dogwood, maackia, ninebark, striped maple and lacebark pine.

Fragrance, though usually associated with flowers, is also a potential feature of the leaves, fruit and even wood of trees and shrubs. Arborvitae, summersweet clethra, crabapple, lilac, wolf willow and viburnum are examples of plants with appealing scents. Situate fragrant plants near your home where the scent can waft into an open window, or near pathways.

Branches as a feature combine elements of form and bark and, like those two features, can become an important winter garden attribute. Branches may have an unusual gnarled or twisted shape (corkscrew hazelnut), bear protective spines or thorns (barberry and hawthorn) or be brightly coloured (golden willow and red-osier dogwood).

Red elderberry

Blue holly

Growth rate and **life span**, though not really aesthetic features of woody plants, are none theless important aspects to consider. A fast-growing tree or shrub that grows 60 cm (24") or more per year will mature quickly and can be used to fill in space in a new garden. A slow-growing species that grows less than 30 cm (12") per year may be more suitable in a space-limited garden.

Short-lived plants are usually quick to mature and reach flowering age, and they often appeal to people who enjoy changing their garden design or who aren't sure exactly what they want. Long-lived trees, on the other hand, are an investment in time. Some trees can take a human lifetime to reach their mature size, and some may not flower until 10 years after planting. You can enjoy a long-lived tree as it develops, and you will also leave a legacy for future generations—your tree may very well outlive you.

Fast-Growing Trees & Shrubs
- Ash
- Birch
- Elderberry
- Forsythia
- Hydrangea
- Lilac
- Linden
- Poplar
- Red-twig dogwood
- Silver maple
- Staghorn sumac
- Virginia creeper

Slow-Growing Trees & Shrubs
- Boxwood
- Chokeberry
- Daphne
- Euonymus
- Fir
- Ginkgo
- Holly
- Oak
- Rhododendron
- Russian cypress
- Yew

Getting Started

Before you fall in love with the idea of having a certain plant in your garden, it is important to consider the growing conditions the plant needs and whether any areas of your garden are suitable. Your tree or shrub will need to not only survive, but thrive, in order for its flowers or other features to reach their full potential.

All plants are adapted to certain growing conditions in which they do best. Choosing plants to match your garden is far more practical than trying to alter your garden to match the plants. Yet it is through the use of trees and shrubs that we can best alter a garden's conditions. Over time, a tree can change a sunny, exposed garden into a shaded one, and a hedge can turn a windswept area into a sheltered one. However, the woody plants you choose must be able to thrive in the garden as it

exists now, or they may not live long enough to produce these changes.

Light, soil conditions and exposure are important factors to guide your selection. As you plan, look at your garden as it exists now, but keep in mind the changes trees and shrubs will bring.

LIGHT

Buildings, trees, fences, the time of day and the time of year influence the amount of light in your garden. Light levels are often divided into four categories for gardening purposes: full sun, partial shade (partial sun), light shade and full shade. Some plants can adapt to a wide range of light levels, but most have narrower preferences.

Full sun locations receive direct sunlight most of the day. An example would be an open location along a south-facing wall.

Heat from the sun may be more intense in one spot than another, depending on, for example, the degree of shelter from the wind. **Partial shade** locations receive direct sun for part of the day and shade for the rest. An unobstructed east- or west-facing wall gets partial shade. **Light shade** locations receive shade most or all of the day, but with some sun getting through to ground level, such as when a small-leaved tree allows dappled light onto the ground beneath it. **Full shade** locations receive no direct sunlight. The north wall of a house is often in full shade.

Hemlock grows well in full sun or full shade.
False cypress prefers full sun.

SOIL

Plants have a vital relationship with the soil in which they grow. Many important plant functions take place underground. Soil holds air, water, nutrients, organic matter and various organisms. Plant roots depend on these resources for growth and use the soil to anchor the plant body. In turn, plants influence soil development by breaking down large clods with their roots and by increasing soil fertility when they die and decompose.

Potentilla adapts well to clay soil (below).

Soil particles come in various sizes. Sand particles are the largest. Water drains quickly from a sandy soil, and nutrients can be rapidly washed away. Sand has many air spaces and doesn't compact easily. Clay particles are the smallest, visible only through a microscope. Water penetrates clay very slowly and drains away even more slowly. Clay holds the most nutrients but has very little room for air and compacts quite easily. Silt particles are smaller than sand particles

Bog rosemary does well in wet soil.

Bittersweet tolerates poor soils.

and larger than clay particles. Most soils are made up of a combination of different particle sizes.

Particle size is one influence on the drainage and moisture-holding properties of soil; slope is another. Knowing how quickly the water drains out of your soil will help you decide whether you should plant moisture-loving or drought-tolerant plants. Rocky soil on a hillside will probably drain quickly and is best for plants that prefer a very well-drained soil. Low-lying areas tend to retain water longer, and some areas may rarely drain at all. Moist areas suit plants that require a consistent water supply; constantly wet areas should be reserved for plants that are adapted to boggy conditions.

In very wet areas, drainage can be improved by adding organic matter to the soil, by installing some form of drainage tile or by building raised beds. Consult with nursery professionals before adding sand to heavy clay soils, or you may create something much like concrete. Working some gypsum into a clay soil along with organic matter will help break it up and allow water to penetrate and drain more easily. Water retention in sandy soil can be improved by adding organic matter.

Another important aspect of soil is the pH—the level of acidity or alkalinity. Soil pH influences the availability of nutrients for plants. A pH of 7 is neutral; lower values (down to 0) indicate acidic conditions, and higher values (up to 14) indicate alkaline conditions. Most plants prefer a neutral soil pH of 6.5 to 7.5. A soil test is highly recommended and is useful for indicating the exact pH and other conditions of your particular soil.

If a soil test reveals a pH problem, your soil can be made more acidic by adding horticultural sulfur or more alkaline by adding horticultural lime. The test results should include recommendations for additive quantities, especially if you let the lab know what plants you intend to grow.

It is much easier to amend soil in a small area than in an entire garden. The soil in a raised bed or planter can be adjusted quite easily to suit a few plants whose soil requirements vary greatly from the conditions in your garden.

Rhododendrons require acidic soil.

Ninebark thrives in alkaline soil.

EXPOSURE

Exposure is a very important consideration in all gardens that include woody plants. Your plants may be exposed to wind, heat, cold, rain and snow, and some species are more susceptible to injury by these forces than others. Buildings, walls, fences, hills and hedges or other woody plants can all influence your garden's exposure.

Kiwi does best in a sheltered location (below).

Wind can cause extensive damage to plants, particularly to evergreens in winter. Plants in windy locations can become dehydrated if no water is available from the frozen ground, and they cannot replace moisture as quickly as it is lost through the leaves. Although the standard recommendation is to keep plants well watered in fall until the ground freezes, it is just as important to prevent drought stress during the heat of summer. Tests have shown that a plant deprived of water in summer suffers greater winter windburn.

Daphne is worth trying in Zone 3.

Young barberry in mulched bed

The goal is to avert plant stresses throughout the growing season. Broad-leaved evergreens, such as rhododendron and holly, are most at risk from winter dehydration, so grow them in a sheltered site.

Strong winds can break weak branches or blow entire trees over. However, woody plants often make excellent windbreaks. Hedges and trees temper the wind's effect without the turbulence found on the leeward side of more solid structures, such as walls or fences. Windbreak trees should be species that can flex in the wind or should be planted far enough from buildings to avoid extensive property damage if they or their branches fall.

Hardiness zones (see map, p. 15, and the Quick Reference Chart, pp. 320–325) indicate whether a species can tolerate the conditions in your area, but they are only guidelines. Daphne is generally listed as a Zone 4 plant but often thrives in sheltered spots in Zone 3. Don't be afraid to try species that are not listed as hardy for your area. Plants are incredibly adaptable and just might surprise you.

Here are some tips for growing out-of-zone plants:
• Before planting, observe your garden on a frosty morning. Areas that escape frost are potential sites for tender plants. Cold air tends to collect in low spots and can run downhill, through breaks in plantings and structures, much as water does.
• Provide shelter from the prevailing wind.
• Plant in groups to create windbreaks and microclimates.
• Mulch young plants in fall, at least for their first two years, with a thick layer of clean organic mulch (see p. 46). Good winter protection requires a minimum depth of 15–20 cm (6–8").
• Water thoroughly before the ground freezes in winter.
• Cover or screen frost-tender shrubs with a layer of burlap or horticultural cloth, or use special insulating blankets available at garden centres. Plants in containers can be dug into the vegetable garden or placed under shelter or against a building for protection.

Purchasing Trees & Shrubs

Having considered the features you like and the range of growing conditions your garden offers, you can select the plants. Any reputable garden centre should have a good selection of popular woody plants. Finding unusual specimens might require a few phone calls and a trip to a specialized nursery. Mail-order nurseries can be a great source of the newest and most unusual plants.

Many garden centres and nurseries offer a one-year warranty on trees and shrubs, but, because they take a long time to mature, always choose the healthiest plants regardless. Never purchase weak, damaged or diseased plants, even if they cost less. Examine the bark and avoid plants with visible damage. Check that the growth is even and appropriate for the species. A shrub should be bushy and branched right to the ground, and a tree should have a strong leader. Observe the leaf and flower buds. If they are dry and fall off easily, the plant has been deprived of moisture. The stem or stems should be strong, supple and unbroken. The rootball should be soft and moist when touched. Avoid plants with dry rootballs.

Woody plants are available for purchase in three forms:

Bare-root stock has roots surrounded only by moist sawdust or peat moss and a plastic wrapping. Reject stock that appears to have dried out during shipping. Keep the roots moist and cool, and

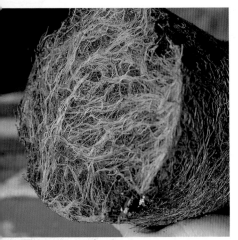

Avoid purchasing root-bound plants.

Purchasing plants in fall lets you see the fall colour.

plant as soon as possible in spring. See p. 34 for information on planting bare-root stock.

Balled-and-burlapped (B & B) stock comes with the roots surrounded by soil and wrapped in burlap, often secured with a wire cage for larger plants. The plants are usually field grown and then dug up, balled and burlapped the year they are sold. It is essential that the rootball remains moist. Large trees are available in this form, but be aware that the soil and rootball can be very heavy, and extra expenses for delivery and planting may apply. Planting can be done almost anytime during the growing season. See p. 35 for information on planting balled-and-burlapped stock.

Container plants are most common at garden centres and nurseries. They are grown in pots filled with potting soil, and they have established root systems. Container stock is easy to plant, establishes quickly after planting and can be planted almost anytime during the growing season. See p. 36 for information on planting container stock.

When choosing a plant, make sure it hasn't been in the container too long. If the roots densely encircle the inside of the pot, then the plant has become root-bound. A root-bound tree or shrub will not establish well, and as the roots mature and thicken, they can choke and kill the plant. Note that sometimes field-grown stock is dug up and sold in containers instead of burlap; ask if you aren't sure. Treat such plants

Temporary winter storage for container plants

like balled-and-burlapped stock when planting.

Bigger is not always better when it comes to choosing woody plants. Smaller plants of a given species often grow up healthier and more robust than larger stock, particularly field-grown (as opposed to container-grown) plants. When a plant is dug up out of the field, the roots are severely cut back.
The smaller the plant, the more quickly it can recover from the shock of being uprooted.

Improper handling can damage woody plants. You can lift bare-root stock by the stem, but do not lift any other trees or shrubs by the trunk or branches. Instead, lift by the rootball or container, or if the plant is too large to lift, place it on a tarp or mat and drag it.

Care during transport is also critical. Even a short trip home

from the nursery can be traumatic for a plant. The heat produced inside a car can quickly dehydrate a tree or shrub. If you have an open vehicle for transport, lay the plant down or cover it to shield it from the wind. Avoid mechanical damage such as rubbing or breaking branches during transport.

Once home, water the plant if it is dry and keep it in a sheltered location until you plant it. Remove damaged growth and broken branches but do no other pruning. Plant your tree or shrub as soon as possible. A bare-root tree or shrub should be planted in a large container of potting soil if it will not be planted outdoors immediately. If you must store a container plant over a cold winter before planting, bury the entire container until spring.

Planting Trees & Shrubs

Before you pick up a shovel and start digging, call Alberta One-Call (www.alberta1call.com), a service that prompts all utility companies to mark the gas, electric, phone and any other underground utility lines. Your local government or county offices usually have the phone numbers handy if you can't locate them. Be careful when digging around underground electric or gas lines, and don't plant trees or shrubs within 90 cm (36") of them. Even if you don't damage anything by digging, the roots may cause trouble in the future, or the plant may need to be cut down if the pipes or wires ever need servicing.

Consider the mature plant size as well. The plant you have in front of you is most likely pretty small. Once it reaches its mature height and spread, will it still fit the space you have chosen? Is it far enough away from the house, the driveway and all walkways? Will it hit the overhang of the house or any overhead power lines?

If you're planting several shrubs, make sure that they won't grow too close together once they are mature. Normally, to determine the spacing, you add the mature spreads and then divide by two. For example, when planting a shrub with an expected spread of 1.25 m (4') next to one with an expected spread of 1.75 m (6'), you would plant them 1.5 m (5') apart. To ensure you will have no gaps when the plants are mature, the spacing in hedges and windbreaks should be just one-half to two-thirds the spread of the mature plants.

Finally, double-check the conditions. Will the soil drainage be adequate? Will the plant get the right amount of light? Is the site very windy? It's important to start with the plant in the right spot and in the best conditions you can give it.

WHEN TO PLANT

For the most part, trees and shrubs can be planted at any time of the year, but some seasons are better for the plants and more convenient than others. Preferred planting times are given at the beginning of each plant entry in this book.

Spring is a great time to plant shrubs and some trees. It gives the trees or shrubs an entire growing season to become established before winter sets in, and the plants can get a good start before the weather turns really hot. Avoid planting during the hottest and driest part of summer, when plants suffer the immediate effects of transplant shock combined with the stress of blistering

IVORY HALO dogwood

sun and heat. For most trees, planting in late summer to early fall is best; you avoid the hottest days of summer and give the plants at least a couple months to establish root systems before they slip into winter dormancy.

Bare-root stock is generally available only in spring and must be planted as soon as possible to avoid moisture loss.

Balled-and-burlapped and container stock can be planted at any time with satisfactory results, but it is always wise to avoid planting in the heat of summer.

The time of day to plant is also a consideration. Avoid planting during the hottest part of the day. Planting in the morning or evening—or on a cloudy, calm day—will be easier on both you and the plant.

It's a good idea to plant as soon as possible after you bring your specimen home. If you have to store the tree or shrub for a short time before planting, keep it out of direct sunlight and ensure the rootball remains moist.

PREPARING THE HOLE

Trees and shrubs should always be planted at the depth at which they were growing, or just above the roots if you are unsure of the depth for bare-root stock. Run your finger down the stem to where the

Sizing up the hole (above), digging the hole (below)

roots just begin to spread out. This area should be just above the soil surface. The depth of the hole should be slightly less than the depth of the rootball or container, or from the bottom of the rootball or container to where the roots begin to spread out.

Be sure that the plant is not set too deep. Planting even 5 cm (2") too deep can cause problems. Most potted field-grown trees are planted deeply in the pot to help keep the freshly dug tree from tipping over, and there may be mulch on top of the soil as well. In this case, it is generally best to scrape off the soil until you find the point where the roots begin to spread out.

The hole should be wide enough to comfortably accommodate the rootball, or even wider. Make the hole for bare-root stock wide enough to completely contain the expanded roots, plus a bit of extra room on the sides.

It is good practice to loosen the soil for a distance beyond the hole with a garden fork or power tiller. This allows the new roots an easier medium to grow into than undisturbed soil, providing an easy transition zone from the rootball soil to the existing on-site soil. The soil around the rootball or in the container is not likely to be the same composition as the soil removed from the hole. Lightly roughening up the sides and bottom of the hole will help with root transition and water flow.

PLANTING BARE-ROOT STOCK

Remove the plastic and sawdust from the roots. Soak the entire root system of bare-root trees and shrubs in a bucket of water for

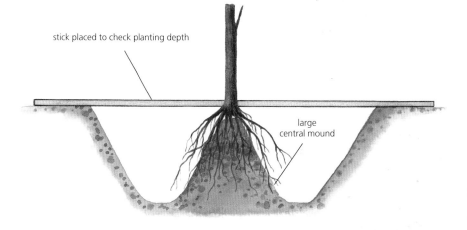

stick placed to check planting depth

large
central mound

Planting bare-root stock

12 hours prior to planting. Make sure the hole is big enough to allow the roots to fully extend. Fan out the roots and centre the plant over the hole's central mound—which is often made cone shaped—using it to help spread out and support the roots.

PLANTING BALLED-AND-BURLAPPED STOCK

Burlap was originally made out of natural fibres. It could be loosened and left wrapped around the rootball to eventually decompose. Modern burlap may or may not be made of natural fibres, and it can be difficult to tell the difference. Synthetic fibres will not decompose and will eventually choke the roots. It is always best to remove any burlap from around the rootball to prevent girdling and to maximize contact between the roots and the soil. If roots are already growing through the burlap, remove as much burlap as you can without damaging these new

roots. If you know the burlap is natural and decide to leave it on, loosen it from the rootball and tuck it below the soil line so it won't wick water away from the roots and into the air.

If a wire basket holds the burlap in place, remove it. You may need to use strong wire cutters to get the basket off. If the tree is very heavy, it may not be possible to remove the base of the basket, but cut away at least the sides, where most of the important roots will be growing.

Once you have removed the basket, set the still-burlapped plant into the hole. Lean the plant over to one side and roll the upper part of the burlap down to the ground. When you lean the plant in the opposite direction, you can often pull the burlap out from under the roots. If the tree is difficult to move once in the hole, you may need to cut away as much burlap as you can instead.

Past horticultural wisdom suggested removing some top branches when planting to make up for roots lost when the plant was dug out of the field. The theory was that the roots could not provide enough water to the leaves, so top growth should be removed to achieve "balance." We now know that the top growth—where photosynthesis occurs and thus where energy is produced—is necessary for root development. The new tree or shrub might drop some leaves, but don't be alarmed; the plant is doing its own balancing. A very light pruning will not adversely affect the plant, but remove only those branches that have been damaged during transport and planting. Leave your new plant to settle in for a year or two before you start any formative pruning.

PLANTING CONTAINER STOCK

Containers are usually made of plastic or pressed fibre and should be removed before planting. Although some containers appear to be made of peat moss, they do not decompose well. The roots may have difficulty penetrating the pot sides, and the fibre will wick moisture away from the roots.

Container stock is very easy to plant (see photos, p. 37). Gently remove or cut off the container and observe the root mass to see whether the plant is root-bound. If roots circle around the inside of the container, they should be loosened or sliced. Any large roots encircling the soil or growing into the centre of the root mass instead of outward should be removed before planting. A sharp pair

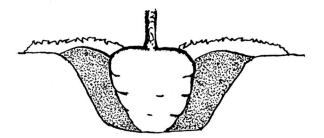

Planting balled-and-burlapped or container stock

1. Gently remove container.

2. Ensure proper planting depth.

3. Backfill with amended soil.

4. Settle backfilled soil with water.

5. Ensure newly planted shrub is well watered.

6. Add a layer of mulch.

Young tree in its new home

Adding organic matter to backfill soil

of hand pruners or a pocket knife will work well for this task.

BACKFILLING

With your bare-root, balled-and-burlapped or container plant in the hole and standing straight up, it is time to replace the soil. A small amount of organic matter

can be well mixed into the backfill to encourage the plant to become established, but too much organic matter creates a pocket of rich soil that the roots may be reluctant to move beyond. If the roots do not venture beyond the immediate area of the hole, the tree or shrub will be weaker and much more susceptible to problems, and the encircling roots could eventually choke the plant. Such a tree will also be more vulnerable to blow-down in a strong wind.

Backfill should generally reach the same depth the plant was grown at previously, or to just below where the roots begin to spread out. If planting into a heavy soil, raise the plant about 2.5 cm (1") to help improve surface drainage away from the crown and roots. The graft unions of grafted stock are generally kept above ground to make it easy to spot and remove suckers sprouting from the rootstock.

When backfilling, it is important to have good root-to-soil contact so the plant will be stable and establish successfully. Large air pockets left behind after backfilling could result in excessive settling and root drying. Use water to settle the soil gently around the roots and in the hole, being careful not to drown the plant. It is a good idea to backfill in small amounts rather than all at once. Add some soil and water it down, repeating the process until the hole has been filled. Stockpile any soil that remains after backfilling and use it to top up the soil around the plant as the backfill settles.

If you are working with a heavy clay soil, make sure the surface drainage slopes away from your new transplant. With other soil types, build a temporary 5–10 cm (2–4") high, doughnut-like mound around the perimeter of the hole to capture extra water. This mound can be made of soil or mulch, such as wood chips. Water into this reservoir for at least the first season. Doing so ensures that water percolates down through the new root mass. The ring of soil or mulch, called a **treewell,** is an excellent tool for conserving water, especially during dry spells. During periods of heavy rain, you may need to breach a soil treewell to prevent the roots from becoming waterlogged. The treewell can be rebuilt when drier conditions resume. In a year or so, once the tree or shrub has become established, the treewell will no longer be needed and should be permanently removed.

To conserve water, mulch around the new planting. Composted wood chips or shredded bark will stay where you put them, unlike pebble bark or peat moss. Do not use too much (7.5–10 cm

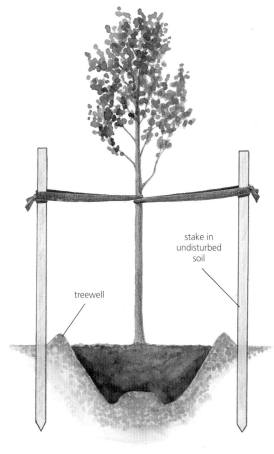

treewell

stake in undisturbed soil

Two-stake method

[3–4"] is adequate) and avoid mulching directly against the trunk or base of the plant to avoid encouraging disease problems.

STAKING

Some trees may need to be staked to provide support while the roots establish. Staking is recommended only for bare-root trees, top-heavy trees over 1.5 m (5') tall or trees planted in windy locations (particularly evergreens, which tend to catch winter winds). The stakes should be removed as soon as the roots have had a chance to become established, which normally takes about a year.

Growing trees and shrubs without stakes is preferable, because unstaked trees develop more roots and stronger trunks. Most newly planted trees can stand on their

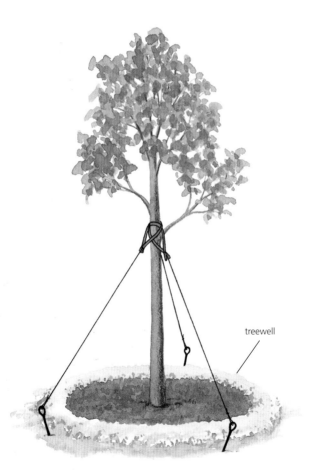

treewell

Three-stake method

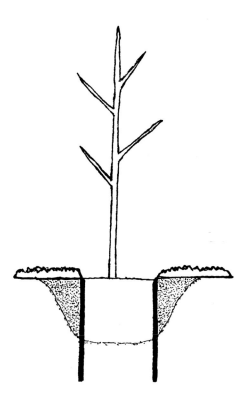

Invisible staking method

own without staking. You can always stake later if you think it is necessary.

Two common methods are used for staking newly planted trees; wood, sturdy plastic or metal stakes can be used in both methods.

The **two-stake** method is suitable for small trees (about 1.5–1.75 m [5–6'] tall) and for trees in low-wind areas. Drive two tall, sturdy stakes firmly into the soil on directly opposite sides of the tree in line with the prevailing wind and outside the rootball; driving the stakes in near the tree can damage the roots and will not provide adequate support. Tie strong cord, rope, cable or wire to the stakes. The end that goes around the trunk should be a wide, belt-like strap of material that will not injure the trunk. Your local garden centre should have ties designed for this purpose, or you can cushion the rope or wire with a section of rubber hose. Attach the straps to the tree about 90 cm–1.25 m (3–4') above the ground.

The **three-stake** method is used for larger trees and for trees in areas subject to strong or shifting winds. This technique is much the same as the two-stake method, but with three short, sturdy stakes evenly spaced around the tree. Attach heavy wire or cable to each stake, again with wide strapping or padding on the end that goes around the trunk. To keep the straps in place, position them just above the lower branches.

A new method for staking container-grown plants does not require the stakes to be removed. **Invisible staking** requires three to five sturdy wooden dowels, 2.5 cm x 5 cm (1" x 2") or 5 cm x 5 cm (2" x 2") stakes—at least twice the depth of the rootball. The larger stakes would be used for larger container stock. Pound these stakes into the ground directly against the rootball to just below the soil surface. The stakes decay over time.

Keep the following points in mind, regardless of the staking method you use:
• Never wrap rope, wire or cable directly around a tree trunk. Always use non-damaging material. Reposition the strapping every two to three months to prevent any rubbing or girdling injury.
• Never tie trees so firmly that they can't move. Young trees need to be able to move in the wind to produce strong trunks and to develop roots more thickly in appropriate places to compensate for the prevailing wind.
• Don't leave the stakes in place too long. One year is sufficient for almost all trees. The stakes should

be there only long enough to allow the roots some time to grow and establish. The tree will actually be weaker if the stakes are left for too long, and over time the ties can damage the trunk and weaken or kill the tree.
• Water your newly planted trees and shrubs early and often, taking care not to drown them. Provide about 22 L (5 gal.) of water three times a week for the first two weeks, then 22 L (5 gal.) on a weekly basis for a few more months to really help the new plants become established.

TRANSPLANTING

If you plan your garden carefully, you should rarely need to move trees or shrubs. The younger the plant, the more likely it is to reestablish successfully when moved to a new location. It typically takes a tree one year for every 2.5 cm (1") of its trunk diameter to become well established after it has been transplanted.

Generally, you can transplant evergreens in spring before growth starts or later in the season after it stops, as long as the transplanting does not take place during a spell of hot weather. Deciduous plants should be transplanted only while dormant—when the branches are bare of leaves. Spring is the best time, but it can also be done in fall. Some woody plants (see the individual species entries) resent being moved once established, and you should avoid transplanting them whenever possible.

When woody plants are transplanted, they inevitably lose most of their root mass. Take care to dig a rootball of an appropriate size. The size of the tree or shrub determines the minimum size of the rootball that must be dug out in order for the plant to survive. As a general guideline, you must excavate a rootball with at least 30 cm (12") of diameter (preferably more) for every 2.5 cm (1") of diameter on the main stem (measured 15–30 cm [6–12"] above the ground).

Rootballs are heavy, and a 60 cm (24") rootball is probably the most the average gardener can manage without heavy equipment. Therefore, trees with trunks more than 5 cm (2") in diameter should be moved only by professionals. Shrubs cannot always be measured as easily as trees, so use your best judgement. Because shrubs mature fairly quickly, starting with a new one may be easier than trying to move a very large specimen.

If it is necessary and feasible to transplant a shrub or small tree, follow these steps:

1) Calculate the size of the rootball to be removed, as described above.

2) Water the rootball area to a depth of 30 cm (12") and allow excess water to drain away. The moist soil will help hold the rootball together.

3) Wrap or tie the branches to minimize branch damage and to make transport from the old site to the new one easier.

4) Slice a long spade or shovel into the soil vertically, cutting a circle the size of the calculated rootball around the plant. Cut down to about 30 cm (12").

Older oaks do not like to be transplanted.

This depth should contain most of the roots for the size of tree or shrub that can be transplanted manually.

5) At this point, most small, densely rooted trees and shrubs can be carefully removed from the hole by leaning on the spade or shovel and prying the plant up and out. If you encounter resistance, you may have missed some roots and should repeat step 4. Once the plant has been freed, place it on a tarp and continue with step 10. Larger trees and shrubs will require additional steps; continue with step 6.

6) Cut another circle one shovel-width outside the first circle, to the same depth.

7) Excavate the soil between the two cut circles.

Spruces also dislike being transplanted when older.

8) When the appropriate rootball depth is reached, carefully cut horizontally under the rootball. When you encounter a root, cut it with a pair of hand pruners or loppers. The goal is to sculpt out a rootball that is standing on a pedestal of undisturbed earth.

9) Spread a tarp in one side of the hole. Gently remove the pedestal and lean the rootball over onto the tarp. Carefully cut any remaining roots in the pedestal. Lift the tree and rootball out of the hole with the tarp, not by the stem or branches.

Mock orange transplants easily.

10) Lift or drag the tarp to the new
location and plant immediately.
See planting instructions given
in preceding sections for information on when to plant, how to
plant, staking, etc. Transplanted
trees and shrubs can be treated
as balled-and-burlapped stock.

Caring for Trees & Shrubs

The care you give your new tree or shrub in the first year or two after planting is the most important. During this period of establishment, it is critical to remove competing weeds, to keep the plant well watered and to avoid all mechanical damage. Be careful with lawn mowers and string trimmers, which can quickly girdle the base of the plant. Whatever you do to the top of the plant affects the roots, and vice versa.

Once established, woody plants generally require minimal care. A few basic maintenance tasks, performed regularly, save time and trouble in the long run.

WEEDING

Weeds can rob young plants of water, light and nutrients, so keep weeds under control to encourage optimal growth of your trees and shrubs. Avoid deep hoeing around woody plants because it may damage shallow-rooted species. A layer of mulch is a good way to suppress weeds. If you believe that you must use commercial weed killers, consult your local nursery or extension agent for advice, and follow the label directions carefully.

MULCHING

Mulch is an important gardening tool. It helps soil retain moisture, it buffers soil temperatures and it prevents soil erosion during heavy rain or strong winds. Mulch prevents weed seeds from germinating by blocking out the light, and it can deter pests and help prevent diseases. It keeps lawn mowers and line trimmers away from plants, reducing the chance of damage. Mulch can also add aesthetic value to a planting.

Organic mulches, such as compost, composted wood chips, bark chips, shredded bark, composted leaves and dry grass clippings, add beneficial nutrients to the soil as they break down over time but must be replenished on a regular basis.

Inorganic mulches, such as stones, crushed brick or gravel, do not break down and so do not have to be replenished. These types of mulches don't provide nutrients, and they can also adversely increase soil temperatures. Some books recommend using black plastic or ground cloth under the mulch, but doing so can disrupt the microbial balance of the soil, prevent worms and other important soil organisms from moving freely to the surface and restrict the movement of oxygen and water into the soil.

For good weed suppression, the mulch layer should be 7.5–10 cm (3–4") thick. Try to maintain a mulch-free zone immediately around the trunk or stem bases. Piling mulch up around the base of a plant may encourage fungal decay and rot.

WATERING

The weather, type of plant, type of soil and time of year all influence the amount of water your trees and shrubs need. Pay attention to the wind; like hot, dry weather, it can quickly dry out your soil and plants so that you will need to water them more frequently. Different plants require different amounts of water; some,

Keep mulch away from the base of your tree or shrub.

such as willow and some birch species, will grow in a temporarily waterlogged soil, whereas others, such as pine, prefer a dry, sandy soil. Sandy soils and slopes retain

SOIL PROBE
You can make a soil probe from a 9 mm (⅜") to 1.25 cm (½") diameter wooden dowel. Carve one end into a point, then cut a groove or paint a mark 30 cm (12") up from that end. Do not finish the wood, because you want it to discolour as it absorbs the soil moisture. Push the rod into the soil 30 cm (12") deep, leave it for up to a minute, then remove the stick. If it has darkened with moisture, you don't need to water. If it is still dry, water immediately. It is quite possible for our heavy clay soils to be dry down to 7.5 cm (3") but plenty wet enough farther down. I have seen many a plant saved from drowning through the use of this simple probe.

less water than heavy clay soils and flat or low areas. Plants need more water when they are getting established in a new location, flowering or producing fruit.

Plants are good at letting us know when they are thirsty. Wilted, flagging leaves and twigs are signs of water deprivation, but excessive water can also cause a plant to wilt. Test for soil moisture by checking at least 5 cm (2") down with your fingers or with a soil probe (see p. 47). If the soil is dry, you will need to take immediate action. It is not healthy for a plant to go into water stress. If you detect moisture, you don't need to water.

Make sure your young trees and shrubs are well watered in fall. Continue to water as needed until the ground freezes. Fall watering is very important for all evergreen plants—once the ground has frozen, the roots can't draw moisture from it, leaving the foliage susceptible to drying out.

Once established, trees and shrubs usually need watering only during periods of excessive drought. To keep water use to a minimum and reduce evaporation losses, avoid watering in the heat of day. Work organic matter into the soil to help the soil absorb and retain water, and apply mulch to help prevent water loss. Collect and use rainwater whenever possible.

FERTILIZING

Most garden soils provide all the nutrients plants need, particularly if you use an organic mulch and mix compost into the soil before planting your garden. Simply allowing leaf litter to remain on the ground after the leaves drop in fall promotes natural nutrient cycling of nitrogen and other elements in the soil.

Not all plants have the same nutritional requirements, however. Some plants are heavy feeders, whereas others thrive in poor soils. Pay attention to the leaf colour of your plants as an indicator of nutritional status. Yellowing leaves, for example, may indicate nutrient deficiency.

When you do fertilize, use only the recommended quantity, because too much can be very harmful. Fertilizer that is applied in too high a concentration can easily burn roots. Synthetic fertilizers are more concentrated than organic fertilizers and therefore have the potential to cause more problems.

Granular fertilizers consist of small, dry particles that can be spread with a fertilizer spreader or by hand. Consider using a slow-release type of granular fertilizer. It may cost a bit more but will save you time and reduce the risk of burn by releasing the nutrients gradually over the growing season. One application per year is normally sufficient. Apply the fertilizer in early spring to provide nutrients for growth.

Fertilizing should be done only to correct a visible nutrient deficiency, to correct a deficiency identified by a soil and tissue test, to increase vegetative, flower or fruit growth or to increase the vigour of a plant that is flagging.

Applying fertilizer incorrectly or in excess does not benefit your plants. In fact, it makes a tree or shrub more susceptible to some pests and diseases and can accelerate a plant's decline.

Do not fertilize trees or shrubs
• when a soil and tissue test indicates sufficient soil nutrients
• if your plants are growing and appear healthy
• if your plants are large and you want to reduce pruning and shearing
• during times of drought, when the roots will not absorb nutrients and excess partially wetted fertilizer can burn root hairs.

If you do not want to encourage fast growth, do not fertilize. Remember that most trees and shrubs do not need fertilizer and that fast growth may make plants more susceptible to problems.

In particular, fall fertilizing with chemical fertilizers is not recommended—the resulting late-season new growth is easily damaged in winter. Organic fertilizers can be applied in fall because they are activated by soil organisms that are not as active in cool weather.

Unnecessary or excessive fertilizer pollutes our local lakes, streams and groundwater. Many homes in Alberta obtain their drinking water from wells, which can be contaminated by fertilizers. Use fertilizers wisely, and both your plants and our environment will benefit.

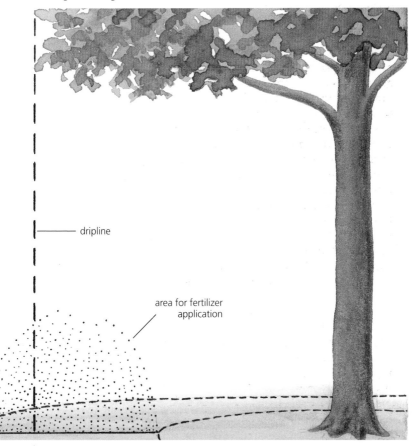

dripline

area for fertilizer application

Pruning

Pruning helps maintain the health and attractive shape of a woody plant. It also increases the quality and yield of fruit, controls and directs growth, and creates interesting plant forms, such as topiary, espalier and bonsai. Pruning is perhaps the most important maintenance task when growing trees and shrubs—and the easiest to mess up. Fortunately for new gardeners, it is not difficult to learn and can even be enjoyable if done correctly from the beginning and continued on a regular basis.

Proper pruning combines knowledge and skill. Knowing how woody plants grow and about the growth habits of your particular plant will help you avoid pruning mistakes that can ruin a plant's shape or make it prone to disease and insect damage.

If you are unsure about pruning, take a pruning course. Courses may be offered by a local garden centre, botanical garden, college or master gardener. Excellent books are also available on the subject.

Another option is to hire a professional, such as an arborist certified by the International Society of Arboriculture (ISA). Certified professionals understand the plants and have the special pruning training and equipment to do a proper job. They might even be willing to show you some pruning basics. Always call a professional to prune trees growing near power lines or other hazardous areas or to prune or cut down large branches and trees that could damage buildings, fences, cars or pedestrians. Many gardeners have injured themselves or others, or caused significant property damage, because they simply didn't have the equipment or the know-how to remove a large branch or tree.

Plants will always try to grow to their genetically programmed potential size. If you are doing a lot of pruning to keep a tree or shrub in check, the plant may be too large for that site. I cannot emphasize enough how important it is to consider the mature size of a plant before you put it into the ground.

WHEN & HOW MUCH TO PRUNE

Aside from removing damaged growth, do not prune for the first year after planting a tree or shrub. After that time, the first pruning should develop the plant's struc-

Proper hand pruner orientation

ture. For a strong framework, do not prune branches that have a wide angle at the crotch (where the branch meets another branch or the trunk), because these branch intersections are the strongest. Prune out branches with narrower crotches while ensuring an even distribution of the main (scaffold) branches. These branches will support all future top growth.

Trees and shrubs vary greatly in their pruning needs. Some plants, such as boxwood, tolerate or even thrive on heavy pruning and shearing, but other plants, such as cherry, may be killed if given the same treatment. Pruning guide-lines are given in each species entry in this book.

The amount of pruning also depends on your motivation. Less work is involved in simply tidying the growth, for example, than in creating intricate topiary.

Many gardeners are unsure about what time of year they should prune. Knowing when a plant flowers is the easiest way to know when to prune. (See p. 56 for information on pruning conifers.) Trees and shrubs that flower before about July, such as crabapple and forsythia, should be pruned after

they finish flowering. These plants form the following year's flower buds in summer and fall. Pruning just after the current year's flowers fade allows plenty of time for the next year's flowers to develop and does not take away any of the current year's blooms.

Late-flowering species, such as peegee hydrangea, can be pruned early in the year instead. These plants form flower buds on new stems as the season progresses, and pruning in spring just before or as the new growth begins to develop encourages the best growth and flowering.

Some plants, such as birch and maple, have a heavy spring flow of sap. As long as proper pruning cuts are made, these trees can still be pruned in spring. If the excessive bleeding is aesthetically unappealing or is dripping onto some thing inappropriately, wait until these species are in full leaf before pruning.

Take care when pruning any trees in early spring, when many canker-causing organisms are active, or in fall, when many wood-rotting fungi release their

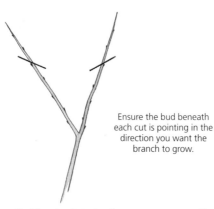

Ensure the bud beneath each cut is pointing in the direction you want the branch to grow.

Cutting back to bud   Cutting to a lateral branch

spores. During cool weather, the plants are fairly inactive and less able to fight off invasion.

Inspect trees and shrubs annually for any dead, damaged, diseased or awkwardly growing branches and to determine what other pruning, if any, is needed. Always remove dead, diseased and damaged branches as soon as you discover them, regardless of the time of year.

THE KINDEST CUT

Trees and shrubs have a remarkable ability to repair their wounds, but it is critical to make proper pruning cuts. A proper pruning cut, though still a wound, minimizes the area where insect and disease attack can occur and takes advantage of the areas on a plant where it can best deal with wounds. The tree or shrub can then heal as quickly as possible, preventing disease and insect damage.

Using the right tools makes pruning easier and more effective. The size of the branch being cut determines the type of tool to use.

Hand pruners should be used for cutting branches up to 2 cm (³/₄") in diameter. Using hand pruners for larger stems increases the risk of damage, and it can be physically strenuous.

Loppers are long-handled pruners used for branches up to 3.75 cm (1¹/₂") in diameter. Loppers are good for removing old stems. Hand pruners and loppers must be properly oriented when making a cut (see photo, p. 51). The blade should be to the plant side of the cut and the hook to the side being removed. If the cut is made with the hook toward the plant, the cut will be ragged and slow to heal.

Pruning saws have teeth specially designed to cut through green wood. They can be used to cut branches up to 15 cm (6") in diameter and sometimes larger. Pruning saws are easier to use and much safer than chainsaws.

Hedge clippers, or shears, are intended only for shearing and shaping hedges.

Make sure your tools are sharp and clean before you begin any pruning task. If the branch you

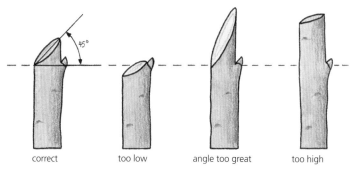

correct   too low   angle too great   too high

Cutting back to a bud

are cutting is diseased, sterilize the tool before using it again. Use denatured alcohol or a solution of 1 part bleach to 10 parts water for cleaning and sterilizing.

TYPES OF PRUNING CUTS
You should be familiar with the following types of pruning cuts.

Cutting back to a bud is used for shortening a branch, redirecting growth or maintaining the size of a tree or shrub. Each cut should be made slightly less than 65 mm ($^1/_4$") above a bud (see diagram, above). If the cut is too far away from or too close to the bud, the

wound will not heal properly. Cut back to buds that are pointing in the direction you want the new growth to grow in (see diagram, p. 52).

Cutting to a lateral branch is used to shorten limbs and redirect growth. The diameter of the branch to which you are cutting back must be at least one-third of the diameter of the branch you are cutting. As with cutting back to a bud, cut slightly less than 65 mm ($^1/_4$") above the lateral branch and line up the cut with the angle of the branch that is to remain (see diagram, p. 52). Whenever possible, make cuts at an angle so that rain won't sit on the open wound.

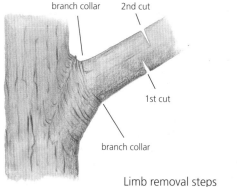

branch collar   2nd cut

1st cut

branch collar

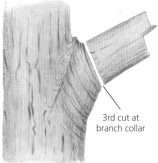

3rd cut at branch collar

Limb removal steps

Removing limbs can be a complicated operation. Because the wound is large, it is critical to cut in the correct place—at the branch collar—to ensure quick healing. The cut must be done in steps (see diagram, p. 53) to avoid damaging the bark.

The first cut is on the bottom of the branch to be removed. This cut should be 30–45 cm (12–18") up from the crotch and should extend one-third of the way through the branch. The purpose of the first cut is to prevent bark from peeling down the tree when the second cut causes the main part of the branch to fall. The second cut is made to the top of the branch, a bit farther along then the first cut. This cut removes most of the branch. The final cut should be made just above the branch collar. The plant tissues at the branch collar quickly create a barrier against insects and diseases. Do not make flush cuts and do not leave stubs; both can be slow to heal.

The use of pruning paint or paste has been much debated. The current consensus is that these substances do more harm than good. Trees and shrubs have a natural ability to create a barrier between living wood and dead or decaying sections. An unpainted cut will eventually heal over, but a cut that has been treated with paint or paste may never heal properly.

Shearing is used to trim and shape hedges. Because some of the normal pruning rules (such as being careful where you cut in relation to buds) are disregarded in shearing, only plants that can handle heavy pruning should be sheared.

Informal hedges take advantage of the natural shape of the plant and require only minimal trimming. These hedges generally take up more room than formal hedges, which are trimmed more severely to assume a neat, even appearance. Formal hedges are generally sheared a minimum of twice per growing season.

For any hedge, make sure all sides are trimmed to encourage even growth. The base of your hedge should always be wider than the top to allow light to reach the

incorrect   Hedge shape   correct

entire hedge and to prevent it from thinning out at the base. A hedge will gradually increase in size despite shearing, so allow room for this expansion when planting.

Thinning, or renewal pruning, is a rejuvenation process that maintains the shape, health and productivity of shrubs. It opens up space for air and light to penetrate and provides room for young, healthy branches and selected suckers to grow. Thinning often combines the first two cuts discussed above, and it is the most frequently performed pruning practice. Plants that produce new growth from ground level (either from the crown or by suckers) can be pruned this way.

A shrub that is thinned annually should have one-quarter to one-third of the growth removed. Cutting the oldest stems encourages new growth without causing excessive stress from loss of top growth. Although some plants can be completely cut back to the ground and seem to suffer no ill effects, it is generally better to remove no more than one-third of the growth.

Follow these four steps to thin most multi-stemmed shrubs:
1) Remove all dead, diseased, damaged, rubbing and crossing branches to branch junctions, buds or ground level.
2) Remove up to one-third of the growth each year, leaving a mix of old and new growth, and cutting unwanted stems at or close to the base. Do not cut stems below ground level because many disease organisms are present in soil.
3) Thin the top of the shrub to allow air and light penetration and to

Thinning cuts

balance the shape. Because removing the oldest stems generally thins out the top as well, this step is not always necessary.
4) Repeat the process each year on established, mature shrubs. Regular pruning of shrubs will keep them healthy and productive for many years.

BRANCH COLLARS
To learn to identify branch collars, look at the branch intersections of an apple or pear tree. There will be a slight swelling at the base of each branch. This swelling is actually trunk tissue and must be protected to ensure quick and complete wound closure. Once you see and feel this collar on an apple or pear tree, you'll have an easier time finding it on other trees. If you aren't sure where a collar ends, err on the side of caution and cut slightly farther out from the trunk.

Sheared arborvitae

PRUNING CONIFERS

Coniferous trees and shrubs, such as spruce, pine and juniper, require little or no pruning other than to fix damage or correct wayward growth. Proper pruning procedures do differ, however, for different conifers.

Fully extended mugo pine candles

Spruce trees have buds all along their stems and can be pruned at almost any time of year. Branches can be pruned back into the last two or three years of growth.

Pines, on the other hand, must be shaped and directed in mid- to late spring, after the danger of frost has passed. At this time, the new growth, called candles, should have almost fully extended but should still be pliable. Pinch the candles by up to half their length before they are fully extended. Pines do not have side buds along their stems, but, when the candles are pinched at the proper time, new buds will set near the pinched end. For bushy, dense growth, pinch all candles by half. Pinching should be done by hand and not with shears or hand pruners. This technique can be time consuming and has a limited effect. It is best to choose a cultivar with a naturally dense, bushy habit that is expected to reach an appropriate size for the space you have.

Yews, junipers and arborvitae can be lightly sheared for hedging. It is best to begin training hedge plants when they are very young. Yews can be pruned heavily during dormancy, but it is better to shear them on an ongoing basis. As specimens, yews can be heavily hand pruned at almost any time to keep their natural shape.

When removing a branch on a conifer, cut it back to the branch collar at the trunk. Before you start cutting, take a good look at a few branches because the collar can be difficult to find on a conifer. Cutting a branch back partway is usually pointless—most conifers, including pine and fir, will not regenerate from old wood.

Juniper can regenerate from old wood, but it takes a long time, and it may result in an oddly shaped plant. To avoid disfiguring the plant, make sure you really need to remove a branch before you do so. Here is another reason to think about mature size before you plant any tree or shrub.

If the central leader on a young conifer is broken or damaged, cleanly remove it and train a new leader in its place. In doing so, you reduce the chance of infection and prevent many opportunistic leaders from competing. Gently place a straight stake next to the main trunk. Do not insert the stake into the ground. Tie the stake to the main trunk, being careful not to girdle the tree by tying it too tightly. Bend the chosen new leader as upright as possible and tie it to the stake. Remove the stake when the new leader is growing strongly upright. Remove or cut the tips of any other leaders that attempt to form.

Older, larger trees may be irreparably damaged by the loss of a leader.

Topping disfigures and stresses trees.

TREE TOPPING

One pruning practice that should never be performed is tree topping. Topping is done in an attempt to control height or size, to prevent trees from growing into overhead power lines, to allow more light onto a property or to prevent a tall tree from potentially toppling onto a building.

Topped trees are ugly, weak and potentially hazardous. A tree can be killed by the stress of losing so much of its live growth, or by the gaping, slow-to-heal wounds that are vulnerable to attack by insects and wood-rotting fungi. The heartwood of a topped tree rots out quickly, resulting in a weak trunk. The crotches on new growth also tend to be weak. Topped trees, therefore, are susceptible to storm damage and blowdown. Hazards aside, topping a tree spoils its aesthetic value and that of the surrounding landscape.

It is much better to completely remove a tree, and start again with one that will grow to a more appropriate size, than to attempt to reduce the size of a large, mature specimen.

SPECIALTY PRUNING

Custom pruning methods are used to create interesting plant shapes.

True topiary made of boxwood

Apple espalier

Spruce and juniper bonsai (below)

Topiary is the shaping of plants into animal, abstract or geometric forms. True topiary uses hedge plants sheared into the desired shape. Species that can handle heavy pruning, such as boxwood, are chosen. A simpler form of topiary involves growing vines or other trailing plants over a wire frame to achieve the desired form. Small-leaved ivy and other flexible, climbing or trailing plants work well for this kind of topiary.

Espalier involves training a tree or shrub to grow in two dimensions instead of three, with the aid of a solid wire or other framework. The plant is commonly trained against a wall or fence, but it can also be freestanding. This method is popularly applied to fruit trees, such as apple, when space is at a premium. Many gardeners consider the forms attractive and unusual, and you may want to try your hand at espalier even if you have plenty of space.

Bonsai is the art of developing miniature versions of large trees and landscapes. A gardener prunes the top growth and roots and uses wire to train the plant to the desired form. The severe pruning creates a dwarfed form. Many books are available on the subject, and courses may be offered at colleges or by horticultural or bonsai societies.

Propagating Trees & Shrubs

Many gardeners enjoy the art and science of starting new plants. Although some gardeners are willing to try growing annuals from seeds and perennials from seeds, cuttings or divisions, they may be unsure how to go about propagating their own trees and shrubs. Many woody plants can be propagated with ease, however, allowing the gardener to buy a single specimen and then clone it, rather than buying additional plants.

Do-it-yourself propagating does more than cut costs. It can become an enjoyable part of gardening and an interesting hobby in itself. As well, it allows gardeners to add to their landscapes species that may be hard to find at nurseries.

A number of methods can be used to propagate trees and shrubs. Many species can be started from seed, which can be a long, slow process, but some gardeners enjoy the variable and sometimes unusual results. Simpler techniques include cuttings, ground layering and mound layering.

CUTTINGS
Cut segments of stems can be encouraged to develop their own roots and form new plants. Cuttings are treated differently depending on the maturity of the growth.

Hydrangea

Willow

Cuttings taken in spring or early summer from new growth are called **greenwood** or **softwood** cuttings. They can actually be the most difficult cuttings to start because they require warm, humid conditions that are as likely to cause the cuttings to rot as to root.

Cuttings taken in fall from mature, woody growth are called **hardwood** or **ripe** cuttings. In order to root, these cuttings require a coarse, gritty, moist and preferably warm soil mix and low, but not freezing, air temperatures. They may take all winter to root. These special conditions make it difficult to start hardwood cuttings unless you have a cold frame, heated greenhouse or propagator.

The easiest cuttings to start are those taken in late summer or early fall from new (but mature) growth that has not yet become completely woody. They are called **semi-ripe**, **semi-mature** or **semi-hardwood** cuttings.

Follow these steps to take and plant semi-ripe cuttings:
1) Take cuttings about 5–10 cm (2–4") long from the tip of a stem, cutting just below a leaf node (the node is the place where a leaf meets the stem). There should be at least two nodes on the cutting. The tip of each cutting will be soft, but the base will be starting to harden.
2) Remove the leaves from the lower half of each cutting. Moisten the stripped end and dust it lightly with rooting hormone powder (consult your local garden centre for the appropriate kind).

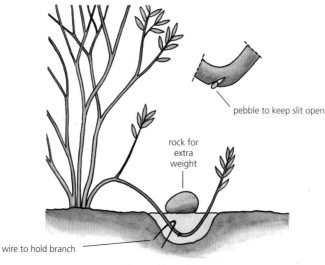

pebble to keep slit open

rock for
extra
weight

wire to hold branch

Ground layering

3) Plant the cuttings directly in the garden, in a cold frame or in pots. The soil mix should be well drained but moist. Firm the cuttings into the soil to ensure that no air spaces will dry out the emerging roots.
4) Keep the cuttings out of direct sunlight and keep the soil moist.
5) Make sure the roots are well established before transplanting. The plants should root by the time winter begins.
6) Protect new plants from extreme cold for the first winter. Plants in pots should be kept in a cold but frost-free location.

Plants for Semi-Ripe Cuttings
Cotoneaster
False cypress
Forsythia
Hydrangea
Potentilla
Russian cypress
Willow

GROUND LAYERING
Layering—ground layering in particular—is the easiest propagation method and the one most likely to produce successful results. Layering allows future cuttings to form their own roots before being detached from the parent plant. In ground layering, a section of a flexible branch is buried until it produces roots. The method is quite simple.

1) Choose a branch or shoot growing low enough on the plant to reach the ground. Remove the leaves from the section of at least four nodes that will be underground. At least another four should protrude above ground at the new growth end.
2) Twist the leafless section of the branch, or make a small cut on the underside near a leaf node. This damage will stimulate root growth. A toothpick or small pebble can be used to hold the cut open.

Chokeberry

Dogwood

3) Bend the branch down to see where it will touch the ground and dig a shallow trench about 10 cm (4") deep at this location. The end of the trench nearest the shrub can slope gradually upwards, but the end where the branch tip will be should be vertical to force the tip up.

4) Use a peg or bent wire to hold the branch in place. Fill the soil back into the trench, and water well. A rock or brick on top of the soil will also help keep the branch in place.

5) Keep the soil moist but not soggy. Roots may take a year or more to develop. Once roots are well established, the new plant can be severed from the parent and planted in a permanent location.

The best shrubs for layering have low, flexible branches. Spring and fall are the best times to start the layer. Many species respond better in one season than the other, but some, such as rhododendron, respond equally well in either.

Plants to Layer in Spring
Chokeberry
Daphne
Dogwood
Lilac
Virginia creeper

Plants to Layer in Fall
Cedar
Blueberry
Euonymus
Forsythia
Hazelnut
Honeysuckle
Saskatoon
Viburnum

Euonymus (below)

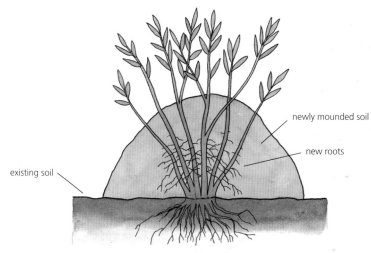

newly mounded soil

new roots

existing soil

Mound layering

MOUND LAYERING

Mound layering is a simple way to propagate low, shrubby plants. With this technique, the shrub is partially buried in a mound of well-drained soil mix. The buried stems will then sprout roots along their lengths. This method can provide many new plants with little effort.

Mound layering should be initiated in spring, once new shoots begin to grow. Make a mound from a mixture of sand, peat moss and soil over half or more of the plant. Leave the branch tips exposed. More soil can be mounded up over the course of summer. Keep the mound moist but not soggy.

At the end of summer (or, for large plants, the following season), gently wash the mound away and detach the rooted branches. Plant them out either directly where you want them or in a protected, temporary spot if you want to shelter them for the first winter.

Plants to Mound Layer
Cotoneaster
Dogwood
Euonymus
Forsythia
Lilac
Potentilla

Cotoneaster

Problems & Pests

Tree and shrub plantings can be both assets and liabilities when it comes to pests and diseases in the garden. Many insects and diseases attack only one plant species. Mixed plantings can make it difficult for pests and diseases to find their preferred hosts and establish a population. At the same time, because woody plants are in the same spot for many years, any problems can become permanent. The advantage is that beneficial birds, insects and other pest-devouring organisms can also develop permanent populations. The plants selected for this book, which include some native plants that have survived the conditions in Alberta for millennia, are generally less susceptible to problems.

For many years, pest control meant spraying or dusting with the goal to eliminate every pest in the landscape. A more moderate approach advocated today is known as IPM (Integrated Pest Management or Integrated Plant Management). The goal of IPM is to reduce pest problems to levels of damage that you can accept.

Consider whether a pest's damage is localized or covers the entire plant. Will the damage kill the plant or does it only affect the outward appearance? Are there methods of controlling the pest without chemicals? The book *Garden Bugs of Alberta* (Lone Pine Publishing, 2008) provides an in-depth look at IPM for insects.

IPM is an interactive system in which observation, identification and assessment are the primary tools. Observing your plants on a regular basis will allow you to assess the severity of any infestation. It will also let you catch problems early, when they are easier to control with minimal effort. Seeing an insect does not mean you have a problem, though. Most insects do no harm, and many are beneficial to your garden as pollinators or predators. Take immediate action against the well-known garden pests you are already familiar with, but wait until you have identified any other insects as harmful before attempting to control them. You may find that an insect you are concerned about is actually eating the ones you don't want.

A good IPM program includes learning what conditions your particular plants need for healthy growth, what pests might affect them, where and when to look for those pests, and how and when to best control them. Keep records of pest damage because your observations can reveal patterns that will be useful both in spotting recurring problems and in planning your maintenance regime. Most problems strike at about the same time each year.

An effective, responsible pest management program has four steps. Cultural controls are the most important. Physical controls should be attempted next, followed by biological controls. Chemical controls should always be the last resort. Chemicals can endanger gardeners and their families and pets, and they kill as many good organisms as bad ones, leaving the whole garden vulnerable to even worse attacks.

Cultural controls are the gardening techniques you use in the day-to-day care of your garden. Perhaps the best defence against pests and diseases is to grow your woody plants in the conditions for which they are adapted. It is also very important to keep your soil healthy, with plenty of organic matter added.

Other cultural controls are equally straightforward. Choose resistant varieties of trees and shrubs that are not prone to problems. Space your plants so they have good air circulation in and around them and are not stressed by competing for light, nutrients and space. Remove plants that are decimated by the same pests every year. Dispose of diseased foliage and branches by burning the material or by taking it to a permitted dump site. Prevent the spread of disease by keeping your gardening tools clean and by tidying up dead plant matter every fall.

Sticky trap

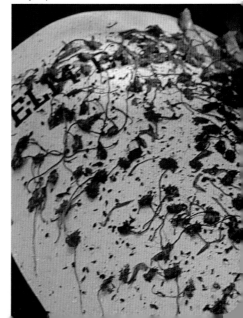

Frogs eat many insect pests.

Predatory ground beetle

of such devices. Physical control of diseases usually involves removing the infected plant or plant parts to keep the problem from spreading.

Biological controls make use of predators that eat pests. Animals such as birds, snakes, frogs, spiders, ladybird beetles, bats and certain bacteria can help keep pest populations manageable. Encourage these creatures to take up permanent residence in your garden. A birdbath and birdfeeder will encourage birds to come to your yard, where they will feed on a wide variety of insect pests. Beneficial insects are probably already living in your landscape, and you can encourage them to stay by planting appropriate alternate food sources. Many beneficial insects eat nectar from plants such as yarrow and daisies. It is often the young and not the adult insects that are predatory. Another form of biological control is the naturally occurring soil bacterium *Bacillus thuringiensis* var. *kurstaki*, or *B.t.k.* for short. Available in garden centres, it breaks down the gut lining of some insects.

Physical controls are generally used to combat insect and mammal problems (for example, picking insects off shrubs by hand, which is not a daunting task if the problem is caught early). Simply drop the offenders into a bucket of soapy water (soap prevents them from floating and climbing out and may suffocate them).

Other physical controls for insects and mammals include traps, barriers, scarecrows and natural repellents that make a plant taste or smell bad to pests. Garden centres offer a wide array

Chemical controls should rarely be necessary, but, if you must use them, many less toxic organic options and more precisely targeted pesticides are becoming available, because consumers demand effective pest-control products that do not harm the environment. One drawback to using any chemical, however, is that it may also kill the beneficial insects that you have been trying to attract.

Organic chemicals are now available at most garden centres. Follow the manufacturer's instructions very carefully. A larger amount or concentration of the insecticide is not any more effective in controlling insect pests than the recommended dosage. Many people think that because a pesticide is organic, they can use however much they want. Although organic sprays are made from natural sources and will more readily break down into harmless compounds rather than accumulate in the environment, they can be as dangerous as synthetic chemical ones. An organic spray kills because it contains a lethal toxin. NEVER overuse any pesticide. Always practice target application, or "spot spraying"; rarely does the whole area or even the whole plant need to be sprayed.

If a particular pest is not listed on the package, the product will not control that pest. It is also important to find out at what stage in an insect's life cycle you will get the best control. Some pests can be controlled only at certain stages. Proper and early identification of pests is vital for finding a quick solution.

Alternatives to commercial chemical pesticides are available or can easily be made at home; horticultural oils and insecticidal soaps, for example, are effective and are safer products to use for pest control (see p. 75).

Cultural, physical, biological and chemical controls are all possible defences to use against insect pests. Many diseases, however, can be dealt with only culturally. It is usually the weakened plants that succumb to diseases,

though some diseases can infect plants regardless of their level of health. Some diseases, such as powdery mildew, are largely a cosmetic concern, but they may weaken a plant enough to make it susceptible to other problems. Prevention is often the only hope. Once a plant has been infected, it (or the infected parts) should generally be destroyed to prevent the disease from spreading.

Any pesticide, whether organic or synthetic, disrupts the balance of microorganisms in the soil profile (containers with sterile planting mix excluded), kills many beneficial insects and sets gardeners on the vicious circle of having to use those products to control their problems. I would like to see all forms of pesticides used on plants eliminated, or at least severely reduced, and people willing to accept some pest damage.

Ladybird beetle

Ladybird larvae are voracious predators of garden pests.

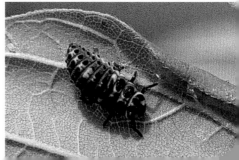

GLOSSARY OF PESTS & DISEASES

Anthracnose
Fungus. Yellow or brown spots on leaves; sunken lesions and blisters on stems; can kill plant.
What to Do. Choose resistant varieties and cultivars; keep soil well drained; thin out stems to improve air circulation; avoid handling wet foliage. Remove and destroy infected plant parts; clean up and destroy debris from infected plants in fall. Applying liquid copper fungicide can minimize damage.

Aphids
Tiny, pear-shaped insects, winged or wingless; can be green, black, brown, red or grey; e.g., woolly adelgids. They cluster along stems and on buds and leaves and suck sap from plants, causing distorted or

Green aphids

stunted growth. Sticky honeydew forms on surfaces, encouraging sooty mould.
What to Do. Squish small colonies by hand; dislodge with brisk water spray from hose. Predatory insects and birds feed on aphids. Spray serious infestations with insecticidal soap (see p. 75) or neem oil according to directions.

Woolly aphids

Beetles
Many types and sizes; usually round, with hard, shell-like outer wings covering membranous inner wings. Some are beneficial: e. g., ladybird beetles or "ladybugs." Others are not: e.g., Japanese beetle, leaf skeletonizers, bark beetles, weevils. Larvae: see Borers, Grubs. Leave wide range of possible chewing damage: make small or large holes in or around

Beetle damage

margins of leaves; consume entire leaf or areas between leaf veins ("skeletonize"); may also chew holes in flowers and eat through root bark. Some bark beetles carry deadly plant diseases.
What to Do. For shrubs, pick beetles off at night and drop them in soapy water; spread an old sheet under small trees and shrubs and shake off beetles to collect and dispose of them; use a broom to reach tall branches. The Hot Pepper Wax brand of insect repellent discourages beetles and may also repel rabbits and deer.

Blight
Fungal or bacterial diseases, many types; e.g., leaf blight,

needle blight, petal blight, snow blight, twig blight. Leaves, stems and flowers blacken, rot and die. See also Fire Blight, Grey Mould. **What to Do.** Thin out stems to improve air circulation; keep mulch away from base of plants; remove debris from garden at end of growing season. Remove and destroy infected plant parts. Sterilize equipment after each cut to avoid reinfecting plant and spreading fungus.

Borers
Variably sized, worm-like larvae of some moths, wasps and beetles; among the most damaging of plant pests. Burrow into plant stems, leaves or roots, under bark and sometimes into heartwood, destroying conducting tissue and structural strength. Burrows are sites where infection and decomposition can begin; some borers carry infection. **What to Do.** Site tree or shrub properly and keep it as healthy as possible with proper fertilizing and watering. May be able to squish borers

within leaves. Remove and destroy bored parts; may need to remove entire plant.

Bugs (True Bugs)
Small insects up to 1.25 cm ($^1/_2$") long; green, brown, black or brightly coloured and patterned. Many are beneficial; a few pests, such as lace bugs, pierce plants to suck out sap. May inject toxins that deform plants; pierced tissues result in sunken areas, leaves that rip as they grow and dwarfed or deformed leaves, buds and new growth. **What to Do.** Remove debris and weeds from around plants in fall to destroy overwintering sites. Spray plants with insecticidal soap (see p. 75) or neem oil according to directions.

Canker
Swollen or sunken lesions on stems or branches, surrounded by living tissue. Caused by many different bacterial and fungal diseases; most enter through wounded wood, sometimes after woodpecker activity. **What to Do.** Maintain vigor of plants; don't wound

or injure trees (e.g., string trimmer damage), especially in spring when canker-causing organisms are most active; control borers and other bark-dwelling insects. Prune out and destroy infected material. Sterilize pruning tools before, during and after use on infected plants.

Case Bearers
see Caterpillars

Caterpillars
Larvae of butterflies, moths and sawflies; e.g., bagworm, budworm, case bearers, cutworm, leaf rollers, leaf tiers, loopers, webworm. Chew foliage and buds; severe infestations can completely defoliate plants. **What to Do.** Removal from plant is best control; use high-pressure water and soap or pick caterpillars off by hand if plant is small enough; cut off and burn large tents or webs of larvae. Control biologically using *B.t.k.* (see p. 66); apply horticultural oil in spring. Slippery or sticky barrier bands on trunks prevent caterpillars from climbing trees to reach leaves.

Caterpillar on hawthorn flowers

Dieback
Plant slowly wilts, browns and dies, starting at branch tips. Can be caused by wide range of disease organisms, cultural problems and nutrient deficiencies.
What to Do. Keep plants healthy by providing optimal growing conditions. Cut off dead tips below dead sections.

Fire Blight
Highly destructive bacterial disease of the rose family, which includes crabapple, cherry, pear, cotoneaster, hawthorn, kerria and serviceberry. Infected areas appear to have been burned. Look for bent twig tips (resembling a shepherd's hook), branches that retain leaves over winter and cankers on plant's lower parts. Disease usually starts at young tips and kills its way down stems.
What to Do. Choose resistant plant varieties. Remove and burn infected parts, making cuts at least 60 cm (24") below infected areas. Sterilize tools after each cut on infected plant. Pollinating birds and insects may reinfect plants through flowers, so wholly infected plants must be removed and burned.

Galls
Unusual swellings of plant tissues (leaves, buds, flowers, fruit, stems or trunks) caused by insects or diseases. Often a specific gall affects a single genus or species.
What to Do. Cut out and destroy galls. Insect galls, which usually contain eggs and juvenile forms, are more unsightly than damaging to the plant; control insects before they lay eggs; otherwise, remove and destroy galls before young insects emerge. Galls caused by disease often require destruction of plant; avoid placing other susceptible plants in same location.

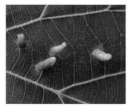
Poplar galls

Grey Mould (*Botrytis* Blight)
Fungal disease. Grey fuzz coats affected surfaces; leaves, flowers or fruit may blacken, rot and die. Common on dead plant matter and on damaged or stressed plants in cool, damp, poorly ventilated areas.
What to Do. Thin out stems for better air circulation; keep mulch away from base of plant, particularly in spring when plant starts to sprout; remove debris from garden in fall; do not overwater. Remove and destroy infected plant parts.

Grubs
Larvae of various beetles. Commonly found underground; usually curled in a "C" shape; white or grey body with white, grey, brown or reddish head. Problematic in lawns; may feed on shallow roots of trees and shrubs. Plant wilts despite regular watering; may pull easily out of ground in severe cases.
What to Do. Throw any grubs found onto a stone path or patio for birds to devour; apply parasitic nematodes or

milky disease spore to infested soil (ask at your local garden centre).

Leafhoppers & Treehoppers

Small, wedge-shaped, green, brown, grey or multi-coloured insects; jump around frantically when disturbed. Suck juice from plant leaves; cause distorted growth; carry diseases such as aster yellows. Treehoppers also damage bark when they slit it to lay eggs.
What to Do. Encourage predators by growing nectar-rich species such as yarrow. Wash insects off with strong spray of water; spray insecticidal soap (see p. 75) or neem oil.

Leaf Miners

Tiny, stubby, yellow or green larvae of some butterflies and moths. Tunnel within foliage, leaving winding trails; tunneled areas are lighter in colour than rest of leaf. Unsightly rather than health risk to plant.
What to Do. Remove debris from area in fall to destroy overwintering sites; attract parasitic wasps with nectar plants such as yarrow.

Leaf miner damage

Remove and destroy infected foliage.

Leaf Rollers

see Caterpillars

Leaf Scorch

Yellowing or browning of leaves begins at tips or edges. Most often caused by drought or heat stress but can also be caused by bacteria.
What to Do. Water susceptible plants during droughts and avoid planting them where excessive heat reflects from pavement or buildings. For bacterial leaf scorch, remove plant and replace with resistant species. To help prevent or ameliorate bacterial leaf scorch: control the insect carriers (leafhoppers and spittlebugs) of scorch bacteria; prune out

scorched shoots as soon as symptoms appear; inject bactericide into the trunk of lightly damaged specimens; fertilize and irrigate as appropriate.

Leaf Spot

Bacterial: small, brown or purple speckles grow to encompass entire leaves; leaves may drop. *Fungal*: black, brown or yellow spots and withering leaves; e.g., black spot, scab, tar spot.
What to Do. Bacterial infection is more severe—must remove entire plant. For fungal infection, remove and destroy infected plant parts; sterilize removal tools; avoid wetting foliage or touching it when wet; remove and destroy debris at end of growing season; spray compost tea (see p. 75) on leaves.

Mealybugs

Tiny crawling insects related to aphids; appear covered with white fuzz or flour. Sucking damage stunts and stresses plant; excreted honeydew promotes sooty mould.
What to Do. Remove by hand on small plants; wash plants with soap and

water; wipe with alcohol-soaked swabs; remove heavily infested leaves; encourage or introduce natural predators such as mealybug destroyer beetle (note: the larvae of this beetle resemble very large mealybugs) and parasitic wasps; spray with insecticidal soap (see p. 75) or horticultural oil.

Powdery mildew

Mildew

Two types, both fungal, but with slightly different symptoms. *Downy mildew*: yellow spots on upper sides of leaves and yellow, white or grey downy fuzz on undersides. *Powdery mildew*: white or grey powdery coating on leaf surfaces that doesn't brush off.

What to Do. Choose resistant cultivars; space plants well; thin out stems to encourage air circulation; tidy any debris in fall. Remove and destroy infected leaves or other parts. For downy mildew, spray foliage with mixture of 75 mL (5 tbsp.) horticultural oil, 10 mL (2 tsp.) baking soda and 4.5 L (1 gal.) water; apply once a week for three weeks. For powdery mildew, spray foliage with compost tea (see p. 75) or very dilute fish emulsion (5 mL to 1 L [1 tsp. per 1 qt.] of water).

Mites

Tiny red, yellow or green, eight-legged relatives of spiders that do not eat insects but may leave fine webbing on leaves and stems; almost invisible to the naked eye; usually found on undersides of plant leaves; e.g., bud mites, spider mites, spruce mites. Suck juice out of leaves, which become discoloured and speckled, then turn brown and shrivel up.

What to Do. Wash off with strong spray of water daily until all signs of infestation are gone. Introduce predatory mites, available at garden centres. Spray plants with insecticidal soap (see p. 75), or spray horticultural oil at a rate of 75 mL to 4.5 L (5 tbsp to 1 gal.) of water; if necessary, spray again in a month or so.

Mosaic
see Viruses

Needle Cast
Fungal disease causing premature needle drop. Spotty yellow areas turn brown; infected needles drop up to a year later.

What to Do. Ensure good air circulation. Clean up and destroy fallen needles; prune off damaged growth. To prevent recurrence, treat plants with Bordeaux mix (a fungicide available at garden centres) twice, two weeks apart, as candles elongate the next spring.

Nematodes
Tiny, translucent worms of various kinds; some, such as predatory and decomposer nematodes, can be beneficial; others damage plants. *Foliar* and *stem*: yellow spots on leaves turn brown; leaves shrivel and wither; lesions appear on stems; problem starts low on plant and works upward. *Root-knot*: plant is stunted and may wilt; yellow spots appear

on leaves; roots have tiny bumps or knots.
What to Do.
Mulch soil; mix in organic matter; clear garden debris in fall; avoid wetting leaves; don't touch wet foliage of infested plants. Can add parasitic nematodes to soil. In extreme cases, remove infested plants.

Psyllids
Plant lice; treat as for aphids (see Aphids).

Rot
Various fungi and bacteria that cause decay of various plant parts; can be fatal. *Crown rot*: affects base of plant; stems blacken and fall over; leaves yellow and wilt. *Heart rot* (wood rot): decays a tree's heartwood; damage often evident only after high winds bring down branches or whole tree. *Root rot*: leaves turn yellow; plant wilts; when dug up, plant shows roots rotted away.
What to Do. Keep soil well drained; avoid damaging plant while working around it; keep mulches away from plant base. Destroy completely infected plants; replant area with different, rot-resistant species or cultivars.

Rust
Fungi. Pale spots on upper leaf surfaces; fuzzy or dusty orange spots on leaf undersides; e.g., blister rust, cedar-apple rust, cone rust.
What to Do.
Choose rust-resistant varieties and cultivars; avoid handling wet leaves; provide plant with good air circulation; clear up garden debris in fall. Remove and destroy infected plant parts. A late-winter application of lime-sulfur can delay infection the following year.

Sawflies
see Caterpillars

Scab
see Leaf Spot

Scale Insects (Scale)
Tiny, shelled insects that suck sap, weakening and possibly killing plant or making it vulnerable to other problems. Juvenile scale insects (crawlers) are mobile, but once a female scale insect pierces a plant with her mouthparts, she stays there for life.
What to Do. Spray water to dislodge crawlers; wipe adults off using alcohol-soaked swabs. Prune off heavily infested branches. Encourage natural predators and parasites. Spray dormant oil in spring before budbreak.

Skeletonizers
see Beetles

Large slug on leaf

Slugs & Snails
Mollusks with slimy, smooth skin; snails have conspicuous, spiral shells, whereas slugs do not; to 20 cm (8") long; grey, green, black, beige, yellow or spotted. Can leave large, ragged holes in foliage and silvery slime trails on and around plants.
What to Do.
Attaching strips of copper to wood around raised beds or to smaller boards placed around susceptible plants will shock them. Pick off by hand in evening and squish with boot or drop in soapy water. Spread wood ash or diatomaceous earth (available

from garden centres—do not use the kind meant for swimming pool filters) around plants; it will pierce their soft bodies and cause dehydration. Lay damp cardboard on ground in evening, then dispose of it and resting slugs in morning. A shallow dish of beer may be effective. Used according to directions, slug baits containing iron phosphate control slugs without harming humans or animals. If slugs damaged your garden late in season, begin controls as soon as green spring shoots appear.

Sooty Mould
Fungus. Thin, black film on leaf surfaces reduces light available to plant.
What to Do. Wipe mould off leaf surfaces; control aphids, mealybugs and whiteflies (their honeydew excretions encourage sooty mould).

Tar Spot
see Leaf Spot

Thrips
Slender insects with narrow, fringed wings; yellow, black or brown. Difficult to see; may be visible if you disturb them by blowing gently on infested flower. Suck plant juices, particularly in flowers and buds, which results in mottled petals and leaves, dying buds and distorted and stunted growth.
What to Do. Remove and destroy infested plant parts; encourage native predatory insects with nectar plants such as yarrow; spray severe infestations with insecticidal soap (see p. 75) or neem oil according to directions. Use blue sticky cards to prevent recurrence. Horticultural oil controls adult thrips.

Viruses
May stunt plants and distort, streak or discolour leaves and flowers. Examples: ash yellows, mosaic virus, ringspot virus.
What to Do. Control disease-spreading insects such as aphids, leafhoppers and whiteflies. Infected plants cannot be treated and must be destroyed.

Weevils
see Beetles

Whiteflies
Tiny, moth-like, white flying insects; live on leaf under-

Mosaic virus

sides; flutter up into air when disturbed. Suck juice out of leaves, causing yellowed foliage and weakened plants; sticky honeydew excretions encourage sooty mould.
What to Do. Destroy weeds inhabited by whiteflies. Attract native predatory beetles and parasitic wasps with nectar plants such as yarrow and sweet alyssum. Make a sticky, flypaper-like trap by mounting a tin can on a stake, wrapping it with yellow paper and covering it with a clear plastic bag smeared with petroleum jelly—discard and replace bag when covered in flies. Spray severe cases with insecticidal soap

(see p. 75); apply horticultural oil.

Wilt
If watering doesn't help a wilted plant, one of two wilt fungi may be to blame. *Fusarium wilt*: plant wilts, leaves turn yellow then die; symptoms generally spread from one part of plant. *Verticillium wilt*: plant wilts, leaves curl up at edges, turn yellow and may drop off; plant may die. Also see Grubs, Nematodes, Rot.
What to Do. Wilt fungi are difficult to control. Choose resistant varieties; clean up debris in fall. Destroy infected plants; solarize (sterilize) soil before replanting (this may help if you've lost an entire bed of plants) —contact your garden centre for assistance; replant with resistant plants.

Witches'-Broom
Twigs become densely clustered together, broom-like, with many dying back in winter. Caused by various microorganisms or insects, on many types of plants. Fungal brooms afflict cherry (*Prunus*) and blackberry (*Rubus*). A virus causes witches'-broom on black locust. Aphids cause honeysuckle witches'-broom. The phytoplasma organisms that cause elm or ash yellows can also cause witches'-broom.
What to Do. Cut out affected portions. Determine the cause and improve plant's growing conditions.

Woolly Adelgids
see Aphids

Worms
see Caterpillars, Nematodes

Pest & Disease Control Recipes

Compost 'Tea'
Mix 500–1000 g (1–2 lb.) of high-quality, fungally dominated compost in 22 L (5 gal.) of water. Let sit for four to seven days, then strain out solids and return them to compost bin. Store liquid out of direct sunlight. For use, dilute until it resembles weak tea. Use during normal watering or apply as a foliar spray to prevent or treat fungal diseases. Do not use this on plants you intend to eat. High-quality compost tea is available commercially in Alberta.

Horticultural Oil
Mix 75 mL (5 tbsp.) horticultural oil per 4.5 L (1 gal.) water and apply as a spray for a variety of insect and fungal problems. If purchased, follow package directions.

Insecticidal Soap
Mix 5 mL (1 tsp.) mild dish detergent or pure soap (biodegradable options are available) with 1 L (1 qt.) water in a clean spray bottle. Spray surfaces of insect-infested plants. Rinse well within one hour of spraying to avoid foliage discolouration.

About This Guide

The trees and shrubs in this book are organized alphabetically by common name. Alternative common names and scientific names are given beneath the main headings and in the index. The illustrated Trees & Shrubs at a Glance (pp. 5–9) allows you to become familiar with the different plants quickly, and it will help you find a tree or shrub if you aren't sure what it's called.

Clearly displayed at the beginning of each entry are the plant's special features, height and spread ranges normally expected in our landscapes, preferred planting forms (balled-and-burlapped, container or bare-root), optimal planting seasons and plant hardiness zones (see map, p. 15).

Our favorite species, hybrids and cultivars are listed in each entry's Recommended section. Many more types are often available, so check with your local garden centre. Some cultivated varieties are known only by the cultivar name proper, shown in single quotation marks (e.g., 'Little Gem'); others are known instead or also by a trade name registered by a particular company. Trade names are shown in small capitals (e.g., BLACK LACE). For all plants, we present the most commonly used name first, with any alternative names following in parentheses.

Where height, spread and hardiness zones not indicated in the Recommended section, use the information under the main heading. The ranges at the beginning of each entry always encompass the measurements for all plants listed in the Recommended section.

Common pests and problems, if any, are also noted for each entry. Consult the Problems & Pests section of the introduction (pp. 64–75) for information on how to address these problems.

The Quick Reference Chart at the back of the book (pp. 320–325) is a handy guide to planning a diversity of features, forms, foliage types and blooming times in your garden.

We refer to seasons only in a general sense. Keep in mind the timing and duration of seasons in your particular area when planning your garden. Hardiness zones, too, can vary locally; consult your local extension agent, horticulturist or garden centre.

The Trees
& Shrubs

Ash

Fraxinus

Features: fall colour, adaptable, fast growing **Habit:** upright or spreading deciduous tree **Height:** 4.5–15 m (15–50') **Spread:** 4.5–10.5 m (15–35') **Planting:** B & B, container, bare-root; spring or fall **Zones:** 2–8

ASHES ARE HANDSOME, VERSATILE, LARGE SHADE TREES. In a large yard, few large deciduous trees surpass an ash for century-long beauty; just be sure to plant it a good distance from the back or side of the house. Be aware that because of the confusing nature of common names, a mountain ash is not an ash; the mountain ash is genus *Sorbus* (p. 224), whereas true ash trees are *Fraxinus*.

Growing

Ashes grow best in **full sun**. Young plants tolerate partial shade. The soil should be **fertile** and **moist,** with plenty of room for root growth. Tolerating drought, poor soil, salt and pollution, these trees adapt to a wide range of conditions, but they are least susceptible to problems when grown in ideal conditions. *F. americana* is more ornamental but less adaptable than *F. pennsylvanica*.

Little pruning is required. Remove dead, damaged, diseased and wayward branches as needed.

Tips

Ashes are popular, quick-growing shade trees. They grow well in the moist soil alongside streams and ponds. *F. americana* is quite large and is best used in spacious areas such as parks.

F. pennsylvanica (both photos)

Recommended

F. americana (white ash) is a large, wide-spreading tree that grows to 12–13.5 m (40–45') tall and 7.5–9 m (25–30') wide. The fall colour ranges from yellow to purple. **'Autumn Blaze'** is a large tree with an oval crown. It was developed in Morden, Manitoba, for the prairies. It bears green foliage that turns purple in fall and has few seeds. (Zones 3–8)

F. **'Mancana'** is a seedless selection with an oval crown. It grows 12–13.5 m (40–45') tall and 6–9 m (20–30') wide. The green foliage turns brilliant yellow in fall. (Zones 3–8)

F. nigra (black ash) is an upright tree with a narrow, open crown.

In gardens, it grows 10.5–12 m (35–40') tall and 6–7.5 m (20–25') wide, but it can grow to about three times larger in the wild. It occurs in naturally wet areas and bogs and performs best in these types of conditions. **'Fallgold'** is a seedless selection, growing 9–10.5 m (30–35') tall and 4.5–6 m (15–20') wide. The disease-resistant leaves turn golden yellow in fall and persist longer than on most other ashes. **'Major's Gold'** is similar to 'Fallgold' but grows only 3–4.5 m (10–15') wide. (Zones 2–7)

F. **'Northern Treasure'** is a cross between *F. nigra* and a hardy Asian species, *F. mandshurica*. It was also developed at Canada's Morden Research Station to grow in the cold prairies. It grows 9–10.5 m (30–35') tall and 4.5–6 m (15–20') wide. The green foliage turns yellow to orange in fall. This selection yields minimal seeds. (Zones 3–8)

F. americana 'Autumn Blaze' (above)

F. pennsylvanica (green ash, red ash) is an irregular, spreading tree. It grows 12–18 m (40–60') tall and 7.5–9 m (25–30') wide. The foliage turns yellow, sometimes with orange or red, in fall. **'Johnson'** (LEPRECHAUN™) is a dwarf of the species, growing only 4.5–6 m (15–20') tall and wide. It has a dense, oval to rounded crown and is a low water user. **'Patmore'** is a superior, disease-resistant, seedless selection with a large, oval crown. It has bright green foliage and grows 13.5 m (45') tall and 10.5 m (35') wide. **'Rugby'** (PRAIRIE SPIRE®) is a hardy, seedless selection. It forms a narrowly pyramidal to oval outline. The foliage is glossy dark green, and the young bark is lightly orange tinged. **'Summit'** is a neat, upright tree. It grows up to 13.5 m (45') tall and spreads about 7.5 m (25'). It becomes bright yellow in fall. (Zones 3–8)

F. pennsylvanica (both photos)

Problems & Pests

Among the many possible problems are rust, leaf spot, canker, dieback, borers, leaf miners, sawflies, webworm, flower gall, scale insects, ash yellows and powdery mildew. The emerald ash borer is a devastating insect. If this imported pest becomes established, it could mean serious problems for all of our ash trees.

Although these trees are susceptible to many problems, healthy trees grown in good conditions are resistant to insect infestation and fungal diseases.

The prized wood of ash has been shaped into tool handles, spears and bows. Baseball enthusiasts will recall the deeply satisfying sound made when Babe Ruth hit his electrifying home runs with ash bats.

Barberry
Berberis

Features: foliage, spring flowers, fruit, spines **Habit:** deciduous shrub
Height: 30 cm–1.75 m (1–6') **Spread:** 45 cm–1.75 m (18"–6') **Planting:** container;
spring or fall **Zones:** 4–8

THE GREAT JOY OF LANDSCAPING WITH SHRUBS LIES IN THE
exploration of the seemingly endless variations in foliage form, texture and
colour. Few shrub families reward this examination as generously as barberries. Whether they are carrying interest throughout a home's foundation
planting or adding season-long colour, height and structure to the perennial
garden, barberries are an essential addition to northern landscapes. The
sturdy, often shiny leaves range from dark green or yellow to red or purple.
When planted in a curving line and sheared, barberries make a good low
deciduous hedge. Pretty much the only objection raised by some homeowners
is that most varieties possess sharp barbs that can prick the skin.

*Extracts from the rhizomes of
Berberis have been used to
treat rheumatic fever and other
inflammatory disorders, as well as
the common cold.*

Growing

Barberries develop the best fall colour when grown in **full sun,** but they tolerate partial shade. Any **well-drained** soil is suitable. These plants tolerate drought and urban conditions but suffer in poorly drained, wet soil.

Barberries respond well to heavy pruning. They make excellent hedges and should be trimmed after they bloom. A plant in an informal border can be left alone or can be lightly pruned. Remove old wood and unwanted suckers in mid- to late winter. Remove dead wood in summer.

Tips

Large barberry plants make excellent hedges with formidable prickles. Barberries can also be included in shrub or mixed borders. Small cultivars can be grown in rock gardens, in raised beds or along rock walls.

B. thunbergii 'Crimson Pygmy'

Recommended

***B*. x 'Tara'** (EMERALD CAROUSEL™) is a rounded shrub with arching branches. It grows 1.25–1.5 m (4–5') tall and wide and has dark green foliage. The foliage turns reddish purple in fall, sooner than on many other barberries. The showy fruit is bright red.

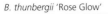

B. thunbergii 'Rose Glow'

B. *thunbergii* cultivar

B. *thunbergii* 'Aurea'

B. thunbergii (Japanese barberry) is a dense shrub with a broad, rounded habit. It grows 90 cm–1.5 m (3–5') tall and spreads 1.25–1.75 m (4–6'). The bright green foliage turns variable shades of orange, red or purple in fall. In summer, glossy red fruit follow the yellow spring flowers. **'Bailgreen'** (JADE CAROUSEL™) is a dense, rounded shrub 90 cm (36") tall and 90 cm–1.25 m (3–4') wide, with jade green foliage. **'Bailone'** (RUBY CAROUSEL™) is a rounded shrub 90 cm–1.5 m (3–5') tall and wide with purple foliage that turns red-purple in fall. **'Concorde'** is a dwarf cultivar with purple foliage. It grows about 45 cm (18") tall. **'Crimson Pygmy'** ('Atropurpurea Nana') is a dwarf cultivar with reddish purple foliage. It grows 45–60 cm (18–24") tall and spreads up to 90 cm (36"). **'Monlers'** (GOLDEN NUGGET™) is a dense, compact plant 30 cm (12") tall and 45 cm (18") wide. Its bright golden yellow foliage develops a good orange fall colour. **'Rose Glow'** has purple foliage variegated with white and pink splotches. It grows 1.5–1.75 m (5–6') tall. **'Sunsation'** is a compact, vasiform shrub 90 cm–1.25 m (3–4') tall and wide, with bright chartreuse foliage in spring that turns more golden with age.

Problems & Pests

Healthy barberries rarely suffer from problems, but stressed plants can be affected by leaf spot, spider mites, aphids, weevils, root rot, wilt, mosaic or scale insects.

Because some barberry species harbour the overwintering phase of the devastating wheat rust fungus, some regions had banned all Berberis. *Many of these regions are now lifting the ban on certain species, including* B. thunbergii, *which have never been proven to harbour the fungus.*

B. thunbergii 'Concorde'

B. thunbergii 'Rose Glow'

Bearberry
Kinnikinnick
Arctostaphylos

Features: late-spring flowers, fruit, foliage **Habit:** low-growing, mat-forming evergreen shrub **Height:** 10–15 cm (4–6") **Spread:** 20 cm–1.25 m (8"–4')
Planting: container; spring or fall **Zones:** 2–7

BEARBERRY IS A TOUGH, MOUNTAIN PLANT AND CAN TOLERATE soil conditions that would cause other plants to fail. It prefers sandy, infertile settings, but being a member of the heath family, whose members include blueberries and rhododendrons, it needs the soil to be amended to a neutral to acidic condition.

This plant's alternative common name, kinnikinnick, is said to be an Algonquian term meaning "smoking mixture," reflecting a traditional use for the leaves.

Growing

Bearberry grows well in **full sun** or **partial shade.** The soil should be of **poor to average fertility, well drained, neutral to acidic** and **moist.** Bearberry adapts to most soils. Generally no pruning is required.

Tips

Bearberry can be used as a ground cover or can be included in a rock garden. Once established, it is a vigorous, wide-spreading grower, but it can be slow to get started. Use mulch to keep the weeds down while the plant is becoming established.

Recommended

A. *uva-ursi* is a low-growing native shrub that grows 10–15 cm (4–6") tall and spreads 20–50 cm (8–20"). White flowers appear in late spring, followed by berries that ripen to bright red. The cultivars share the white flowers and red fruit but also have leaves that turn bright red in winter. **'Vancouver Jade'** has arching stems; it grows 15 cm (6") high and spreads 45 cm (18"). This cultivar is resistant to the leaf spot that can afflict bearberry.

Problems & Pests

Possible problems include bud and leaf galls as well as fungal diseases of the leaves, stems and fruit.

At first glance you might mistake bearberry for a cotoneaster, but bearberry hugs the ground closely and has small, urn-shaped flowers.

A. uva-ursi (both photos)

Beauty Bush
Kolkwitzia

Features: late-spring flowers **Habit:** suckering deciduous shrub **Height:** 1.75–2.75 m (6–9') **Spread:** 1.75–2.75 m (6–9') **Planting:** container; spring or fall **Zones:** 4–8

ZONE 4 PLANTS ARE BEING TRIED AND GROWN MORE AND MORE in Alberta, and beauty bush is one that puts on a grand show when it comes into bloom. The whole shrub is covered in flowers. Beauty bush tends to fade into the background after it finishes blooming. Not so with DREAM CATCHER. The golden-hued foliage is wonderful from spring to fall, and you still get the late-spring flower show. Well worth trying.

Growing

Beauty bush flowers most profusely in **full sun**. DREAM CATCHER does best in filtered sunlight or **partial shade** because its yellow foliage may suffer in full sun. The soil should be **fertile** and **well drained**. This shrub prefers an acidic soil but adapts to soils of various pH levels.

Prune out one-third of the old wood each year after flowering is complete. Old, overgrown plants can be cut right back to the ground if they need rejuvenation.

Tips

Beauty bush is used in shrub borders and woodland gardens. It can be grown as a specimen, especially in a decorative container where the pH of the soil is more easily controlled.

Recommended

K. amabilis is a large shrub with arching branches. Clusters of bell-shaped pink flowers are borne in late spring or early summer. DREAM CATCHER ('Maradco') has bronze-tipped, golden yellow foliage that turns golden-orange in fall, and bears light pink flowers in spring. It can grow 1.75–2.75 m (6–9') tall and wide.

Problems & Pests

Beauty bush is resistant to most pests and diseases, but it may get aphids or leaf spot.

Please remember that DREAM CATCHER *and other patented plants cannot be propagated and sold without a licence.*

K. amabilis (above & below)

The name Kolkwitzia *honours Richard Kolkwitz, a German professor of botany;* amabilis, *appropriately, is Latin for "lovely."*

Birch

Betula

Features: foliage, fall colour, habit, bark, winter and early-spring catkins **Habit:** open deciduous tree **Height:** 3.75–15 m (12–50') **Spread:** 3–7.5 m (10–25') **Planting:** B & B, container; spring or fall **Zones:** 2–8

FOR FOUR-SEASON INTEREST (never forget that we have long winters up here), birch trees are important small to mid-sized deciduous trees to plant, grow and enjoy. In winter, the sculptural form and attractive bark are tremendous landscape assets.

Some people make birch syrup from the sap of sweet birch. The heavy flow of sap in spring is tapped, and the sap is boiled down in the same way that maple sap is for maple syrup.

Growing

Birches grow well in **full sun, partial shade** or **light shade.** The soil should be of **average to rich fertility, moist** and fairly **well drained.** Some birch species naturally grow in wet areas, such as along streams, but don't like to grow in places that remain wet for prolonged periods. Provide supplemental water to all birches during periods of extended drought.

Minimal pruning is required. Remove any dead, damaged, diseased or awkward branches as needed. Any pruning of live wood should be done in late summer or fall to prevent the excessive bleeding of sap.

Tips

Birch trees are generally grown for their attractive, often white and peeling bark. The bark contrasts nicely with the dark green leaves in summer and with the glossy red or chestnut-coloured younger branches and twigs in winter. Yellowish catkins dangle from the branches in early spring.

These trees are often used as specimens. With their small leaves and open canopy, birches provide light shade that allows perennials, annuals or lawns to flourish beneath them. Birch trees are also attractive when grown in groups near natural or artificial water features. Most varieties need quite a bit of room to grow, though upright varieties such as 'Chickadee' and 'Fargo' serve small spaces well.

B. pendula is common and popular but its weeping cultivars are poor

B. nigra

B. papyrifera

B. papyrifera

choices for gardens because of their susceptibility to pests and diseases, particularly the fatal bronze birch borer. If you plan to grow or already have one of these trees, consult a tree specialist to begin a preventive program.

Recommended

B. **'Crimson Frost'** is an upright tree with a broad crown that does well in heavy clay soil. It grows 7.5–10.5 m (25–35') tall and 3–6 m (10–20') wide and has exfoliating white bark with cinnamon hues. The deep reddish purple foliage varies from crimson to orange-yellow in fall. It is interesting but is prone to borers. (Zones 4–7)

B. nigra (black birch, river birch) is an upright tree with an oval crown. It grows 4.5–7.5 m (15–25') tall, 3.75–5.5 m (12–18') wide and has shaggy, cinnamon brown bark that flakes off in sheets when it is young but thickens and becomes ridged as it matures. River birch is disease resistant and also resists bronze birch borer. (Zones 3–8)

B. papyrifera (canoe birch, paper birch) has creamy white bark that peels off in layers, exposing cinnamon-coloured bark beneath. It grows to about 9–12 m (30–40') tall and 4.5–7.5 m (15–25') wide, and dislikes hot summer weather. **'Chickadee'** is a slow-growing, dense, narrowly pyramidal tree that has exceptionally white bark. It grows 9–12 m (30–40') tall and 4.5–7.5 m (15–25') wide, and is quite narrow when young. (Zones 2–7)

B. pendula (European white birch) is an upright, pyramidal to rounded tree with graceful, arching branches. It generally grows to a height of 12–15 m (40–50') but can grow taller in ideal conditions. The tree spreads about half the height. **'Laciniata'** ('Dalecarlica') has more pendulous branches than the species, and the foliage is deeply cut. **'Youngii'** is a small, dome-shaped specimen that grows 3.75–6 m (12–20') tall and 6–7.5 m (20–25') wide, and has interesting, weeping branches. It is often grafted as a standard.

***B. platyphylla* 'Fargo'** (DAKOTA PINNACLE) is a columnar, heat-tolerant selection with glossy, dark green foliage that turns yellow in fall. It grows 9–12 m (30–40') tall and 2.5–4.5 m (8–15') wide and is resistant to bronze birch borer. (Zones 3–7)

Problems & Pests

The bronze birch borer is a destructive insect that can quickly kill weakened trees. It is drawn to white-barked forms. Dieback in the top branches indicates that the insect has

B. nigra

done its damage. Tree-care companies may be able to stave off the tree's demise but not if wilting is already observed.

Aphids love birch trees. Other potential problems include birch skeletonizers, leaf miners and tent caterpillars.

Birch trees were once a common part of spring fertility rituals in Europe. The maypole, for example, was often a skinned birch.

B. pedula 'Youngii'

Bittersweet

Celastrus

Features: fast growth, fruit, fall colour **Habit:** deciduous twining vine or sprawling groundcover **Height:** 3 m (10') **Spread:** 90 cm–1.75 m (3–6') **Planting:** B & B, container; spring, fall **Zones:** 2–8

BITTERSWEET IS A ROUGH-AND-TUMBLE, LOW-MAINTENANCE, vining shrub with a wilder appearance than other plants in the landscape. The plant's chief attribute is its highly decorative fruit, which bursts forth in clusters in fall. Lengths of vine with fruit attached are commonly used in dried flower arrangements. Look for *C. scandens* 'Indian Brave/Maid' (male and female are sold together); these two cultivars are likely your best choice. They grow up to 6 m (20') tall and have proven hardy to Zone 2.

Growing

Bittersweet grows well in **full sun** and tolerates partial shade. It adapts to almost any **well-drained** soil. Poor soil is preferred because rich soil can create a monster. American bittersweet needs little to no pruning.

Male and female flowers usually bloom on separate plants. For assured fruit production, in addition to regular watering, both males and females need to be planted close together, so they are often sold together in one pot.

Tips

Bittersweet is a great choice for the edge of a woodland garden or in naturalized areas. It can quickly cover old trees, fences, arbours, trellises, posts and walls. Used as a groundcover, it can mask piles of rubble and old tree stumps. It also effectively controls erosion on hard-to-maintain slopes.

Be careful—the vines can girdle the stems of young trees or shrubs, sometimes damaging or killing them.

Recommended

C. scandens (American bittersweet, staff vine) is a vigorous, twining vine with glossy, dark green foliage that turns bright yellow in fall. With solid support, it can climb to 3 m (10') or more. Small, undistinguished, yellow-green to whitish flowers bloom in late spring. The showy fruit has bright red arils surrounding the orange seeds. The male and female pair of **'Indian Brave'** and **'Indian Maid'** ('Indian Maiden') grow to 3 m (10') tall and are hardier than the species.

C. scandens (above & below)

Problems & Pests

Aphids, leafhoppers, scale, canker, fungal leaf spot and powdery mildew can be occasional problems for bittersweet.

All parts of bittersweet are said to be poisonous. However, the inner bark was used as an emergency food by some Native cultures, and other plant parts were used as medicine. The fruits are winter food for grouse, pheasant, quail, rabbits and squirrels.

Black Locust
False Acacia
Robinia

Features: foliage, flowers, fast growth, spiny branches **Habit:** open deciduous tree **Height:** 2.5–15 m (8–50') **Spread:** 3–12 m (10–40') **Planting:** B & B, container; spring or fall **Zones:** 3–8

HERE IS ANOTHER TREE SPECIES MAKING AN INROAD IN THE Alberta gardening world. The species itself may not be available, so look for the cultivars. It is perhaps not the best tree for the front yard, but if you need a tough customer for a disturbed or recently flooded site, black locust may work. Its dense wood is good for the fireplace.

Growing

Black locust prefers **full sun**. It does best in **average to fertile, moist** soil but adapts to any soils that aren't constantly soggy. It tolerates infertile or salty soils, drought and pollution. Avoid growing this tree in exposed locations because heavy wind can cause the weak branches to break.

It is best to train black locust trees when they are young. Prune young trees to have a central leader and well-spaced branches. Remove suckers as well as branches that will form a narrow crotch. Large cuts on *Robinia* species do not heal well and should be avoided. Prune in late summer to avoid excessive bleeding.

Tips

Black locust is best used in difficult situations, where other trees have failed to thrive. It can also be used in shelterbelts and as a firewood source.

All parts of this tree contain poisonous proteins. The bean-like seeds should never be eaten.

Recommended

R. pseudoacacia is an upright, suckering and self-seeding deciduous tree. It generally grows 9–15 m (30–50') tall and 6–12 m (20–40') wide, likely towards the shorter, narrower end of the range here in Alberta. It has deeply furrowed bark and produces dangling clusters of fragrant white flowers in early summer. **'Frisia'** has golden yellow foliage that turns yellow-green in summer and orange-gold in fall. **'Purple Robe'**

B. pseudoacacia 'Frisia'

Black locust has been used to reforest waste areas, such as mine spoils, where few other trees could survive.

has pinky purple flowers. TWISTY BABY ('Lace Lady') is a small, often grafted selection with contorted and twisted branches. It grows 2.5–3 m (8–10') tall and 3–4.25 m (10–14') wide and produces few to no flowers. The twisted branches make a good winter garden feature.

Problems & Pests

Even though this tree is outside of its natural range, it can still experience problems. Locust borer is the most troublesome but is not likely to be found outside of its natural range. Occasional problems may occur with caterpillars, leaf miners, scale insects, twig borers, weevils, whiteflies, canker, leaf spot, powdery mildew, root and heart rot, *Verticillium* wilt and witches' broom virus.

Blueberry
Vaccinium

Features: mid-spring to early-summer flowers, fruit, foliage **Habit:** bushy deciduous shrub **Height:** 30 cm–1.5 m (1–5') **Spread:** 60 cm–1.5 m (2–5') **Planting:** container; spring, fall **Zones:** 3–7

BLUEBERRIES CAN BE CHALLENGING SHRUBS TO GROW IN Alberta; many of our soils are slightly alkaline and require a good deal of amendment to provide the conditions blueberries love. You can enjoy abundant white spring flowers, appealing, glossy green summer foliage, fiery orange, red or purple fall foliage and the added bonus of homegrown fruits if you have (or can create) acidic soil in a spot that receives full-day sun.

The edible, deliciously tart berries of Vaccinium *species can be used to makes pies, syrups and wines.*

Growing

Blueberries grow best in **full sun** but tolerate partial shade. The soil should be **peaty, acidic, moist** (especially when producing fruit) and **well drained**. Blueberries are frost hardy.

Little pruning is required. Deadhead the shrubs after flowering unless you want the berries.

Tips

Blueberries can be used in a woodland garden or in a shrub or mixed border. Some people grow them just for the fruit and include them in the vegetable garden or with other fruit-bearing plants. Planting two different varieties together provides better cross-pollination and fruit production.

Recommended

V. corymbosum 'Northland' (highbush blueberry, swamp blueberry) is an upright, dense, well-branched shrub that grows 90 cm–1.5 m (3–5') tall and wide. It has bright green foliage that turns orange in fall. It produces hanging clusters of white, sometimes pink-tinged, flowers in late spring to early summer. The fruit is spherical, small, dark blue and wild tasting.

V. **Half-High Hybrids** are hybrids of *V. angustifolium* and *V. corymbosum* that were developed at the University of Minnesota and can handle our cold winters. **'Northblue'** is a compact shrub with abundant large, dark blue fruit. It grows 50–75 cm (20–30") tall and 75–90 cm (30–36") wide. It has glossy, dark green foliage

V. corymbosum 'Northland'

and is a vivid deep red in fall. **'Northcountry'** grows 45–60 cm (18–24") tall and 75 – 90 cm (30"–36") wide. The dark green foliage turns bright red and orange in fall. The sky blue fruit is mild and sweet. **'Northsky'** is a small, compact plant that grows 30–45 cm (12–18") tall and 60–90 cm (24–36") wide. It has glossy, dark green foliage that turns dark red in fall. Its sweet fruit is sky blue.

Problems & Pests

Occasional problems with caterpillars, scale insects, grey mould, leaf gall, bud gall, crown rot, root rot, powdery mildew or rust are possible but not frequent.

Bog Rosemary
Marsh Rosemary
Andromeda

Features: foliage, flowers **Habit:** low-growing evergreen shrub **Height:** 30–60 cm 12–24") **Spread:** 60–90 cm (24–36") **Planting:** container; spring, fall **Zones:** 2–6

BOG ROSEMARY IS A TRAGICALLY UNDERUSED SMALL SHRUB that is slowly gaining popularity. Its chief asset is wonderful, powder blue foliage that retains its colour all season. The plant's low stature and naturally mounded form make it ideal for use as a front-of-the-border accent plant in foundation plantings, and it can be effective in rock gardens. Bog rosemary is perfectly hardy across the coldest areas of our region and possesses extremely attractive, light pink, urn-shaped flowers that persist over several months in early summer.

In Greek mythology, Andromeda was the daughter of Cassiopeia. She angered Poseidon and was chained to a rock in the ocean—an isolation reminiscent of wild bog rosemary, which grows on moss hummocks in a boggy "sea."

Growing

Bog rosemary grows well in **full sun** or **light shade**. The soil should be **high in organic matter, acidic, moist** and **well drained**.

It is not winter's cold, but the heat and humidity of summer that will most likely adversely affect this shrub; give it light shade in a cooler area to protect it from summer heat if your garden tends to get hot and humid.

Tips

Include this pink- or white-flowered plant in a rock garden or woodland garden, by a water feature or as a groundcover underneath other acid-loving shrubs.

Do not make a tea with or otherwise ingest bog rosemary—it contains andromedotoxin, which can lower blood pressure, disrupt breathing and cause cramps and vomiting.

Recommended

A. polifolia is an attractive plant that bears light pink flowers in late spring and early summer. It grows 30–60 cm (12–24") tall and spreads up to 90 cm (36"). The thick, leathery foliage is dark green. **'Blue Ice'** has icy, slate blue foliage and light pink flowers. Growing 30–40 cm (12–16") tall, it reaches a width of 90 cm (36").

Problems & Pests

Bog rosemary rarely suffers from any pests or diseases.

A. polifolia (above & bottom)

'Blue Ice' (centre)

Boxwood

Buxus

Features: foliage, habit **Habit:** dense, rounded evergreen shrub
Height: 60–90 cm (24–36") **Spread:** equal to height or slightly more
Planting: B & B, container; spring **Zones:** 4–8

ALTHOUGH I AM NOT TOTALLY CONVINCED THAT BOXWOODS
are hardy in Alberta, they are worth trying. Boxwoods are good deciduous
shrubs for clipping into low, dense, formal hedges, and for singular placement
in both foundation and perennial beds. Some gardeners forego the shears and
allow these typically small, rounded, densely foliated shrubs the chance to
grow jagged and wild.

Growing

Boxwoods prefer **partial shade** but adapt to full shade or to full sun if kept well watered. The soil should be **fertile** and **well drained**. Once established, boxwoods are drought tolerant. They can exhibit a low tolerance of extremes of heat and cold, and may do best in a sheltered spot.

Do not disturb the earth around boxwoods once they are established because their roots are close to the surface. Using mulch is beneficial.

Boxwoods can sprout new growth from old wood. Plants that have been neglected or are growing in a lopsided manner can be cut back hard in spring. By the end of summer, the exposed areas will have filled in with new green growth.

Tips

A slow rate of growth and small, densely packed leaves that form an even surface place boxwoods among the most popular plants for creating topiary. When left unpruned, boxwood shrubs form attractive, rounded mounds. They make excellent background plants in a mixed border. Brightly coloured flowers show up well against the even, green surface. Dwarf cultivars can be trimmed into small hedges for edging garden beds or walkways and are a good choice for containers.

Boxwood foliage contains toxic compounds that, when eaten, can cause severe digestive upset.

B. m. 'Green Velvet' (above & below)

Recommended

B. microphylla* var. *koreana* x *B. sempervirens cultivars have been developed, and some have inherited the best attributes of each parent—hardiness and pest resistance on the one hand and attractive foliage year-round on the other. **'Green Velvet'** is a hardy cultivar developed in Canada. It has glossy foliage and a rounded habit, growing up to 90 cm (36") in height and spread.

Problems & Pests

Leaf miners, mites, psyllids, scale insects, leaf spot, powdery mildew and root rot can affect boxwoods.

The wood of Buxus, *particularly the wood of the root, is very dense and fine grained, making it valuable for carving. Its common name arises from its use for ornate boxes.*

Buffaloberry

Shepherdia

Features: showy fruit, silvery to reddish brown scales, attractive bark and foliage **Habit:** rounded to upright deciduous shrub **Height:** 90 cm–4.75 m (3–16') **Spread:** 90 cm–3.75 m (3–12') **Planting:** container, bare-root; spring or fall **Zones:** 3–8

BUFFALOBERRIES ARE TOUGH, NATIVE SHRUBS that are an excellent choice for plantings that are low maintenance and use little water. They are also quite attractive with their silvery scales and attractive bark, and with judicious and gentle pruning, they can be lovely specimens.

Birds enjoy the fruit of buffaloberries. The spines don't stop them.

Growing

Buffaloberries grow well in **full sun to partial shade** in **well-drained, moisture-holding** soils, and prefer slightly alkaline, calcitic soils. They adapt to most soil conditions. Plants tolerate poor, dry soils, winds and salt spray.

Minimal pruning is required, but the shrubs can be pruned for shaping in late winter to early spring while the plants are still dormant. Be cautious and avoid the spines.

Tips

Buffaloberries can be used for informal hedges and windbreaks, and as screening. They are good for naturalizing, and silver buffaloberry can be used for erosion control. With their toughness, buffaloberries are worth trying as container shrubs.

Buffaloberries can fix nitrogen in the soil, which helps provide for their nutrient requirements as well as those of other close-by plants. Plants are dioecious, so male and female plants must be grown in close proximity if you want the fruit.

Recommended

S. argentea (silver buffaloberry) is a large, spiny, rounded to upright shrub that has kinked, spreading branches and fine, silvery leaves with silver-brown scales. It grows 1.75–3.75 m (6–12') tall and 3–3.75 m (10–12') wide, and can form thickets. The small and somewhat inconspicuous pale yellow flowers bloom in early spring. The scarlet red berries are edible but sour and also have silvery scales.

S. argentea (above & below)

S. canadensis (Canada buffaloberry, russet buffaloberry) is a dense, rounded shrub that grows 90 cm–1.75 m (3–6') tall and wide with upright stems and dark green leaves that have silvery undersides with red-brown scales. The early spring flowers are light yellow-green, and the inedible fruit is bright red with silvery scales. The branches and twigs also have reddish brown scales.

Problems & Pests

There are no significant problems.

Bush Honeysuckle
Diervilla

Features: habit, flowers, foliage, adaptability **Habit:** low, thicket-forming decidu-ous shrub **Height:** 90 cm–1.25 m (3–4') **Spread:** 90 cm–1.5 m (3–5') **Planting:** container; spring through fall **Zones:** 3–8

BUSH HONEYSUCKLE IS AN EXCELLENT CHOICE FOR NATURALIZING the spaces under a mature tree canopy, and its shallow, fibrous root system works well anywhere soil erosion is a problem. The small, trumpet-shaped, yellow flowers that appear in midsummer won't knock your socks off, but the attractive bronze-green foliage (often turning red in fall) and fast growing pace make bush honeysuckle a good choice for massing across large areas and for transitioning from lawn to woodlands.

Growing

Bush honeysuckle grows best in **full sun** or **partial shade** but tolerates full shade. Any **well-drained** soil will do. This shrub tolerates dry, rocky soil.

Pruning is rarely required, but the plant can be cut back to within 15–30 cm (6–12") of the ground in early spring as the buds begin to swell.

Tips

Bush honeysuckle is hard to beat for difficult and low-maintenance locations. Often used to stabilize banks or to fill in hot, dry flowerbeds close to the house, this plant can also be added to mixed or shrub borders or to woodland gardens.

Recommended

D. lonicera (bush honeysuckle, northern bush honeysuckle) is a low, suckering shrub. It grows 90 cm–1.25 m (3–4') tall and spreads 90 cm–1.5 m (3–5') or more. Small, yellow flowers are borne in midsummer.

D. lonicera

Problems & Pests

Although these easy-care shrubs rarely suffer any problems, poor air circulation can encourage powdery mildew.

The bush honeysuckles used to be grouped with Weigela *but have recently been assigned to their own genus.*

D. sessifolia 'Butterfly'

Caragana
Caragana

Features: late-spring flowers, foliage, habit **Habit:** prickly, weeping (grafted) or upright to rounded deciduous shrub **Height:** 60 cm–6 m (2–20') **Spread:** 90 cm –5.5 m (3–18') **Planting:** container, B & B, bare-root; spring or fall **Zones:** 2–8

CARAGANAS ARE "TOUGH-AS-NAILS" PLANTS THAT DO WELL IN our province. *C. arborescens* is often seen in shelterbelts and may not be the most ornamental shrub one could plant; however, its cultivars and related species are worthy of consideration. *C. frutex* 'Globosa' is a fine, small shrub, and though it cannot be counted on to flower each year, this is not a problem if the idea is to keep it clipped as a low hedge. Its bluish green foliage holds up well throughout the growing season, which cannot be said of all caraganas.

Growing

Caraganas prefer **full sun** and soil of **average to high fertility.** These plants adapt to just about any growing conditions, and they tolerate dry, exposed locations, especially *C. pygmaea. C. frutex* grows in all but very wet soils.

Prune out awkward or damaged shoots as needed to maintain a neat shape. Rejuvenate unruly or overgrown plants by pruning them to within 15 cm (6") of the ground. To control the spread of a weeping specimen that has been grafted, you can prune back to near the graft at the top of the main trunk; if you prune below the graft, the weeping habit will be lost.

C. arborescens 'Walker'

Caraganas bear pea-like pods that ripen to brown in summer. Hear them rattle in the wind in late summer, and listen for popping sounds as they burst.

Tips

Caraganas are grown as windbreaks and as formal or informal hedges. They can be included in borders, and weeping forms are often used as specimen plants. *C. pygmaea* is an excellent low-barrier plant.

C. arborescens 'Sutherland'

Recommended

C. arborescens (common caragana, Siberian peashrub) is a large, twiggy, thorny shrub that grows up to 5.5 m (18') tall and spreads up to 4.5 m (15'). The branches may be upright or arching. Yellow, pea-like flowers are borne in late spring. **'Lorbergii'** has fine, fern-like foliage with narrow leaflets and narrower flowers than the species. **'Pendula'** has long, weeping branches. It is generally grafted to a standard that may be 90 cm–1.75 m (3–6') in height; the spread is equal or greater.

C. arborescens

C. pygmaea

'Sutherland' is a narrow plant with many upright, unbranched stems. Weeping forms are often grafted onto it. 'Walker' is a similar weeping form with fine, feathery foliage.

C. frutex (Russian peashrub) is an upright, spreading, suckering shrub about 1.75 m (6') tall and 1.25–1.5 m (4–5') wide. It rarely produces spines and has finer foliage than *C. arborescens*. It is not as attractive to pests as the other peashrubs listed here. It bears yellow flowers in late spring and early summer. 'Globosa' develops a rounded form that is branched to the base. It grows 90 cm (36") tall and wide.

C. microphylla (little-leaf peashrub) is similar to but smaller and more dense than *C. arborescens*. It is a spiny, upright, rounded plant that grows 1.75–3 m (6–10') tall and wide. The leaflets are smaller and shinier than those of *C. arborescens*, and turn yellow in fall. When mature, this species is drought tolerant. 'Silver Spires' has fern-like, silvery green foliage and is more upright than the species, growing 2.5–3 m (8–10') tall and 1.25–1.5 m (4–5') wide. It has showy yellow flowers and red seedpods.

C. pygmaea (pygmy caragana) is a dense, mounding, spiny plant 60–90 cm (24–36") tall and 1.25–1.75 m (4–6') wide. It displays yellow blooms in late spring and early summer. (Zones 3–8)

C. 'Roborovskyi' (*C. roborovskyi*) develops a globe form that bears silver-green foliage and bright yellow late-spring flowers. It is available as a

grafted standard that grows 1.25–
2.5 m (4–8') tall and 90 cm–1.25 m
(3–4') wide.

Problems & Pests

The foliage can be somewhat prone
to black spot, particularly during
moist or humid summers. Aphids,
spider mites and leafhoppers may
disfigure young foliage but are generally not a problem.

*The tough, durable caraganas are
native to Siberia and Mongolia.
They are a good choice for difficult
locations and regions, such as
anywhere in Alberta. Because
caragana roots fix nitrogen in the
soil, these plants have been used
in soil-improvement programs.*

C. arborescens (above & below)

Cedar
Arborvitae
Thuja

Features: foliage, bark, form **Habit:** small to large evergreen shrub or tree
Height: 30 cm–9 m (1–30') **Spread:** 30 cm–4.5 m (1–15') **Planting:** B & B,
container; spring or fall **Zones:** 2–8

FEW EVERGREEN GENERA OFFER SUCH A WIDE VARIETY IN
height, growth habit and colouration as *Thuja*, and, once established, these
plants suffer little winter burn, making them even more appealing to Alberta
gardeners. Be aware that when grown in partial shade, they can become loose
and somewhat wispy over time. Try to provide five solid hours of direct sunlight daily.

*Crush some cedar foliage between
your fingers to enjoy the wonderful
aroma. Be cautious, though, if you
have sensitive skin—the pungent
oils may irritate.*

Growing

Cedars prefer **full sun**. The soil should be of **average fertility, moist** and **well drained**. These plants enjoy humidity and are often found growing near marshy areas. Cedars perform best in locations with some **shelter** from the wind, especially in winter when the foliage can easily dry out, giving entire plants a rather drab brown appearance.

T. occidentalis cultivars (all photos)

These plants take well to pruning and are often grown as hedges. Although they may be kept formally shaped, they are also attractive if clipped to maintain a loose but compact shape and size.

Tips

Large varieties of cedar make excellent specimen trees, and smaller cultivars can be used in foundation plantings, shrub borders and formal or informal hedges.

Deer enjoy eating the foliage of *T. occidentalis*. If deer are a problem in your area, you may wish to avoid using this plant.

Recommended

In the wilds of the American Midwest and northeastern states, *T. occidentalis* often grows to about 18 m (60') tall and 3–4.5 m (10–15') wide. In cultivation in Alberta, it grows to about half this size or less. The following cultivars may be slightly less cold hardy than the species. **'Brandon'** is a dense, columnar plant with medium to dark green foliage. It grows 3–5.5 m (10–18') tall and 90 cm–1.25 m (3–4') wide

T. occidentalis 'Skybound' (above)

T. occidentalis 'Emerald' (below)

and does best with protection from drying winds. **'Emerald'** ('Smaragd') can grow 3–4.5 m (10–15') tall, spreading about 1.25 m (4'). This cultivar is small and cold hardy; the foliage does not lose colour in winter. **'Gold Champion'** has yellow foliage and grows about 90 cm (36") tall, with an equal spread. **'Golden Globe'** has a dense, rounded habit with golden-tipped foliage that turns slightly bronze in winter. It grows 60–90 cm (24–36") tall and wide. **'Holmstrup'** is small and upright, with whorls of tightly compact foliage. It grows 1.75–3 m (6–10') tall and 60–90 cm (24–36") wide. **'Little Gem'** is a globe-shaped dwarf with dark green foliage. It grows 90 cm (36") tall and 1.25–1.75 m (4–6') wide. **'Little Giant'** is a rounded, bright green cultivar. It grows 60–90 cm (24–36") tall, with an equal spread. **'Skybound'** is another dense, columnar selection that grows 3–5.5 m (10–18') tall and 90 cm–1.25 m (3–4') wide. It bears lustrous dark green foliage and is quite hardy.

'**Techny**' is a hardy cultivar with a broad, pyramidal form. It grows 3–6 m (10–20') tall and 1.5–2.5 m (5–8') wide and keeps its bluish green colour all winter. '**Teddy**' has feathery, blue-green foliage that turns purple to bronze in winter. It grows 30–45 cm (12–18") tall and 30–60 cm (12–24") wide. '**Wareana**' is a broadly pyramidal, well-branched plant that has thick, dark green to blue-green foliage that can develop a purple sheen in winter. It grows 1.5–3 m (5–10') tall and wide. '**Woodwardii**' is a globe form that grows 90 cm–1.5 m (3–5') tall and wide.

Problems & Pests

Leaf miners, red spider mites, scale insects, blight, canker and heart rot are possible, albeit infrequent, problems. Leaf miner damage may resemble winter browning—hold branch tips up to the light and look for tiny caterpillars feeding inside. Trim and destroy infested foliage before June.

T. occidentalis 'Little Gem'

Many diverse cedar cultivars are available, from pyramidal forms that make excellent specimens, or yellow types that add colour to the winter landscape, to dwarf, globe-shaped forms for the mixed border or rock garden.

T. occidentalis 'Techny'

Cherry
Plum, Almond
Prunus

Features: spring to early-summer flowers, fruit, bark, fall foliage **Habit:** upright, rounded, spreading or weeping deciduous tree or shrub **Height:** 60 cm–12 m (2–40') **Spread:** 60 cm–12 m (2–40') **Planting:** B & B, container, bare-root; spring **Zones:** 2–8

THIS LARGE GENUS OF TREES INCLUDES MANY EDIBLE "STONE" fruits—apricots, peaches and nectarines, plus those drawing our attention here: cherry, plum and almond. Most are native to the Northern Hemisphere, and a few varieties thrive in even the coldest portions of Alberta. Although not all bear edible fruit (birds likely have a different viewpoint), the plants mentioned below have numerous terrific uses. Compact sizes, wonderful forms, breathtaking spring blooms and vivid fall colours make these trees and shrubs worth much consideration.

Growing

These plants prefer **full sun** and **moist, well-drained** soil of average fertility. Plant them on shallow mounds when possible to encourage drainage. Shallow roots will come up from the ground if the trees aren't getting enough water.

Most plants listed here need little or no pruning when grown individually. Simply remove damaged growth and wayward branches. Specific pruning requirements are noted below. Most pruning should take place after flowering is complete and the leaves have fully emerged.

Tips

These trees and shrubs make beautiful specimens. Many are small enough to include in almost any garden. Use small species and cultivars in borders, or group to form informal hedges or barriers. *P. fruticosa*, *P. tomentosa* and *P.* x *cistena* can be trained as hedges.

Cherries can be short-lived. If you plant a pest-susceptible species, enjoy it while it thrives but be prepared to replace it once problems surface.

Recommended

P. besseyi (western sand cherry) is an erect to prostrate shrub that grows 60 cm–1.25 m (2–4') tall and wide, bearing small clusters of white flowers in early to mid-spring and spherical to slightly oblong, black to red-yellow fruit. Fall foliage is reddish orange. This shrub tolerates hot, dry conditions and is an effective plum pollinator. Prune one-third of the old wood to the ground each year and remove wayward suckers. (Zones 3–8)

P. virginiana 'Schubert'

P. x *cistena* (purple-leaf dwarf plum, purple-leaf sand cherry) is an upright shrub that grows 90 cm–1.75 m (3–6') high, with an equal or lesser spread. It has deep purple leaves, mid- to late-spring, fragrant, white or slightly pink flowers and purple-black fruit. (Zones 3–8)

P. 'Evans' is a small tree with dark green foliage that grows 3–4.5 m (10–15') tall and 2.5–3.75 m (8–12') wide. It has white flowers in spring

P. tomentosa

P. pensylvanica (above & below)

followed by bright red, semi-sweet, edible fruit in mid- to late summer. **'Evans'** and **'Carmine Jewel'** can be pruned minimally if grown strictly for ornamental purposes. The University of Saskatchewan suggests that the plants can be pruned in late winter to early spring before the plants break dormancy to encourage growth for good fruit production. Thin the branches so fruit is accessible for harvest and so that sunlight can reach it, but remove no more than 25% of the branches per year. Keep the weeping branches; those are the ones most likely to have good fruit production. (Zones 3–8)

P. fruticosa (Mongolian cherry; *P. eminens*) is a rounded shrub that grows 90 cm–1.25 m (3–4') tall and wide and has attractive, glossy, dark green foliage. Allow room for growth because it spreads well by suckers. This shrub has white blooms in spring and produces tart, dark red edible fruit. Prune one-third of the old wood to the ground each year and remove wayward suckers. (Zones 3–8)

P. x kerrasis **'Carmine Jewel'** is a University of Saskatchewan Department of Plant Sciences introduction. It is a hardy, multi-stemmed, rounded shrub that grows 1.75–2.5 m (6–8') tall and wide, with dark green foliage. It bears white flowers in spring and tart, dark red, edible fruit in mid-summer. New USask *P. x kerrasis* releases to look for include **'Crimson Passion,' 'Cupid'** and **'Juliet.'**

P. maackii (Amur chokecherry) is a rounded to broadly pyramidal, single to multi-stemmed tree that grows

7.5–10.5 m (25–35') tall and wide.
Fragrant, white, mid-spring flowers
give way to red fruit that ripens to
black. The peeling, glossy reddish
to golden brown bark provides year-
round interest. GOLDRUSH ('Jefree')
has a more upright growth habit,
reaching 7.5 m (25') tall and 6 m (20')
wide. It has more resistance to frost-
cracking of the bark than the species.
(Zones 2–6)

P. mandshurica (Manchurian apricot; *P. armeniaca* var. *mandshurica*) is
a small, frost-resistant tree with a
rounded, spreading crown. It grows
4.5–6 m (15–20') tall and wide, bearing pale pink flowers in spring, and
spherical, red-yellow fruit. **'Westcot'**
(*P.* x 'Westcot') is a good apricot
hybrid for the Prairies. It has large,
mild, sweet tasting, yellow fruit with
a light red blush that is ripe in mid- to
late summer. (Zones (3)4–8)

P. nigra (Canada plum) is an upright
tree with a narrow, oval-shaped
crown. It grows 4.5–6 m (15–20')
tall and 3–4.5 m (10–15') wide,
producing small clusters of white,
sometimes pink-tinged, flowers. The

P. x cistena

grey, plate-like bark flakes off like
scales. The fruit is yellow-red to red.
'Princess Kay' grows 3–4.5 m (10–15')
tall and 2.5–3.75 m (8–12') wide and
has fragrant, white, double flowers. It
produces little or no fruit but blooms
freely at a young age. The bark is
dark red-brown to almost black,
with contrasting white lenticels. Fall
foliage is orange to red. (Zones 2–6)

P. x cistena

P. nigra 'Princess Kay' (above)
P. tomentosa (below)

P. x *nigrella* '**Muckle**' (muckle plum) is an oval to rounded shrub with upright branches and attractive dark green foliage that turns a wonderful orange in fall. It grows 3–4.5 m (10–15') tall and 2.5–3 m (8–10') wide and bears vivid pink flowers that come from bright red buds. It is a hybrid of *P. nigra* and *P. tenella*. (Zones 3–8)

P. padus var. *commutata* (mayday) is a large, rounded, spreading tree that grows 9–12 m (30–40') tall and wide. The new leaves are bright to bronzy green, maturing to dark green and turning red or yellow in fall. Cylindrical, slightly drooping clusters of fragrant white flowers bloom in spring, followed by small, glossy black fruit. '**Ethel**' is a slightly smaller selection and has pink flowers. (Zones 3–8)

P. pensylvanica (pin cherry) is a fast-growing tree with a rounded, spreading crown and yellow to red fall colour. It grows 4.5–6 m (15–20') tall and 3–4.5 m (10–15') wide and has attractive, peeling, reddish orange bark. Small clusters of white flowers in mid- to late spring yield small, light red fruit that birds enjoy. This species likes very moist soil, performing well by streams and in light boggy conditions. (Zones 2–6)

P. tenella (Russian almond) is an upright suckering shrub with medium to dark green foliage with orangey fall colour. It grows 90 cm–1.5 m (3–5') tall and wide, and bears rose pink to deep pink flowers in early spring followed by showy tan to red fruit in summer. Because of its suckering habit, the best use for this shrub is in natural settings where it can form thickets. (Zones 2–7)

P. tomentosa (Nanking cherry) grows 1.75–2.5 m (6–8') tall and wide. It has pink buds that yield fragrant, white flowers in mid-spring and tart, edible, bright red fruit in midsummer. The exfoliating, shiny, reddish bark is attractive in winter. Prune out some of the lower branches so the bark is more visible, or leave the branches to gracefully sweep the ground. (Zones 2–7)

P. x triloba **'Multiplex'** (double-flowering plum) is an upright, spreading shrub that grows 1.75–3 m (6–10') tall and wide and has three-lobed, dark green foliage that turns orange in fall. It has abundant, showy, light to medium double pink flowers in early spring before the leaves emerge. The plant is hardy to Zone 2, but the flower buds are not.

P. virginiana (chokecherry) is a small, suckering tree with an oval, rounded or pyramidal crown and dark green foliage. It grows 4.5–7.5 m (15–25') tall and wide. Small, dense clusters of white flowers bloom in late spring, followed by small, red fruits that mature to purple. **Var. *melanocarpa*** ('Melanocarpa') has black fruit. **'Midnight'** is a non-suckering selection that has deep purple foliage. **'Schubert'** is a more pyramidal selection whose dark green leaves turn dark red-purple in summer.

Problems & Pests

Aphids, borers, caterpillars, leafhoppers, mites, nematodes, scale insects, canker, crown gall, fire blight, powdery mildew and viruses can be problematic. Root rot can occur in poorly drained soils.

P. tomentosa

Cut some cherry stems in February, mash the bottom ends with a hammer and arrange them in a vase indoors for an early burst of fragrant blooms.

P. virginiana 'Schubert'

Chokeberry

Aronia

Features: flowers, fruit, fall foliage **Habit:** suckering deciduous shrub
Height: 90 cm–1.75 m (3–6') **Spread:** 90 cm–2.5 m (3–8') **Planting:** container,
bare-root; spring or fall **Zones:** 3–8

CHOKEBERRIES ARE TOUGH, EASY-TO-GROW SHRUBS WITH MANY
attractive features, and they deserve to be widely used in our landscapes.
Chokeberries have shiny, dark green foliage, good fall colour, fragrant, lovely
white flowers, attractive, glossy fruit and a handsome, upright form.

*High in vitamins, especially vitamin C,
chokeberry fruit is used as a local
(alternative to citrus in parts of Russia.*

Growing

Chokeberries grow well in **full sun** or **partial shade,** with the best flowering and fruiting and strongest branches in full sun; in partial shade the weight of the fruit may cause the branches to splay downward. The soil should be of **average fertility** and **well drained,** but these plants adapt to most soils and generally tolerate poor, wet or dry soil. *A. arbutifolia* 'Brilliantissima' prefers moist to wet soil.

Up to one-third of a mature chokeberry's oldest stems can be pruned out annually.

Tips

Chokeberries are useful in a shrub or mixed border. They also make interesting, low-maintenance specimens. Left to their own devices, they can colonize a fairly large area.

Recommended

A. arbutifolia *(Photinia floribunda;* aronia, red chokeberry) is an upright shrub, 90 cm–1.75 m (3–6') tall and 90 cm–1.25 m (3–4') wide, with white flowers in late spring and persistent, waxy, bright red fruit. Shades of orange and red colour the fall leaves. **'Brilliantissima'** has bright red fall foliage.

A. melanocarpa (black chokeberry) is an upright, suckering

Too bitter even for birds unless fermented, chokeberry fruit usually persists all winter. Copious amounts of sugar are needed when making jam or juice.

A. melanocarpa

shrub that grows 90 cm–1.75 m (3–6') tall and 1.75–2.5 m (6–8') wide, bearing white flowers in late spring and early summer. Ripening in fall, the dark fruit persists through winter. The foliage turns red to purplish red in fall. **'Autumn Magic'** has bright red to purple fall foliage. IROQUOIS BEAUTY ('Morton') is a compact cultivar just 90 cm (36") tall and slightly wider than it is tall.

Problems & Pests

Major problems are rare, but fungal leaf spot is possible.

Cotoneaster
Cotoneaster

Features: foliage, early-summer flowers, persistent fruit, variety of forms **Habit:** deciduous groundcover or shrub **Height:** 15 cm–3 m (6"–10') **Spread:** 1.25–3 m (4–10') **Planting:** container; spring, fall **Zones:** 2–8

TALL VARIETIES OF COTONEASTERS HAVE BEEN POPULAR HEDGE plants in Alberta for generations, but when it comes to relatively low-growing, horizontal deciduous shrubs, there are few alternatives better than the short, spreading varieties. *C. adpressus* features wonderful, bluish green groundcover foliage that turns a rich red in fall. For tall hedges, the classic *C. lucidus* takes to shearing well, and it can be planted only 45 cm (18") apart. The absence of suckering adds to the value of cotoneasters when used for hedges; the width is up to you, not the plant. Attractive red to black fruit is a prime feature of all cotoneasters.

C. x 'Hessei'

Growing

Cotoneasters grow well in **full sun** or **partial shade**. The soil should be of **average fertility** and **well drained**.

Although pruning is rarely required, these plants tolerate even hard pruning. Prune cotoneaster hedges in mid- to late summer to see how much you can trim off while still leaving some of the ornamental fruit in place. Hard pruning encourages new growth and can rejuvenate plants that look worn out.

Tips

Cotoneasters can be included in shrub or mixed borders. The low spreaders work well as groundcovers, and shrubby species can be used to form hedges. Some low growers are grafted onto standards and grown as small weeping trees.

Although cotoneaster berries are not poisonous, they can cause stomach upset if eaten in large quantities. The foliage may be toxic.

Recommended

C. acutifolius (Peking cotoneaster) is a rounded to erect shrub with arching branches that grows 1.5–3 m (5–10') tall and wide. It has dull, grey green to dark green foliage, and it produces pink-tinged, white flowers in summer. The small, red fruit is egg-shaped. Fall turns the leaves orange-yellow. (Zones 4–8)

C. adpressus (creeping cotoneaster) is a low-growing, deciduous species that is used as a groundcover. It grows only 15–30 cm (6–12") high and spreads up to 2.5 m (8') wide. Red-tinged, white flowers are pro-

duced in summer. In fall, the foliage turns reddish purple and the fruit ripens to red. (Zones 3–6)

C. apiculatus (cranberry cotoneaster) is a deciduous species that forms a mound of arching, tangled branches. It grows about 60–90 cm (24–36") high and spreads up to 2.5 m (8'); sometimes it is available in a grafted tree form. Small, pink flowers bloom in late spring. The bright red fruit persists until winter. (Zones 4–7)

C. x 'Hessei' is a tidy, low-growing, deciduous cultivar with an irregular branching habit. It grows 30–60 cm (12–24") tall and spreads 1.5–1.75 m (5–6'). Dark pink flowers appear in late spring and are followed by fruit that ripens to bright red. The leaves turn burgundy in fall. This cultivar is resistant to spider mites and fire blight. (Zones 4–7)

C. acutifolius (above), *C. apiculatus* (below)

C. integerrimus (European cotoneaster) forms a dense, tangled mound of stems, 90 cm–1.5 m (3–5') tall and 1.25–1.75 m (4–6') wide. It has dull, dark green foliage and produces rose-tinged, white flowers in spring. It bears persistent, small, red to red-purple fruit. (Zones 2–7)

C. lucidus (hedge cotoneaster) is an erect to rounded shrub with glossy, dark green foliage and superb yellow to red fall colour. It grows 1.5–2.5 m (5–8') tall and is usually slightly less wide. Small, pink-tinged, white flowers appear in mid- to late spring and are followed by small, persistent, shiny black fruit. This species is an excellent hedge plant and also looks great when left in its natural form. (Zones 2–7)

Problems & Pests

These plants experience occasional attacks of pear slugs, fire blight and silver leaf. Lace bugs, scale insects, slugs, snails, spider mites, canker, powdery mildew or rust can also affect cotoneasters.

C. acutifolius (above)

C. lucidus (below)

Try a mix of low-growing cotoneasters as a bank planting or use a shrubby type as a foundation plant.

Crabapple
Malus

Features: spring flowers, late-season and winter fruit, fall foliage, habit, bark **Habit:** small to medium, rounded, mounded or spreading deciduous tree **Height:** 2.5–10.5 m (8–35') **Spread:** 90 cm–9 m (3–30') **Planting:** B & B, container; spring, fall **Zones:** 2–8

OF ALL THE ORNAMENTAL TREES, CRABAPPLES ARE THE MOST popular with northern gardeners. The available varieties range from small and compact to quite large, and their mid-May show of big, beautiful blooms is a joy to behold. Many crabapples fall into the small tree category, making them ideal for small yards and for multiple plantings throughout large properties. Many varieties introduced over the past 20 years have combined good winter hardiness with much improved disease resistance.

Growing

Crabapples prefer **full sun** but tolerate partial shade. The soil should be of **average to rich fertility, moist** and **well drained**. These trees tolerate damp soil.

Crabapples require little pruning but adapt to aggressive pruning. Remove damaged or wayward branches and suckers when necessary. Vertical branches should be removed because they won't flower as much as horizontal branches. The next year's flower buds form in early summer, so any pruning done to form the shape of the tree should be done by late spring, or as soon as the current year's flowering has finished.

Tips

Crabapples make excellent specimen plants. Many varieties are quite small, so there is one to suit almost any size of garden. Some forms are small enough to grow in large containers. The flexibility of the young branches makes crabapples good choices for creating espalier specimens along walls or fences.

If planted in full sun, crabapples mature into magnificent, fully rounded focal points of the landscape.

Many pests overwinter in the fruit, leaves or soil at the base of the tree, so one of the best ways to prevent the spread of crabapple pests and diseases is to clean up all the leaves and fruit that fall off the tree. Clearing away the pests' winter shelter helps keep their populations under control.

Recommended

The following are just a few suggestions from among the hundreds of crabapples available. When choosing a species, variety or cultivar, look for disease resistance. Ask for information about new resistant cultivars at your local nursery or garden centre.

All of the following crabapples flower in mid- to late spring, unless otherwise noted.

M. x *adstringens* (rosybloom crabapples) are upright, oval to rounded trees that grow about 4.5–6 m (15–20') tall and 3.75–4.5 m (12–15') wide unless noted otherwise. They are crosses between varieties of *M. baccata* and *M. pumila*. **'Kelsey'** bears semi-double pink flowers and persistent, dark purple fruit. The spring foliage is reddish, turning a bronze-green in summer. **'Pink Spires'** is a narrow, upright tree that grows 4.5–6 m (15–20') tall and 3–3.75 m (10–12') wide. It has dark lavender buds and lavender-pink flowers, which fade with age. The bright purple-red fruit is persistent. Tinged red in spring, the green foliage becomes bronzy in fall. **'Royalty'** is fire blight resistant and has red new growth that turns glossy dark purple in summer, then orange

Some gardeners use crabapple fruit to make preserves, cider or even wine.

in fall. Red-pink to red-purple flowers are followed by small, bright to dark red, persistent fruit. **'Selkirk'** is a fire blight resistant, rounded to vasiform tree that grows 6–7.5 m (20–25') tall and wide, bearing bronze green foliage and pink flowers, followed by persistent, bright red fruit. **'Strathmore'** has a more upright, narrow form and produces bronzy red foliage and rose-pink to red flowers. **'Thunderchild'** is another fire blight resistant selection that has dark purple foliage that turns orange yellow in fall. The rosy pink flowers are followed by small red fruit.

M. baccata is a hardy, rounded tree that grows about 6–7.5 m (20–25') tall and wide. The dark green foliage is lighter green underneath and turns yellow in fall. Abundant pink buds open to showy white flowers, followed by small, yellow to red fruit. This species is susceptible to fire blight. **'Columnaris'** has a narrow upright form, spreading 1.25–1.75 m (4–6') wide. (Zones 2–7)

M. **'Dolgo'** is a vigorous, hardy tree that grows 7.5–10.5 m (25–35') tall and 6–9 m (20–30') wide. The fragrant white flowers appear from light pink buds, and the tree may flower heavily only in alternate years. It has yellow fall foliage and bright purple-red fruits. It has fair to good disease resistance. (Zones 2–7)

M. **'DreamWeaver'** is a small, upright, columnar tree that grows 3 m (10') tall and 90 cm (36") wide and bears bright pink, spring flowers and small purple fruit in fall.

The attractive, glossy, dark bronze-green to purple foliage turns yellow in fall. (Zones 3–8)

M. **'Makamik'** is a rounded, spreading tree that grows 6–7.5 m (20–25') tall and 4.5–6 m (15–20') wide and has bronze foliage that arises from dark red flower buds. Fall colour is orange-yellow. The large, semi-double, rose pink to rose red flowers bloom early and are followed by abundant, persistent, showy purple-red fruit. 'Makamik' is pest and disease resistant. (Zones 3–8)

M. **'Morning Princess'** is a small, upright tree that grows 3–4.5 m (10–15') tall and wide, and has weeping branches. It bears pink-red flowers and has small, round, purple fruit. The semi-glossy, green-tinged purple foliage turns darker purple in fall.

M. **'Radiant'** is a rounded tree that grows 4.5–6 m (15–20') tall and

wide with reddish purple foliage that ages to bronzy green and turns orangey yellow in fall. It has dark red flower buds and fragrant, deep pink flowers, followed by small, persistent, bright to dark red fruit. It is resistant to scab.

M. 'Red Jade' is a small, graceful, rounded to spreading, weeping tree, growing 2.5–3.75 m (8–12') tall and 3.75–6 m (12–20') wide, with glossy, medium to bright green foliage that turns yellow in fall. It produces large, lightly pink-tinged, white flowers that arise from pink to rose-pink flower buds, and small, shiny, red to dark red fruit. This tree is resistant to cedar-apple rust, fire blight and mildew. It is hardy to the warmer parts of Zone 3. (Zones 3–8)

M. 'Royal Beauty' is a spreading, weeping tree with good disease resistance. It grows 3 m (10') tall and 3–4.5 m (10–15') wide, has bronze-red foliage and bears deep pink flowers followed by persistent, dark red fruit in fall. (Zones 3–8)

M. 'Snowcap' is an upright, rounded tree with medium green foliage that turns orange-yellow in fall. It grows 4.5–6 m (15–20') tall and 3.75–4.5 m (12–15') wide, and has white flowers that arise from red flower buds. The small red fruit persists into winter. (Zones 3–8)

M. 'Spring Snow' is a rounded, fruitless selection that grows 6–7.5 m (20–25') tall and 3–4.5 m (10–15') wide, bearing fragrant, bright white flowers. It has glossy, bright green foliage and is heat tolerant. (Zones 3–8)

Problems & Pests

Aphids, Japanese beetles, leaf rollers, leaf skeletonizers, scale insects and tent caterpillars are insect pests to watch for, but the damage is largely cosmetic. Leaf drop caused by apple scab is the most common problem with susceptible cultivars. Cedar-apple rust, fire blight, leaf spot or powdery mildew can also be problematic, depending on the weather.

To help your crabapples become the much-admired mature specimens that they are capable of being, be sure to properly prune them while they are young.

Currant

Ribes

Features: spring flowers, foliage, fruit **Habit:** upright deciduous shrub **Height:** 90 cm–1.75 m (3–6') **Spread:** 90 cm–1.75 m (3–6') **Planting:** container; spring, fall **Zones:** 2–7

CURRANTS ARE EUROPEAN NATIVE SHRUBS OFFERING MUCH OF value to northern gardeners. *R. alpinum* is a great choice for a dense, clipped, formal hedge or informal hedge. The larger species are great in a foundation planting, mixed beds and shrub beds. The selections with edible fruit have a place in your food gardens.

Growing

Currants grow well in **full sun to partial shade** in **moist, well-drained** soil of **average fertility** that is **rich in organic matter.** They tolerate drought. With these plants you should avoid overhead watering.

Unless you want fruit, cut each flowering shoot back to a strong bud or branch after flowering; up to one-third of the growth can be removed annually. Hedges can be trimmed back after flowering.

Tips

Currants can be used in shrub or mixed borders, or at the edge of a woodland garden. Alpine currant makes an excellent hedge, remaining branched to the ground.

The female flowers and showier male flowers of *R. alpinum* are borne on separate plants; you will need both if you want the fruits.

Recommended

R. alpinum (alpine currant) is a dense, bushy, rounded shrub, 90 cm–1.25 m (3–4') tall and wide, bearing early, bright green foliage, clusters of chartreuse flowers and persistent scarlet fruit. It tolerates shade and urban conditions.

R. aureum (golden currant) is an upright, open, 1.75 m (6') tall and wide shrub with slightly arching stems and mid- to blue-green foliage that turns red in fall. The spicy yellow flowers may be tinged red. The fruit is purple-black.

R. nigrum **'Consort'** is an upright, spineless shrub that grows 90 cm–1.75 m (3–6') tall and 90 cm–1.25 m (3–4') wide. It has dark green foliage that is odorous when bruised or crushed, and turns yellow, orange or red in fall. Hanging clusters of white flowers give way to round, sweet, black fruit that is high in antioxidants. It is self-fertile but will likely produce better when cross-pollinated. This cultivar is resistant to white pine blister rust. (Zones 3–7)

R. 'Pixwell' is a rounded to spreading gooseberry that grows 90 cm–1.25 m (3–4') tall and wide, and has small

R. alpinum

The edible red currants (R. rubrum) *produce mouth-watering fruit that can be eaten right off the bush or used for jellies, jams and pies.*

thorns and glossy green foliage. It bears green flowers that may be red-tinged, and abundant, sweet, juicy fruit that starts off green but turns purple when ripe. (Zones 3–7)

R. rubrum **'Red Lake'** is a vigorous, well-branched, mounding shrub, 90 cm–1.25 m (3–4') tall and wide. It bears large, bright translucent red fruit. A late frost may damage the flowers.

Problems & Pests

Anthracnose, aphids, caterpillars, dieback, downy mildew, leaf spot, powdery mildew, rust and scale insects can all be problematic. Some currants, including *R. aureum,* are alternate hosts for white pine blister rust, a devastating pine fungus, and are banned in many communities.

Daphne
Daphne

Features: foliage, fragrant spring flowers **Habit:** upright, rounded or low-growing evergreen, semi-evergreen or deciduous shrub **Height:** 15 cm–1.25 m (6"–4') **Spread:** 60 cm–1.25 m (2–4') **Planting:** container; early spring or early fall **Zones:** 4–7

ALTHOUGH DESERVING OF THEIR REPUTATION FOR BEING somewhat of a challenge to grow, daphnes are well worth the extra effort, even if just for their long, oval, variegated foliage and soft, dainty flowers. Daphnes highly deserve a place within the perennial garden or can be used as focal points near the front of shrub borders. The key to success in growing these shrubs is to prepare neutral to slightly alkaline soil that drains freely. Daphnes most often die because of overwatering, so it's best to water them once a week the first month after planting, then cut back to once every two weeks during periods of no rain. Once established, these plants prefer life on the dry side.

Growing

Daphnes grow best in **full sun** but tolerate partial shade. The soil should be of **average fertility** and **well drained**. Loose, sandy soils work well. Avoid overfertilizing or overwatering. A layer of mulch keeps the roots cool, and daphnes overwinter best when covered with a thick layer of snow or mulch.

The neat, dense growth needs little pruning. Remove damaged or diseased branches right away. Spent inflorescences can be removed, if desired, once flowering has finished. To preserve the natural growth habit of the shrub, cut the flowering stems back to where they join main branches.

Tips

Daphnes can be included in shrub or mixed borders. *D. cneorum* makes an attractive groundcover in a rock garden or woodland garden. Plant daphnes near paths, doors, windows or other places where the wonderful scent can be enjoyed.

Although generally considered hardy only to Zone 4, daphnes often thrive as smaller plants in even colder climates. They do, however, have a strange habit of dying suddenly, and experts have various theories to explain why. The best advice is to plant them in well-drained soil and then leave them alone. Avoid any disturbance that could stress the plants, and don't move them after they have been planted.

D. x *burkwoodii* 'Carol Mackie'

All parts of daphnes are toxic if eaten, and the sap may cause skin irritations. Avoid planting these species where children may be tempted to sample the berries.

Recommended

D.* x *burkwoodii (Burkwood daphne) is a semi-evergreen, upright shrub that grows 60 cm–1.25 m (2–4') in height and spread. It bears fragrant, white or light pink flowers in late spring and sometimes again in fall. **'Carol Mackie'** is a common cultivar; its dark green leaves have creamy margins.

D. cneorum (garland flower, rose daphne) is a low-growing, evergreen shrub. It grows 15–30 cm (6–12") tall and can spread up to 1.25 m (4'). The fragrant, pale to deep pink or white flowers are borne in late spring.

Problems & Pests

Aphids, scale insects, crown rot, root rot, leaf spot, twig blight and viruses can affect daphnes, and plants grown in poor conditions can be more susceptible to these problems. Diseased daphnes may wilt and die suddenly.

Dogwood
Cornus

Features: late-spring to early-summer flowers, fall foliage, fruit, habit
Habit: deciduous large shrub or small tree **Height:** 60 cm–4.5 m (2–15')
Spread: 60 cm – 4.5 m (2–15') **Planting:** B & B, container; spring to
summer **Zones:** 2–8

IT IS IMPORTANT TO DESIGN YOUR LANDSCAPE WITH A THOUGHT
toward the winter months because we have a relatively large number of days
falling between November 1 and April 30 when the only green is provided
by the evergreen conifers. Don't abandon ship in winter—grow dogwoods.
Red- and yellow-twigged varieties are a must in the north, giving much
needed colour to our white winter world. They happen to look good in
summer as well. *C. alternifolia* is a great choice for adding a focal point to a
moist, lightly shaded area. Although its bark is grey, the magnificent form
adds graceful elegance year-round.

Growing

Shrub dogwoods prefer **full sun** or **partial shade,** with the best stem colours developing in full sun. *C. alternifolia* prefers **light to partial shade**. The soil should be of **average to hig**h fertility, rich in organic matter, neutral to slightly acidic and well drained. Shrub dogwoods adapt to most soils but prefer moist soil. *C. sericea* tolerates wet soil.

C. alternifolia requires little pruning. Simply remove damaged, dead or awkward branches in early spring.

C. alba and *C. sericea*, which are grown for the colourful stems that are so striking in winter, need ongoing rejuvenation pruning to maintain a steady supply of colourful young growth. *C. racemosa* also responds well to rejuvenation pruning. A drastic, but effective, method to encourage new growth is to cut back all stems to within

C. alba IVORY HALO® (above), *C. alternifolia* (below)

C. alba 'Sibirica'

a few buds of the ground in early spring. To make up for the loss of the top growth, feed the plant once it starts growing. A less drastic approach is to cut back only the oldest branches (the ones that have lost the most colour) up to about one-third of the stems, to within a few buds of the ground early each spring.

Tips

C. alternifolia makes a wonderful specimen plant and is small enough to include in most gardens. Use dogwoods along the edge of a woodland garden, in a shrub or mixed border, alongside a house or near a pond, water feature or patio. Shrub dogwoods look best in groups rather than as single specimens.

Recommended

C. alba (red-twig dogwood, Tartarian dogwood, Tatarian dogwood) is a shrub grown for the bright red

C. alba 'Bud Yellow'

stems that provide winter interest; green all summer, they turn red as winter approaches. This species can grow 1.5–2.5 m (5–8') tall, with an equal spread. The cultivars generally grow 1.25–1.75 m (4–6') tall and wide. The species prefers cool climates and can develop leaf scorch and canker problems if the weather gets very hot. **'Argenteo-marginata'** ('Elegantissima') has grey-green leaves with creamy margins. **'Bud's Yellow'** has bright yellow stems and is disease resistant. **'Gouchaultii'** is usually wider than it is tall. It has green foliage with yellow margins that may have pink to purple tinges. IVORY HALO® ('Bailhalo') is a compact, rounded shrub with creamy white edges to its green foliage. **'Kesselringii'** has bronze-green foliage that turns red-purple in fall, and dark purple stems. **'Prairie Fire'** bears golden-yellow spring foliage that turns yellow-green in summer

C. sericea 'Cardinal'

C. alternifolia

and bright red in fall. The stems are orange-red. **'Sibirica'** (Siberian dogwood) has pinkish red to bright red winter stems. (Zones 2–7)

C. alternifolia (pagoda dogwood) has a rounded to spreading form and can be grown as a large, multi-stemmed shrub or a small tree with a single stem. It grows 3–4.5 m (10–15') tall and wide, but can grow larger in ideal conditions. The branches have an attractive layered appearance. Clusters of small, white flowers appear in early summer. This species prefers light shade. (Zones 3–8)

C. racemosa (gray dogwood) is an erect, multi-stemmed shrub that grows 2.5–3 m (8–10') tall and wide and spreads by rhizomes to form colonies. It has dark green foliage and attractive grey bark on mature stems. In late spring it bears abundant clusters of white flowers at the stem tips. (Zones 3–8)

C. sericea cultivar

C. racemosa

Use the strong horizontal branching of pagoda dogwood for contrast with vertical lines in the landscape.

C. sericea (*C. stolonifera;* red-osier dogwood, red-twig dogwood) is a widespread, vigorous native shrub that has bright red stems and spreads by stolons. It grows 1.75–3 m (6–10') tall, spreads up to 3.75 m (12') and bears clusters of small, white flowers in early summer. The fall colour is red or orange. **'Cardinal'** has pinkish red stems that turn bright red in winter. **'Flaviramea'** (yellow-twig dogwood) has bright yellow-green stems. **'Kelseyi'** is a compact, mounded to round selection that grows 60–90 cm (24–36") tall and wide. It has glossy, dark green foliage and red fall colour. **'Silver and Gold'** has variegated (white-and-green) leaves and yellow-green stems.

C. alba 'Sibirica'

Problems & Pests

The many possible problems include aphids, borers, leafhoppers, nematodes, scale insects, thrips, weevils, anthracnose, blight, canker, leaf spot, powdery mildew and root rot.

Piano keys and spindles have been made from the heavy, hard wood of some dogwoods.

C. sericea cultivars

Douglas-Fir

Pseudotsuga

Features: foliage, cones, habit **Habit:** conical to columnar (with age) evergreen tree **Height:** 12–18 m (40–60') **Spread:** 4.5–7.5 m (15–25') **Planting:** container; spring, fall **Zones:** 3–8

WHEN CHOOSING LARGE, DENSE EVERGREENS FOR YOUR YARD, give Douglas-fir serious consideration; at all stages of its growth, it is a majestic, beautiful tree. Douglas-fir possesses a more rugged, less uniform appearance than do spruce, particularly as it approaches maturity. A single specimen set a proper distance from the house is stunning, and its dense, billowy form plays well with spruce and pines when combined in large evergreen stands.

According to legend, the unique three-pronged bracts of Douglas-fir cones are the hind feet and tails of tiny mice trying to hide inside them.

Growing

Douglas-fir prefers **full sun**. The soil should be of **average fertility, acidic, moist** and **well drained,** but Douglas-fir adapts to most soils with good drainage. Pruning is generally not required.

Tips

The species can be grown as a single large specimen tree or in groups of several trees. The smaller cultivars can be grown in smaller gardens as specimens or as part of shrub or mixed borders. Purchase plants grown from local seed sources for the best performance.

Recommended

P. menziesii subsp. *glauca* (Rocky Mountain Douglas-fir) is native to southwestern Alberta and is likely the one you will find available at nurseries. It is not as imposing as its larger West Coast kin, growing 12–18 m (40–60') tall and 4.5–7.5 m (15–25') wide. Some new seedling varieties on the market are a striking blue, much like Colorado blue spruce.

P. menziesii (above & below)

Problems & Pests

Canker, leaf cast (the needle version of leaf spot), borers, weevils, spruce budworm and other caterpillars, scale insects, adelgids or aphids can cause occasional problems.

Elderberry
Elder
Sambucus

Features: early-summer flowers, fruit, foliage **Habit:** large, bushy deciduous shrub
Height: 1.5–6 m (5–20') **Spread:** 1.5–6 m (5–20') **Planting:** bare-root, container; spring or fall **Zones:** 3–9

ELDERBERRIES ARE FANTASTIC ORNAMENTAL SHRUBS, ESPECIALLY
the newer varieties, which are proving popular with homeowners, and some
of the best have proven hardy in Zone 3. *S. nigra* 'Gerda' and 'Eva' are knock-
outs, featuring purplish black (yes, black) foliage and huge, lemon-scented,
pink flowers in June.

*Elderberry fruit attracts birds
to the garden and can be used
to make wine or jelly.*

Growing

Elderberries grow well in **full sun** or **partial shade**. Cultivars grown for burgundy or black leaf colour develop the best colour in full sun, but cultivars with yellow leaves show their finest colour in light or partial shade. The soil should be of **average fertility, moist** and **well drained**. Established plants tolerate dry soil.

S. canadensis 'Aurea'

Although elderberries do not require pruning, they can become scraggly and untidy if ignored. They tolerate even severe pruning. Plants can be cut back to within a few buds of the ground in early spring. This treatment controls the spread of these vigorous growers and encourages the best foliage colour on specimens grown for this purpose.

If you desire flowers and fruit as well as good foliage colour, remove only one-third to one-half of the growth in early spring because flowers are not produced on new growth. Fertilize or apply a layer of compost after pruning to encourage strong new growth.

Tips

Elderberries can be used in shrub or mixed borders, in natural woodland gardens or next to ponds or other water features. Plants with interesting or colourful foliage can be used as specimen plants or to create focal points.

Both the flowers and the fruit of *S. canadensis* and *S. nigra* can be used to make wine. The berries are also popular for pies and jelly—or try them in place of blueberries in scones or muffins. Cooking elderberry

S. nigra 'Gerda' BLACK BEAUTY

S. racemosa

fruits before eating them is recommended. Raw, they are not really edible and can cause nausea, vomiting, diarrhea and gastrointestinal pain, particularly in children. Although less tasty, the fruit of *S. racemosa* can be used for similar purposes, but the berries of most other *Sambucus* species are considered inedible. All parts of elderberries other than the berries are toxic.

Recommended

S. canadensis (S. nigra subsp. *canadensis;* American elderberry) is a shrub about 1.75–3 m (6–10') tall, with an equal spread. The white flowers of midsummer give way to dark purple berries. A widespread native across the eastern and central US, this species is generally found growing in damp ditches and alongside rivers and streams. **'Aurea'** has yellow foliage and red fruit. (Zones 4–8)

S. racemosa (above)

S. nigra 'Gerda' BLACK BEAUTY (below)

S. nigra (*S. nigra* subsp. *nigra;* European elderberry, black elderberry) is a large shrub that can grow 3.75 m (12') tall and wide. The yellowish white to creamy white flowers of early summer give way to purple-black fruit. **'Eva'** (BLACK LACE) is an upright selection that grows 1.75–3 m (6–10') tall and 1.25–1.75 m (4–6') wide and has deeply lobed, dark purple to black foliage. It bears large clusters of lemon-scented, pink flowers followed by dark red fruit. **'Gerda'** (BLACK BEAUTY) has dark foliage that gets blacker as the season progresses. It bears pink flowers and grows 1.75–3 m (6–10') tall, with an equal spread. **'Guincho Purple'** grows 2.5–3.75 m (8–12') tall and wide and has purple-red stems. The purple-green foliage fades to dark green in summer and turns red in fall. The flowers are tinged pink. **'Madonna'** grows 1.75–3 m (6–10') tall and wide, and it has dark green foliage with wide, irregular, golden yellow margins. (Zones 4–8)

S. racemosa (European red elderberry, red elderberry) is native to Alberta. It grows 2.5–4.5 m (8–15') tall, with an equal spread. This shrub bears pyramidal clusters of white flowers in spring, followed by bright red fruit. **'Plumosa Aurea'** has golden-yellow, deeply cut foliage. **'Sutherland Gold'** has deeply cut, yellow-green foliage. It grows 1.5–3 m (5–10') tall and wide. (Zones 3–7)

S. canadensis (above & below)

Problems & Pests

Borers, canker, dieback, leaf spot or powdery mildew may occasionally affect elderberries.

The versatile elderberries can be cut back hard each year or trained into a small tree.

Elm

Ulmus

Features: habit, fall colour, bark **Habit:** variable, rounded to vase-shaped deciduous tree **Height:** 9–24 m (30–80') **Spread:** 7.5–18 m (25–60') **Planting:** container, B & B, bare-root; spring or fall **Zones:** 2–8

THERE ARE GOOD REASONS WHY ELMS WERE ONCE CHOSEN TO grace yards, streets and boulevards across Alberta: they are gorgeous, magnificent trees. We are incredibly fortunate that the elm trees in Alberta have not suffered the same fate as many across Canada and the US. Dutch elm disease wiped out millions of elms across America beginning in the 1960s; but it didn't take them all, and from those very trees that shrugged off the attack, new, disease-resistant elms have been developed.

Growing

Elms grow well in **full sun** or **partial shade**. They adapt to most soil types and conditions but prefer a **fertile, moist** soil. Elms tolerate urban conditions, including salt from roadways.

Pruning, which is rarely needed, can be done in fall. Remove damaged, diseased or dead growth as needed. The elm bark beetle, which spreads Dutch elm disease, is attracted to wounds and freshly cut elm wood. Avoid pruning between early April and late July, when the beetle is active. Do not transport or store elm firewood. Immediately burn, bury or chip all wood from tree removal or pruning.

U. americana

Tips

Elms are large trees that are attractive when given plenty of room to grow on large properties and in parks. Siberian elm is not the most ornamental tree, but it is loved by wildlife. It is best used in large spaces and out-of-the-way areas where the weak wood will not be an issue.

Recommended

U. americana (American elm) is a long-lived, large, vase-shaped native tree with pendulous branches and a large, rounded to oval crown. It usually grows 18–24 m (60–80') tall and spreads 9–18 m (30–60'). The shiny, dark green foliage turns golden yellow in fall. With age, the thick, grey bark becomes deeply furrowed. This species is susceptible to Dutch elm disease, but disease-resistant cultivars are becoming available.

'Brandon' is a slightly smaller, more compact version of the species tree, reaching 15 m (50') tall and 12 m (40') wide. The foliage has excellent yellow fall colour.

U. pumila (Siberian elm) is a fast-growing tree that reaches a height of 9–15 m (30–50') and grows 7.5–12 m (25–40') wide, with a rounded to spreading crown and small, medium to dark green foliage that turns yellow in fall. It has weak wood and will drop branches in a strong wind. It is resistant to Dutch elm disease.

Problems & Pests

In addition to the fatal Dutch elm disease fungus, elms can suffer attack from aphids, borers, bark and leaf beetles, caterpillars, Japanese beetles, leafhoppers, leaf miners, canker, dieback, leaf spot, powdery mildew, rot or *Verticillium* wilt.

Euonymus
Euonymus

Features: foliage, corky stems, habit **Habit:** deciduous or evergreen shrub, small tree, groundcover or climber **Height:** 60 cm–3 m (2–10') **Spread:** 60 cm–3 m (2–10') **Planting:** B & B, container; spring, fall **Zones:** 3–8

EUONYMUS IS AN INTERESTING, UNDERUSED, SOMEWHAT DIVERSE genus of plants that we should use more here in Alberta. Only a handful of trees and shrubs match the fiery fall colour of *E. alata*. Its smaller cultivars are outstanding for providing fall contrast, especially when mixed with dense evergreens and plants with yellow fall colour. The shrubs are good in summer as well, with arching, textured branches that host delicate, soft green foliage. *E. nana* var. *turkistanica* has a fine texture and decent fall colour, good for adding variety to shrub and mixed beds.

Growing

Euonymus prefers **full sun** but tolerates **light** or **partial shade.** It also tolerates heavy shade but with diminished fall colour. Soil of **average to rich** fertility is preferable, but any moist, well-drained soil will do.

Use only hand pruners (or loppers for larger wood) to prune any euonymus species. *E. alata* and *E. nana* var. *turkistanica* require little pruning except to remove dead, damaged or awkward growth as needed. Remove older stems of *E. alata* to the base to thin congested shrubs. *E. alata* tolerates severe pruning and can be used as a hedge. *E. fortunei* is a vigorous, spreading plant that can be trimmed as required to keep it within the desired growing area. It tolerates severe pruning.

Tips

E. alata adds season-long colour in a shrub or mixed border, as a specimen, in a naturalistic garden or as a hedge. The smaller cultivars can be used to

E. alata (above)

E. alata (below), E.nana (centre)

E. fortunei 'Emerald 'n' Gold'

The name euonymus translates as "of good name"—rather ironic, given that all parts of these plants are poisonous and can cause severe stomach upset.

create informal hedges. *E. fortunei* can be grown as a shrub in a border or as a hedge. It is an excellent substitute for boxwood. Its trailing habit also makes it suitable as a groundcover or container plant. *E. nana* var. *turkistanica* can be mixed into shrub and mixed beds or used as an informal hedge and for group planting.

Recommended

E. alata (burning bush, winged euonymus) is an open, mounding, deciduous shrub. It grows 1.75–3 m (6–10') tall and wide or slightly wider. The foliage turns vivid red in fall, but only with five or more hours of sunlight per day. The small, red fall berries are somewhat obscured by the bright foliage. The corky ridges or "wings" that grow on the stems and branches provide winter interest. This widespreading plant can be invasive. **'Compacta'** has denser, more compact growth and has less prominently corky ridges on the branches. During unusually cold winters, it may suffer winter damage. FIRE BALL® ('Select') is a hardier selection of 'Compacta' that suffers no winter damage. It provides brilliant red fall colour.

E. alata 'Compacta'

E. fortunei (wintercreeper euonymus) is the progenitor of a wide and attractive variety of evergreen cultivars that can be prostrate, climbing or mounding and often have attractive variegated foliage. **'Emerald 'n' Gold'** is a bushy selection 60 cm (24") tall and 90 cm (36") wide. It has green leaves with wide, gold margins. The foliage turns pinky red during winter and spring. (Zones 4–8)

E. nana **var.** *turkistanica* (dwarf narrow-leaved burning bush) is an upright, dense, fine-textured shrub with narrow, semi-evergreen, dark green foliage that turns pinkish to purple-green in fall. It grows 60–90 cm (24–36") tall and wide. The pendent, showy pink fruits split open to reveal orange seeds.

E. nana var. *turkistanica*

E. alata FIRE BALL®

Problems & Pests

The two worst problems are crown gall and scale insects, both of which can prove fatal to the affected plant. Other possible problems include aphids, leaf miners, tent caterpillars, leaf spot and powdery mildew.

E. alata *achieves the best fall colour when grown in full sun.*

False Cypress
Chamaecyparis

Features: foliage, habit, cones **Habit:** rounded to mounding evergreen shrub or narrow pyramidal tree **Height:** 60 cm–9 m (2–30') **Spread:** 60 cm–6 m (2–20') **Planting:** container; spring or fall **Zones:** 3–8

CHAMAECYPARIS IS A SPLENDID GENUS OF EYE-CATCHING TREES and shrubs that are starting to catch on here in Alberta. A site sheltered from the drying winds is best because these plants are susceptible to winter burn. False cypresses are worthy of trying in our province, and nurseries are now beginning to carry these plants.

Growing

False cypresses prefer **full sun;** growth in shaded areas may be sparse or thin. The soil should be **fertile, neutral to acidic, moist** and **well drained**; alkaline soils are tolerated.

No pruning is required on specimen trees. Plants grown as hedges can be trimmed anytime during the growing season. Avoid severe pruning because new growth will not sprout from old wood. To tidy shrubs, rub off or pull dry brown foliage from the base by hand.

Tips

The dwarf and slow-growing cultivars are used in shrub or mixed borders, in rock gardens, as foundation plants and as bonsai.

As with the related cedar and junipers, the foliage of false cypresses may be irritating to sensitive skin. Wear gloves and long sleeves when planting or pruning.

Recommended

C. pisifera (Japanese false cypress, Sawara cypress) is a pyramidal tree in youth, becoming open with age. It is native to Japan and may grow 6–9 m (20–30') tall and 4.5–6 m (15–20') wide in our climate. **'Mops'** (var. *filifera* 'Mops,' 'Golden Mops') is a rounded to mounding, dwarf threadleaf variety that grows slowly to 60–90 cm (24–36") tall and wide in 10 years, and it may be 1.75–2.5 m (6–8') tall and 2.5–3 m (8–10') wide with age. It has bright gold, thread-like foliage that holds its colour well. **'Squarrosa'** (moss false cypress) has less pendulous foliage than the other cultivars. Young plants grow densely, somewhat resembling fuzzy stuffed animals. The growth becomes more relaxed and open with maturity. There are a number of variants of this cultivar featuring different sizes, forms and foliage colours. **'Sungold'** is a dense, rounded to mounding shrub with long, thread-like branches and thread-like foliage that is gold when young and fades to a lime chartreuse with age. It eventually reaches 1.75–2.5 m (6–8') tall and 2.5–3 m (8–10') wide. (Zones 4–8)

C. thyoides **'Heather Bun'** ('Heatherbun') is a compact, mounded to round shrub that grows 1.75–3 m (6–10') tall and 1.25–1.5 m (4–5') wide. The soft, blue-green foliage turns purplish in winter.

Problems & Pests

False cypresses are not prone to problems, but they can occasionally be affected by spruce mites, blight, gall or root rot.

C. thyoides 'Heather Bun'

False Spirea
Ural False Spirea
Sorbaria

Features: summer flowers, foliage **Habit:** suckering deciduous shrub
Height: 90 cm–1.75 m (3–6') **Spread:** 90 cm–1.75 m (3–6') or more
Planting: container; anytime **Zones:** 2–7

FOR NATURALIZING LARGE AREAS, AND FOR CONTROLLING SOIL
erosion on slopes, false spirea is an excellent choice, but because of its
suckering habit, it remains a little-used shrub in garden settings. It does
have some noteworthy features though: the foliage is virtually blemish-
free, feathery and tropical-like, with each leaf having up to two dozen
narrow, rough-textured, 5–10 cm (2–4") long leaflets. The spring
growth is tinged a rich red. Also, the midsummer show of long
clusters of white flowers resembles gargantuan astilbes
in bloom, and false spirea is incredibly hardy.

*False spirea can help prevent soil
erosion on the steep banks of a ditch*

Growing

False spirea grows equally well in **full sun, partial shade** or **light shade**. The soil should be of **average fertility, high in organic matter, moist** and **well drained,** but this plant is adaptable and can tolerate hot, dry periods.

Pruning false spirea is both easy and important. Each year after flowering, remove about one-third of the oldest growth. When necessary, rejuvenation pruning can be done in spring as the buds begin to swell—cut the entire plant back to within a few buds of the ground. To help prevent excessive spread, use a barrier in the soil and remove any suckers whenever they appear in undesirable places.

Remove the faded brown seedheads if you find them unattractive.

Tips

Use false spirea in large shrub borders, as a barrier plant, in naturalized gardens or in lightly shaded woodland gardens. This plant can be aggressive, but its spread is most troublesome in small gardens.

Recommended

S. sorbifolia is a large, many-stemmed, suckering shrub that is

S. sorbifolia (above & below)

native to Asia. It grows 1.25–1.75 m (4–6') tall and 1.75 m (6') or more wide, producing long clusters of many tiny, fluffy, white or cream flowers in midsummer. This plant is very cold hardy. SEM is a compact selection that grows 90 cm–1.25 m (3–4') tall and wide. Young foliage is pink to pink-red and changes to light green in summer.

Problems & Pests

False spirea has no serious problems but can fall victim to fire blight in stressful conditions.

Fir

Abies

Features: foliage, cones, form **Habit:** narrow, pyramidal or columnar evergreen tree or shrub **Height:** 30 cm–15 m (1–50') **Spread:** 60 cm–7.5 m (2–25') **Planting:** B & B, container; spring **Zones:** 3–7

FIRS OFFER A GOOD SELECTION OF ATTRACTIVE AND UNUSUAL evergreen trees sure to add beauty to any northern landscape. *A. balsamea* is an excellent choice when you want a tall but relatively narrow evergreen, and it can be planted as near as 4.5 m (15') from a house. The dwarf varieties provide gardeners the opportunity for creative expression. They have wide-ranging forms and needle colourations that assure year-round interest and add distinction to shrub borders, foundation plantings and mixed gardens.

Fir and spruce superficially resemble each other, but fir needles are flat, whereas spruce needles are sharply pointed. Also, fir cones sit on top of the branches, whereas spruce cones hang downwards.

Growing

Firs usually prefer full sun but tolerate partial shade. The soil should be rich, neutral to acidic, cool, moist and well drained. *A. balsamea* tolerates wet soil. *A. concolor* prefers a loose, sandy soil and does not tolerate heavy clay.

These trees generally don't tolerate extreme heat or polluted, urban conditions, but *A. concolor* accepts such situations far better than do other *Abies*.

No pruning is required. Remove dead or damaged growth as needed.

Tips

Firs make impressive specimen trees for large areas. The natural species tend to be too large for the average home garden. Several compact or dwarf cultivars can be included in shrub borders or used as specimens.

A. nordmanniana (above), *A. balsamea* 'Nana' (below)

Recommended

A. balsamea (balsam fir) is quite pyramidal when young but narrows as it ages. A slow-growing tree native to the northeastern US, it can reach 9–15 m (30–50') in height with a spread of 4.5–6 m (15–20'). **'Nana'** is a slow-growing, dense, rounded shrub with dark green needles that have silvery white undersides. It grows 30–60 cm (12–24") tall and 60–90 cm (24–36") wide. This coneless dwarf cultivar is more suitable to a small garden than the much larger parent species. It benefits from some afternoon shade from the hot sun. (Zones 3–6)

A. concolor (silver fir, white fir) is an impressive specimen that grows 7.5–12 m (25–40') tall and spreads 4.5–7.5 m (15–25') in garden conditions. A whitish coating on the needles gives the tree a hazy blue appearance. **'Candicans'** is a narrow, upright tree

A. balsamea (above), *A. concolor* 'Candicans' (below)

with silvery blue needles. **'Compacta'** is a dwarf cultivar that makes an attractive specimen tree. It grows to 1.25–1.75 m (4–6') in height and spread. It has whiter needles than the species. (Zones 3–7)

A. koreana (Korean fir) is slow growing and small, by evergreen standards, with a height of 4.5–9 m (15–30') and a spread of 3–6 m (10–20'). Even young trees produce the unusual, attractive purple-blue cones. **'Horstmann's Silberlocke'** ('Silberlocke') has unusual, twisted needles that show off the silvery stripes on their undersides. (Zones 4–7)

A. nordmanniana is a narrow pyramidal to columnar tree that grows 9–15 m (30–50') tall and 4.5–6 m (15–20') wide, with dense, glossy, dark green foliage and tiered branches to the ground. It produces large, cylindrical, reddish brown cones. (Zones 4–7)

A. concolor 'Candicans'

Problems & Pests

Firs are susceptible to problems with aphids, bagworm, bark beetles, spruce budworm, needle blight, root rot or rust.

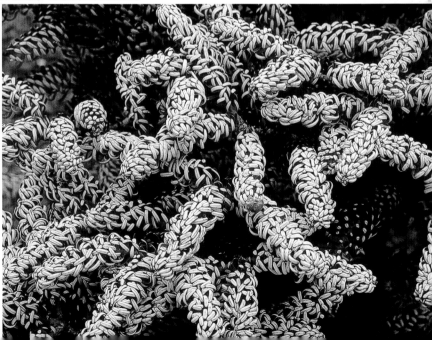
A. koreana 'Horstmann's Silberlocke'

Forsythia

Forsythia

Features: early- to mid-spring flowers **Habit:** spreading deciduous shrub with upright to arching branches **Height:** 1.25–1.75 m (4–6') **Spread:** 1.25–1.75 m (4–6') **Planting:** B & B or container in spring or fall; bare-root in spring **Zones:** 3–8

FORSYTHIAS ARE TRULY THE HARBINGERS OF SPRING. THE CHEERY, bright yellow blooms bring much needed colour while much of the rest of the landscape remains in drab disarray. The summer foliage cannot be considered outstanding, but these plants can quickly develop a wild, irregular growth habit that fits well into a naturalized setting.

Growing

Most forsythias grow best in **full sun** but tolerate light shade. The soil should be of **average fertility, moist** and **well drained.**

Correct pruning is essential to keep forsythias attractive, but prune young plants only minimally. Flowers are usually produced on growth that is at least two years old. Mature plants should be thinned annually, removing old wood back to vigorous shoots and removing one or two of the oldest stems to the ground. Pruning should take place after flowering has finished.

Tips

Forsythias are gorgeous early-season bloomers. Include them in shrub or mixed borders among other plants that can take over once the forsythias have finished flowering.

Forsythias quite happily survive in Zone 3. The flowers buds, however, which form in summer, are vulnerable to winter cold. In the coldest areas, a tall shrub may flower only on the lower half that was buried in a protective layer of snow. As long as there is dependable snowfall, simply pile some salt-free snow over your hardy cultivar in winter to enjoy flowers each spring.

Recommended

F. ovata (early forsythia) is an upright, spreading shrub that grows 1.25–1.75 m (4–6') tall and wide. This species has the hardiest buds, and its flowers open in early spring. It is a parent to the following hybrids. *F.* x **'Northern Gold'** was developed

in Canada to produce cold-hardy, bright yellow flowers—even after –33° C (–28° F) temperatures. This upright shrub becomes more arching as it matures. *F.* x **'Northern Sun'** is hardy to –35° C (–30° F) and bears clear yellow flowers. It has a spreading habit.

Problems & Pests

Most problems are not serious; they may include root-knot nematodes, leaf spot and stem gall.

F. x 'Northern Gold'

Genista
Woadwaxen
Genista

Features: flowers, habit, low-maintenance **Habit:** upright and spreading, or mounded deciduous shrub with arching branches **Height:** 30–90 cm (12–36") **Spread:** 60–90 cm (24–36") **Planting:** container, bare-root; spring or fall **Zones:** 3–8

GENISTAS ARE GREAT LITTLE SHRUBS FOR SANDY SOILS, OR REALLY any well-drained soil that is low in fertility. They have the ability to fix atmospheric nitrogen into nodules on their roots—with some help from a few species of symbiotic soil bacteria. Not only do they help feed themselves, they help feed other plants that are growing nearby. With their low maintenance requirements and small stature, both species listed below could make good container specimens.

The stems, leaves and flowers of G. tinctoria *yield a decent yellow dye with the best yellows coming from the flowers.*

Growing

Genistas grow best in **full sun** in **light, well-drained, low to moderately fertile** soil. They tolerate partial shade and poor soils but are not tolerant of wet soils, and overly fertile soils will decrease flowering. Genistas do not transplant well and should be set in place while the plants are still young.

Genistas need minimal to no pruning. Dead, diseased or awkward branches can be removed after flowering is complete or after the first big flush of blooms is done.

Tips

Genistas can be used in mixed and shrub beds, in foundation plantings, as groundcovers when planted closely (especially on dry slopes) and as specimens. *G. lydia* is a good plant for the rock garden.

Recommended

G. lydia (Lydia woadwaxen) is a slow-growing, mounded shrub with arching branches and grey-green stems. It bears bright yellow flowers

G. lydia (above & below)

in abundance in late spring to early summer. It grows 30–60 cm (12–24") tall and 60–90 cm (24–36") wide.

G. tinctoria (dyer's greenwood) is a slow-growing, upright, spreading shrub with minimally branched, green stems and narrow, light green foliage. It grows 60–90 cm (2–3') tall and wide and bears erect clusters of yellow flowers through summer and sporadically into fall. (Zones 2–8)

Problems & Pests

Problems are rare, but scale insects and powdery mildew may occur.

Ginkgo
Maidenhair Tree
Ginkgo

Features: summer and fall foliage, habit, bark **Habit:** deciduous tree, conical in youth but variable with age **Height:** 9–18 m (30–60') **Spread:** 4.5–9 m (15–30') **Planting:** B & B, bare-root, container; spring or fall **Zones:** 3–8

GINKGO IS ONE OF THE OLDEST AND LEAST-CHANGED TREES, appearing the same today as it did 150 million years ago. A ginkgo is a tremendous asset to the landscape from the first year the tree is grown. Ginkgo is a slow grower in Alberta, and it can take many years before the tree reaches maturity. Have patience, and enjoy this unique tree.

Ginkgo appears to have been saved from extinction by its long-time use in Asian temple gardens. Today, this "living fossil" grows almost entirely in horticultural settings.

Growing

Ginkgo prefers **full sun**. The soil should be **fertile** and **well drained;** this tree adapts to most soil types. It also tolerates urban conditions and cold weather. Little or no pruning is necessary.

Tips

Although its growth is slow, ginkgo can mature into a tall, handsome tree with a somewhat loose, cascading canopy. It is a good specimen tree for parks and larger gardens. It can also be used as a street tree.

G. biloba (all photos)

A plant can be either male or female. Choose a male; the rarely sold female ginkgo produces a fruit that drops, rots, makes a mess and is rather malodorous.

Recommended

*G. **biloba*** varies in habit; it eventually grows 9–18 m (30–60') tall and 4.5–9 m (15–30') wide or possibly wider. A few cool fall nights usually turn the clam-shaped leaves an attractive buttery yellow. **'Autumn Gold,'** a broadly conical male cultivar, grows 9–15 m (30–50') tall and spreads 4.5–9 m (15–30'). Its fall colour is bright golden yellow.

Problems & Pests

This tree seems to have outlived most of the pests that might have afflicted it. Leaf spot may affect ginkgo, but it doesn't cause any real trouble.

The unique leaves of ginkgo resemble those of maidenhair fern (inset)

Hawthorn
Crataegus

Features: late-spring or early-summer flowers, fruit, foliage, thorny branches
Habit: rounded to spreading deciduous tree or large shrub, often with a zigzagged, layered branch pattern **Height:** 3.75–6 m (12–20') **Spread:** 3.75–6 m (12–20')
Planting: B & B, container; early spring **Zones:** 3–7

HAWTHORNS ARE SPECTACULAR ORNAMENTAL TREES FOR HOT, sunny spots. Be careful not to plant hawthorns that are susceptible to cedar-apple rust too close to junipers or cedars.

The thorniness of most hawthorns can be an asset, blocking access with an impenetrable hedge or repelling burglars from windows.

Growing

Hawthorns grow well in **full sun.**
They adapt to any well-drained soil,
are moderate to low water users and
tolerate urban conditions.

Hawthorns can be pruned much like
crabapples. Cut out crossing interior
limbs and dead inner wood of dormant plants in late winter to early
spring. Also prune to keep branches
away from pedestrian walkways.
Hawthorn hedges can be pruned
after flowering, in fall or in late winter to spring. Remove any diseased
growth immediately. Wear leather
gloves and safety goggles when pruning hawthorns.

Tips

Hawthorns can be grown as specimen plants or hedges in urban sites
and exposed locations. Hawthorns
have long, sharp thorns, which may
make them unsuitable for yards
with children.

Recommended

C. arnoldiana (Arnold's hawthorn)
is a dense, thorny, non-suckering
large shrub or small tree with a
rounded to wide-spreading crown
and upright to horizontal branches.
It has glossy, dark green foliage and
yellow fall colour. It grows 3.75–6 m
(12–20') tall and wide, bearing
showy clusters of white flowers in
spring, followed by abundant red
fruit that persists well into fall.

C. x *mordenensis* is a dense, upright
tree, 3.75–6 m (12–20') tall and wide,
with a rounded to oval crown, white
flowers and red fruit. The following
cultivars are highly resistant to

C. x *mordenensis* 'Snowbird'

*Hawthorn fruits are edible but dry
and seedy. Some people make jelly
from them. A liqueur can be made
using fermented berries and brandy.*

cedar-apple rust. **'Snowbird'** is hardier than the original hybrid species.
It bears double flowers and sparse
pinkish red fruit. **'Toba'** grows up to
4.5 m (15') tall and wide and is resistant to leaf spot. It has a twisted
trunk, large, sturdy branches and
fragrant, white, double flowers that
age to pink. The fall foliage is yellow-
orange.

C. succulenta (fleshy hawthorn) is
a thorny tree with a rounded to
spreading crown. It grows 4.5–6 m
(15–20') tall and wide, and has
glossy, dark green foliage. It bears
showy, white flowers in spring, followed by bright red, fleshy fruit. It is
the most edible fruit of the species
listed here.

Problems & Pests

Pear slug and cedar-apple rust are
the most prevalent problems.

Hazelnut
Filbert
Corylus

Features: early-spring catkins, nuts, foliage, habit **Habit:** large, dense deciduous shrub or small tree **Height:** 1.25–3.75 cm (4–12') **Spread:** 1.25–3.75 cm (4–12') **Planting:** B & B, container; spring, fall **Zones:** 3–8

HAZELNUTS NOT ONLY LOOK GOOD, BUT MANY KINDS YIELD tasty nuts—if you can beat the squirrels to them, that is. The large leaves are a nice background for shrubs with finer foliage. *C. avellana* 'Contorta' is a lovely accent plant with twisted stems that add winter interest. All varieties develop a wide, wild, irregular shape that can be moderated with pruning as the shrubs gain maturity.

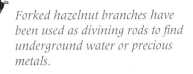

Forked hazelnut branches have been used as divining rods to find underground water or precious metals.

Growing

Hazelnuts grow equally well in **full sun** or **partial shade.** The soil should be **fertile** and **well drained.**

These plants require little pruning but tolerate it well. Entire plants can be cut back to within 15 cm (6") of the ground to encourage new growth in spring. On grafted specimens of *C. avellana* 'Contorta,' straight-growing suckers that come up from the roots can be easily spotted and cut out.

Tips

Use hazelnuts as specimens or in shrub or mixed borders. *C. americana* and *C. cornuta* are good choices for naturalized areas and woodland gardens.

An alternative name for
C. avellana *'Contorta,' Harry Lauder's walking stick comes from the gnarled, twisted cane the famous vaudeville comedian used.*

C. avellana 'Contorta' (above), *C. americana* (below)

C. avellana 'Contorta'
C. cornuta

Male and female flowers are produced on the same plant, but planting at least three plants assures better nut production. The male flowers are the long, showy, dangling catkins; the nuts arise from the rather inconspicuous female flowers.

Recommended

C. americana (American hazelnut, American filbert) is a rounded, multi-stemmed, suckering shrub that gets leggy with age. It grows 1.75–3 m (6–10') tall and 1.25–1.75 m (4–6') wide, and features showy catkins in early spring and dark green foliage that turns orange-yellow in fall. The edible nuts are enclosed in attractive, hairy, papery, frilled bracts that turn from green to brown when ripe. (Zones 4–8)

C. avellana (European filbert, European hazelnut) grows as a large shrub or small tree that reaches a height of 3–4.5 m (10–15') and spreads up to 3.75 m (12'). It bears long, dangling male catkins in late winter and early spring. Various cultivars are more commonly grown than the species. **'Contorta'** (corkscrew hazelnut, Harry Lauder's walking stick), perhaps the

Although all hazelnuts bear edible nuts, C. avellana *and* C. maxima *are two of the most common commercial species. They are grown both for the delicious nuts themselves and for the extracted oil.*

best-known cultivar, grows 2.5–3
m (8–10') tall and wide. The
twisted, contorted stems and leaves
are a particularly interesting feature
in winter, when the bare stems are
most visible.

C. cornuta (beaked hazelnut) is a
small, suckering shrub that grows
1.25–2.5 m (4–8') tall and wide with
slender, angled twigs and large,
bright green foliage that turns yellow
in fall. Small, yellowish, pendant
male catkins are borne in fall, open-
ing in spring to pollinate the inconspicuous, reddish female flowers.
The edible nuts are enclosed in a
hairy, leafy, husk that extends two to
three times the length of the nut and
resembles a beak, and they ripen in
late summer to early fall.

C. maxima var. *purpurea* (purple
giant filbert) adapts to many soils
and makes a fine addition to the
spring garden. Growing 3–3.75 m
(10–12') tall, with an equal spread,
this variety adds deep purple leaf
colour. The rich colour develops best
in full sun, but it usually fades to
dark green with the heat of summer.

Problems & Pests
Bud mites, Japanese beetles, tent caterpillars, webworm, blight, canker,
fungal leaf spot, powdery mildew or
rust may cause occasional problems.

C. maxima var. purpurea

C. americana

Hemlock
Eastern Hemlock
Tsuga

Features: foliage, habit, cones **Habit:** evergreen, pyramidal tree or low-growing to prostrate shrub **Height:** 1.5–9 m (5–30') **Spread:** 60 cm–4.5 m (2–15') **Planting:** B & B, container; spring, fall **Zones:** 3–8

HEMLOCKS ARE AN EXTREMELY ATTRACTIVE GENUS OF GRACEFUL, charming trees and shrubs that deserve to be used more often in the moister areas of our province. They are among the few evergreens that prefer partial shade. If you like plants that develop a broad, weeping form, no evergreen would be better a choice than 'Pendula.' For a vertical accent plant in foundation plantings, perennial gardens or areas where a dense evergreen hedge is needed in less than full sun, 'Monler' is superb—in partial shade it performs much better than any cedar.

Unlike the unrelated herb that killed Socrates, hemlocks of the genus Tsuga *are not poisonous.*

The genus name, Tsuga *(pronounced SOO-gah), is derived from a Japanese word meaning "tree-mother."*

Growing

Hemlocks generally grow well in any light from **full sun to full shade;** 'Monler' is susceptible to winter burn and should remain mostly shaded in winter. The soil should be **humus rich, moist** and **well drained.** These drought-sensitive plants grow best in cool, moist conditions. Avoid roadways because hemlocks are sensitive to air pollution and salt damage.

Hemlock trees need little pruning, but they respond well to it. The cultivars can be pruned to control their growth as required. Trim hemlock hedges in summer.

Tips

With their delicate needles, hemlocks are among the most beautiful evergreens to use as specimen trees—or shape them to form hedges. Small cultivars may be included in a shrub or mixed border. The many dwarf forms are especially useful in small gardens.

Recommended

T. canadensis (eastern hemlock) is a graceful, narrowly pyramidal tree with horizontal to pendulous branches. It grows 6–9 m (20–30') tall and spreads about 3–4.5 m (10–15') wide in cultivation. Many cultivars are available, including groundcovers and dwarf forms. **'Albospica'** has dark green foliage with white tips. **'Monler'** (EMERALD FOUNTAIN) is an upright plant 1.75–3 m (6–10') tall and 60–90 cm (24–36") wide that prefers partial shade. Great for screening, it has dark green

T. canadensis

Don't use hemlock boughs as holiday decorations. The needles drop quickly once the branches are cut.

foliage and weeping branches. **'Pendula'** is a small, upright, weeping form that grows 1.5–4.5 m (5–15') tall, with an equal spread.

Problems & Pests

Stress-free hemlocks have few problems. Aphids, mites, scale insects, weevils, woolly adelgids, grey mould, needle blight, rust or snow blight may cause trouble.

Holly

Ilex

Features: glossy, sometimes spiny leaves; fruit, habit **Habit:** erect to spreading evergreen shrub **Height:** 1.25–1.75 m (4–6') **Spread:** 1.25–1.75 m (4–6') **Planting:** B & B, container; spring or fall **Zones:** 4–8

ALTHOUGH WE CAN'T GROW THE CLASSIC EVERGREEN
I. aquifolium (English holly) that is so popular in Europe, we can grow some of its hardier relatives. Blue hollies are hardy to Zone 4 when planted in a sheltered, well-drained site. The plants' location is critical to their success, even with the most hardy selections. A sheltered location on the north or east side of the home is ideal.

Showy, scarlet holly berries look tempting, especially to children, but they are not edible.

Growing

Hollies prefer **full sun** but tolerate partial shade. The soil should be of **average to rich fertility, humus rich, acidic** and **moist**. Apply a summer mulch to keep the roots cool and moist. Evergreen hollies are susceptible to winter burn, so plant them where they do not receive much, if any, winter sun or wind.

Hollies require little pruning. Simply remove damaged growth in spring. Plants grown as hedges can be trimmed in summer.

Tips

Hollies can be used in groups, in woodland gardens and in shrub and mixed borders or shaped into hedges.

All hollies have male and female flowers on separate plants. To guarantee berries, one male plant growing within 3 m (10')' of any compatible female plant should be sufficient.

Recommended

I. x *meserveae* (blue holly) is an erect to spreading, dense, evergreen shrub. This holly tolerates pruning and makes a formidable hedge or barrier. The glossy red fruit persists past fall. Many cultivars have been developed. Often available in male and female pairs, they can be mixed or matched. **'Blue Prince'** and **'Blue Princess'** have glossy, dark blue-green foliage with spiny margins, and 'Blue Princess' bears red fruit prolifically. These cultivars grow 1.25–1.75 m (4–6') tall, with an equal spread. 'Blue Princess' may grow slightly larger than 'Blue Prince.'

I. x *meserveae* 'Blue Princess' (above)

Problems & Pests

Aphids may attack young shoots. Scale insects or leaf miners can present problems, as can root rot in poorly drained soils.

I. x *meserveae* 'Blue Prince' (below)

Honeysuckle

Lonicera

Features: flowers, habit, fruit **Habit:** rounded, upright deciduous shrub or twining climber **Height:** 60 cm–4.25 m (2–14') **Spread:** 60 cm–3.75 m (2–12') **Planting:** container, bare-root; spring **Zones:** 2–8

HONEYSUCKLES ARE LONG-LIVED, DROUGHT RESISTANT AND easy to grow, and they have done well in many Alberta landscapes for many years. The colourful, tropical-like, often fragrant spring blooms of *Lonicera* are reason enough to grow these popular shrubs and vines. Although these plants can survive and expand in partial shade, flowering will be diminished, so grow them in full sun for the best blooms. All the shrub varieties mentioned below make marvelous clipped or informal deciduous hedges and windbreaks.

Honeysuckle flowers are often pleasantly scented, and they attract hummingbirds as well as bees and other pollinating insects.

Growing

Honeysuckles grow well in **full sun** and tolerate partial shade. The soil should be **average to fertile** and **well drained**. Climbing honeysuckles prefer a **humus-rich, moist** soil.

Shrub honeysuckles benefit from annual thinning (renewal pruning) after flowering is complete. Trim hedges twice a year (usually in early summer and again in mid- to late summer) to keep them neat. To control their direction or size, trim back climbing honeysuckles in spring.

Tips

Shrub honeysuckles can be used in mixed borders, in naturalized gardens and as hedges; some are large and take up a lot of space when mature. Climbing honeysuckles can be trained to grow up a trellis, fence, arbour or other structure; to fill the space provided, they can spread as widely as they climb.

L. x *xylosteoides* 'Claveyi'

Recommended

***L. x brownii* 'Dropmore Scarlet'** (scarlet trumpet honeysuckle) is a twining, climber that bears pinkish

L. x *xylosteoides* 'Miniglobe'

red to orange flowers for most of summer. This vine grows 2.5–3.75 m (8–12') tall and is one of the cold-hardiest climbing honeysuckles. (Zones 3–8)

L. caerulea **var.** *edulis* (blue honey-suckle, Haskap) is an upright shrub with stiff, arching stems, growing 1.25–1.75 m (4–6') tall and 90 cm–1.25 m (3–4') wide. It bears small, yellowish white flowers in early spring, followed by sweet, cylindrical to rounded, dark purple-blue fruit. You will need to plant two varieties that bloom together for pollination.

Choosing the right honeysuckle, planting it in the proper site and pruning it regularly make all the difference when it comes to enjoying your plant.

'**Borealis**' and '**Tundra**' are University of Saskatchewan releases that have abundant, good quality fruit.

L. x '**Mandarin**' is a vigorous twining climber that grows 3–4.25 m (10–14') tall with purple-brown young stems. Young foliage has a coppery colour, turning glossy, dark green in summer. Clusters of long, trumpet-shaped flowers bloom in late spring to early summer and are red-orange on the outside and a yellowish orange on the inside. There is sporadic blooming all summer. (Zones (3)4–8)

L. maximowiczii var. *sachalinensis* (Sakhalin honeysuckle) is a rounded shrub, 1.25–1.75 m (4–6') tall and wide, with arching to horizontal branches and green foliage that is coppery tinged when young and yellow in fall. It bears showy dark purple flowers. The fruit is red. (Zones 3–8)

L. tatarica (Tatarian honeysuckle) is a large, bushy, suckering, deciduous shrub. It grows 1.75–3.75 m (6–12') tall with an equal spread and bears pink, white or red flowers in late spring and early summer. '**Arnold Red**' is a dense shrub with arching branches and blue-green foliage that bears fragrant, red flowers and bright red fruit. It is resistant to Russian aphid. (Zones 3–8)

L. x *xylosteoides* is an erect, rounded, well-branched shrub that grows 1.75–3 m (6–10') tall and wide. It has blue-green foliage and bears pink to light red flowers in late spring to early summer. The fruit is yellow to red. '**Claveyi**' (Clavey's Dwarf)

L. tatarica

grows 90 cm–1.5 m (3–5') tall and wide. '**Miniglobe**' has improved hardiness and disease resistance, and grows 60 cm–1.25 m (2–4') tall and wide. (Zones 3–8)

Problems & Pests

Occasional problems with aphids, leaf miners, leaf rollers, scale insects, blight or powdery mildew can occur.

Plant a honeysuckle vine in a pot and let it climb up a front stair railing.

L. tatarica 'Arnold's Red'

Horsechestnut
Buckeye
Aesculus

Features: late-spring or summer flowers, foliage, spiny fruit **Habit:** rounded or spreading deciduous tree or shrub **Height:** 4.5–12 m (15–40') **Spread:** 4.5–12 m (15–40') **Planting:** B & B, container; spring or fall **Zones:** 3–8

AESCULUS IS A DIVERSE GROUP OF EXTREMELY ATTRACTIVE TREES and shrubs featuring unusual, often rugose foliage, billowing forms and a wide variety of sizes, habits and bloom colours. As is always recommended, note the proper botanical name *(Aesculus)* in your research and shopping because both "buckeye" and "horsechestnut" are bandied about as common names in the trade. Ohio buckeye is hardy across the province. The other two species mentioned below need a warmer microclimate to grow successfully.

Growing

Aesculus species grow well in **full sun** or **partial shade.** The soil should be **fertile, moist** and **well drained.** These plants dislike excessive drought.

Little pruning is required. Remove wayward branches in winter or early spring.

Tips

Aesculus are best suited as specimen and shade trees for large gardens. Their roots can break up nearby sidewalks and patios. The heavy shade of these trees is excellent for cooling buildings but makes it difficult to grow grass beneath the trees; use a shade-loving groundcover instead.

All parts of *Aesculus* plants, especially the seeds, are toxic. People have been poisoned when they confused the nuts of these trees with edible sweet chestnuts (*Castanea* species).

A. x *carnea* (above), *A. hippocastanum* (below)

A. glabra (above)

A. hippocastanum (below)

Recommended

A. x *carnea* (red horsechestnut) is a dense, rounded to spreading tree that grows 7.5–10.5 m (25–35') tall, with an equal spread. It is smaller than common horsechestnut but needs more regular water in summer. Spikes of dark pink flowers are borne in late spring and early summer. The light brown fruit is slightly prickly. **'Briotii'** bears large, lobed leaves and stunning red flowers. (Zones 4–8)

A. *glabra* (Ohio buckeye) is an oval to rounded tree with a dense canopy. It grows 4.5–7.5 m (15–25') tall and wide. The flowers are not very showy, and the fruit is less spiny than that of other *Aesculus* species. Ohio buckeye is susceptible to scorch and looks best when grown in damp, naturalized situations, such as next to a stream or pond. (Zones 3–7)

A. *hippocastanum* (common horsechestnut) is a large, rounded

tree, 9–12 m (30–40') tall and wide, that branches right to the ground if grown in an open setting. White flowers with yellow or pink marks, borne in spikes up to 30 cm (12") long, appear in late spring. Spiky, light brown fruit follows. (Zones (3)4–7)

Problems & Pests

Scale insects, anthracnose, canker, leaf scorch, leaf spot, powdery mildew and rust can all cause problems. Stressed plants are most susceptible to disease.

Horsechestnut and buckeye flowers attract hummingbirds to the garden. Although the seeds are poisonous to people, squirrels eat them with no apparent harm.

The seeds of horsechestnuts and buckeyes are used in many floral displays and dried Christmas arrangements.

A. x *carnea* (above), *A. glabra* (below)

Hydrangea

Hydrangea

Features: flowers, habit, fall foliage of some species **Habit:** mounding deciduous shrub, woody climber or spreading shrub or small tree **Height:** 60 cm–3 m (2–10') **Spread:** 60 cm–2.5 m (2–8') **Planting:** container; spring or fall **Zones:** 3–8

HYDRANGEAS ARE WORTHY, BLOOMING SHRUBS AND ILLUSTRATE the importance of knowing the species of the shrubs you buy, not just the genus. In Alberta, we now have three hydrangea species to choose from. *H. macrophylla* blooms on old wood (last year's bud set), which is why blooming is spotty or nonexistent following severe winters. In contrast, *H. arborescens* and *H. paniculata* bloom on new wood (spring bud set), which is why they bloom every year. Improper pruning may result in no flowers, so pay close attention to the pruning instructions below.

Growing

Hydrangeas grow well in **full sun** or **partial shade.** *H. arborescens* tolerates heavy shade. Shade or partial shade reduces leaf and flower scorch in hot summer areas. The soil should be **of average** to **high fertility, humus rich, moist** and **well drained.** These plants perform best in cool, moist conditions.

H. macrophylla responds to the level of aluminum ions in the soil, which depends on the pH. In acidic soil, the flowers tend to be blue, whereas the same plant grown in an alkaline soil tends to have pink blooms. Most cultivars develop their best colour in either one soil type or the other.

Pruning requirements vary from species to species. See the Recommended section for specific suggestions.

Tips

Hydrangeas have many uses in the landscape. Include them in shrub or mixed borders, use them as specimens or informal barriers or plant them in groups or containers.

H. paniculata

A hydrangea inflorescence (flower cluster) consists of inconspicuous fertile flowers or showy sterile flowers or both. Mophead (or hortensia) inflorescences consist almost entirely of showy, sterile flowers clustered together to form a globular, snowball-like shape. The showy sterile flowers form a loose ring around the smaller fertile ones, giving this flatter inflorescence a delicate, lacy appearance. Both types are well worth growing.

H. arborescens 'Annabelle'

H. paniculata 'Grandiflora' (above)

H. arborescans 'Annabelle' (below)

Recommended

H. arborescens (smooth hydrangea, wild hydrangea) forms a rounded shrub 60 cm–1.25 m (2–4') tall and wide. It looks most attractive if grown as a perennial and cut right back to the ground in fall; the new growth that forms from the base each year bears the flowers. The flowers of the species are not flashy, but its cultivars have large, showy blossoms. **'Annabelle'** bears large, ball-like mophead clusters of white flowers from early to midsummer. A single inflorescence may be up to 30 cm (12") in diameter. More compact than the species, this cultivar is useful for brightening up a shady wall or corner of the garden. However, it often collapses under its own weight, especially after rain.

H. macrophylla (bigleaf hydrangea) is a rounded or mounding shrub that grows 60 cm–1.25 m (2–4') tall and wide. It flowers from mid- to late summer on the previous season's growth, and a severe winter or late-spring frost can kill this species back to the point where no flowering occurs. Prune flowering shoots back to the first strong buds once flowering has finished or early the following spring. On mature, established plants you can remove one-third of the oldest growth yearly or as needed to encourage vigorous new growth. ENDLESS SUMMER bears deep pink mophead flower clusters over a long season on current and the previous year's growth. The only bigleaf hydrangea reliably hardy to Zone 4, it survives cold winters and late-spring frosts well. It grows to 90 cm (3') tall and wide.

H. paniculata (panicled hydrangea) is a spreading to upright shrub that usually grows 90 cm–1.5 m (3–5') tall and wide, but can grow to 3 m (10') tall and 2.5 m (8') wide in an ideal location. It bears white flowers from late summer to early fall. This species requires little pruning. When young, it can be pruned to encourage a tree-like or shrub-like habit, and the entire shrub can be cut to within 30 cm (12") of the ground each fall to encourage vigorous new growth the following summer. **'Grandiflora'** (Pee Gee hydrangea) is the most common hydrangea in Alberta. The mostly sterile, white flowers are borne in mophead clusters up to 45 cm (18") long, fading to pink with age. **'Limelight'** bears upright mophead clusters of light chartreuse flowers. **'Pink Diamond'** bears large lacecap clusters of white flowers that turn an attractive deep pink in fall. **'Quickfire'** blooms about a month earlier than other hydrangeas. The pinkish white flowers fade to a deep rosy pink. It is hardy to Zone 4.

H. macrophylla ENDLESS SUMMER (above)

H. paniculata 'Pink Diamond' (below)

'Tardiva' bears 15 cm (6") long clusters of sterile and fertile flowers, blooming later than the species and other cultivars.

Problems & Pests

Occasional problems for hydrangeas include grey mould, slugs, powdery mildew, rust, ringspot virus and leaf spot. Hot sun and excessive wind can dry out the petals and turn them brown.

Juniper
Juniperus

Features: foliage, variety of colours, sizes and habits **Habit:** evergreen, conical or columnar tree, rounded or spreading shrub, or prostrate groundcover **Height:** 10 cm–12 m (4"–40') **Spread:** 60 cm–4.5 m (2–15') **Planting:** B & B, container; spring or fall **Zones:** 2–8

JUNIPERS ARE EXTREMELY DURABLE EVERGREEN SHRUBS AND are indispensable in Alberta landscapes. These plants run the gamut from evergreen, low-growing, spreading groundcovers to wide, arching, mid-sized shrubs to tall, pyramidal trees. When properly grown, they rarely suffer winter burn. There are many, many junipers to choose from, so consider visiting a large nursery that carries at least two dozen varieties (some carry 40 or more).

The blue "berries" (actually fleshy cones) of junipers are used to season meat dishes and to give gin its distinctive flavour. They also make a nice addition to potpourri.

Growing

Junipers prefer **full sun** but tolerate light shade. Ideally, the soil should be of **average fertility** and **well drained,** but these plants tolerate most conditions. Make sure to keep newly planted junipers well watered.

Although these evergreens rarely need pruning, they tolerate it well and can be used for topiary. Trim them in summer as required to maintain their shape or limit their size.

Tips

The wide variety of junipers available offers endless uses. They make prickly barriers and hedges, and they can be used in borders, as specimens or in groups. The larger species make good windbreaks, whereas the low-growing species work well in rock gardens and as groundcovers.

It is a good idea to wear long sleeves and gloves when handling junipers because the prickly foliage gives some gardeners a rash. Juniper "berries" are poisonous if eaten in large quantities.

Recommended

J. chinensis (Chinese juniper) is a conical tree that grows 6–12 m (20–40') tall and spreads 3–4.5 m (10–15'). It is rarely grown; its many cultivars, which lend themselves to use in small gardens, are preferred. MINT JULEP ('Monlep') is a compact, vase-shaped shrub with arching branches. It grows 1.25–1.75 m (4–6') tall and 1.75–2.5 m (6–8') wide and has bright, mint green foliage. (Zones 3–8)

J. chinensis

J. virginiana 'Blue Arrow'

J. squamata
J. scopulorum 'Moonglow"

J. communis (common juniper) is a native species that is widespread over the Northern Hemisphere. It grows in two distinct forms: a spreading shrub or a small, columnar tree. The variably sized plants may reach 60 cm–6 m (2–20') in height and 90 cm–2.5 m (3–8') in width. The most common form we see in Alberta is a low, spreading shrub 60–90 cm (24–36") tall and 1.25–1.75 m (4–6') wide. Many cultivars take advantage of, and improve on, one growth form or the other. *Var. depressa* 'AmiDak' (BLUEBERRY DELIGHT) is a dense, low-growing, spreading shrub that reaches a height of 30–45 cm (12–18") and can be up to 1.5 m (5') wide. The dark green needles have silver-blue lines on top, and the foliage colour is retained well through winter. This cultivar produces a plethora of berry-like blue cones. 'Effusa' grows 20–30 cm (8–12") tall and 1.25–1.75 m (4–6') wide, and has dark green foliage that persists through winter. (Zones 2–6)

J. horizontalis (creeping juniper) is a prostrate, creeping groundcover that is native to Alberta and boreal regions across North America. It grows 30–60 cm (12–24") tall and spreads up to 2.5 m (8'). The blue-green foliage develops a purple hue in winter. This juniper looks attractive cascading down rock walls, but a susceptibility to diseases often makes it relatively short lived. 'Bar Harbor' grows to 30 cm (12") tall and has blue-green foliage that is more blue than green. The foliage takes on purple shades in winter. 'Blue Chip' grows 20–25 cm (8–10") tall and spreads 1.75–3 m (6–10') wide. The silvery blue foliage is lightly tinged with purple in winter. **'Blue Prince'** grows only 15 cm (6") tall and 90 cm–1.5 m (3–5') wide, bearing dense, intensely blue foliage that holds its colour in winter. **'Hughes'** is a low, graceful, spreading selection that grows 30–40 cm (12–16") tall and 1.25–1.75 m (4–6') wide and has silver-blue foliage that turns purplish in fall. ICEE BLUE ('Monber') has stunning, dense silver-blue foliage that turns an attractive purple in fall. It grows 10–15 cm (4–6") tall and 1.25–1.75 m (4–6') wide. **'Prince of Wales'** bears bright green foliage with a bluish cast that turns light purple in winter. This mat-like shrub is just 10–15 cm (4–6") tall but 1.5–2.5 m (5–8') wide. The centre opens with age. **'Wiltonii'** ('Blue Rug') has trailing branches and silvery blue foliage. Very low growing, it is just 10–15 cm (4–6") tall but spreads 1.75–2.5 m (6–8'). (Zones 3–8)

J. sabina (Savin juniper) is a variable, spreading to erect shrub. It grows 30 cm–1.25 m (1–4') tall and 3 m (10') wide. Many popular cultivars are available. **'Arcadia'** has

J. sabina CALGARY CARPET

dense, gently arching branches and bright green foliage. It grows 30–45 cm (12–18") tall and 1.25–1.75 m (4–6') wide, and it is resistant to twig blight. **'Blue Danube'** is a spreading, vasiform shrub with arching branches and dark blue-green foliage. It grows 60–90 cm (2–3') tall and 1.25–1.75 m (4–6') wide. **'Broadmoor'** is a low spreader with erect branchlets. It grows 60–90 cm (2–3') tall and spreads up to 3 m (10'). **'Buffalo'** has feathery, bright green foliage that holds its colour well in winter. It grows 30 cm (12") tall and spreads about 2.5 m (8').

J. sabina 'Broadmoor'

CALGARY CARPET® ('Monna') is a low, spreading plant about 30 m (12") tall and 1.25–1.5 m (4–5') in spread. **'Skandia'** is a grey-green sister plant to 'Arcadia' with a similar growth habit. It grows 30–40 cm (12–16") tall and 1.25–2.5 m (4–8') wide and is also resistant to twig blight. **'Tamariscifolia'** (tam juniper) forms low, wide mounds 40–50 cm (16–20") tall and 90 cm–1.75 m (3–6') wide. The feathery, dark green foliage is blue-green when young. **'Tamariscifolia New Blue'** is a new selection of 'Tamariscifolia' that has deep blue-green foliage. (Zones 3–7)

J. scopulorum (Rocky Mountain juniper) is a rounded or spreading tree or shrub that grows 4.5–6 m (15–20') tall and spreads 90 cm–2.5 m (3–8'). The species is highly prone to twig blight; the cultivars are less susceptible. **'Blue Heaven'** is an upright, pyramidal tree that grows 3–6 m (10–20') tall and 90 cm–1.75 m (3–6') wide. It has beautiful silver-blue foliage year-round and an abundance of cones. **'Cologreen'** is a

J. scopulorum 'Wichita Blue'

J. horizontalis 'Blue Chip'

dense, cone-shaped, upright selection that grows 3–4 m (10–13') tall and 1.5 m (5') wide and has bright green foliage. 'Medora' is a dense, upright, columnar shrub that grows slowly 3–4.5 m (10–15') tall and 60 cm–1.25 m (2–4') wide. It has blue-green foliage. 'Moonglow' has intensely silver-blue foliage. It is a dense, cone-shaped shrub growing 3–6 m (10–20') tall and 1.5–3 m (5–10') wide. 'Skyrocket' is a narrow, columnar tree with grey-green needles. It grows up to 6 m (20') tall but spreads only 30–60 cm (12-24").
'Table Top Blue' is an unusual, dense, flat-topped shrub with attractive silver-blue foliage. It grows 1.25–1.5 m (4–5') tall and 1.5–1.75 m (5–6') wide. 'Tolleson's Weeping' has arching branches and pendulous, string-like, silvery blue foliage. It is sometimes grafted to create a small, weeping standard tree. This cultivar can be used in a large planter.
'Welchii' is a columnar to cone-shaped shrub growing 2.5–3.75 m (8–12') tall and 1.5–1.75 m (5–6') wide. The blue-green foliage has a silvery sheen when new. 'Wichita Blue' ('Wichita') is an upright pyramidal cultivar that grows 4.5–6 m (15–20') tall and spreads about 1.25 m (4'). It has attractive silvery blue foliage. (Zones 3–7)

J. squamata (singleseed juniper) forms a prostrate or low, spreading shrub or a small, upright tree. It grows up to 9 m (30') tall and spreads 90 cm–7.5 m (3–25'). Rarely grown, it is less popular than its cultivars. 'Blue Star' is a compact, rounded shrub with silvery blue needles. It grows 30–90 cm (12–36") tall

J. chinensis MINT JULEP

and spreads about 90 cm–1.25 m (3–4'). 'Holger' is a compact, spreading plant that grows 45–90 cm (18-36") tall and 1.5–1.75 m (5–6') wide. It has blue-green foliage that is golden yellow when young, providing a nice contrasting effect. (Zones 4–7)

J. virginiana (eastern redcedar) is a durable tree of variable form, from upright to wide-spreading. It can grow 6–9 m (20–30') tall but may grow taller, and it spreads 2.5–3.75 m (8–12'). This species is native to most of eastern and central North America. 'Blue Arrow' is a narrow selection that has bright blue foliage. It grows 3.75–4.5 m (12–15') tall and only 60–90 cm (24–36") wide. (Zones 3–8)

Problems & Pests

Although junipers are tough plants, they can suffer occasional problems caused by aphids, bagworms, bark beetles, leaf miners, mites, scale insects, canker, caterpillars, cedar-apple rust or twig blight.

Kiwi

Actinidia

Features: early-summer flowers, edible fruit, foliage, habit **Habit:** woody, climbing deciduous vine **Height:** 4.5–6 m (15–20') **Spread:** 60–90 cm (24–36")
Planting: spring, fall **Zones:** 3–8

KIWIS ARE USEFUL, VIGOROUS, COLD-HARDY WOODY VINES
that are becoming more popular with Alberta gardeners. The foliage mostly
covers the small, white, fragrant flowers, but the flowers are not why this
vine is grown. Kiwis climb up fences, trellises, walls (with support) and trees
with vigor. Some gardeners might consider them unwieldy, but pruning will
take care of that. Kiwis are a great choice for covering fences, trellises and
pergolas in partial shade. The sweet fruit is a bonus!

*These kiwi species offer hairless fruits
high in Vitamin C, potassium and
fibre. They make good substitutes
for the commercially available
brown, hairy-skinned fruit of
A. chinensis (A. deliciosa).*

Growing

Kiwis grow best in **full sun**, but they also grow well in partial shade. The soil should be **fertile** and **well drained.** These plants require **shelter** from strong winds.

Prune in late winter. The plants can be trimmed to fit the area they've been given. If greater fruit production is desired, the side shoots can be cut back to two or three buds from the main stems.

Tips

These vines need a sturdy structure to twine around. Given a trellis against a wall, a tree or some other upright structure, kiwis will twine upwards all summer. They can also be grown in containers.

Both male and female vines are needed to produce fruit. All species listed here have fragrant, white flowers that are borne in small clusters in early summer, and small, smooth-skinned, yellowish green fruit.

Recommended

*A. **arguta*** (bower actinidia, hardy kiwi) grows 4.5–6 m (15–20') high, but it can be trained to grow lower through the judicious use of pruning shears. The heart-shaped leaves are dark green. **'Issai'** is a vigorous, self-pollinating female vine with dark green foliage and fragrant white flowers in early summer. The sweet fruit is borne on mature plants and is seedless with no other kiwi to cross-pollinate. The species bears more fruit with a male pollinator present. It is not quite as cold hardy as the species.

A. arguta (above & below)

Problems & Pests

Kiwis are occasionally afflicted with fungal diseases, but they are not a serious concern.

Larch

Larix

Features: summer and fall foliage, cones, habit **Habit:** pyramidal deciduous conifer **Height:** 9–18 m (30–60') **Spread:** 3.75–9 m (12–30') **Planting:** B & B, container; early spring **Zones:** 1–7

EVERGREEN OR DECIDUOUS? MANY PEOPLE WOULD guess that larches belong in the former category because of their cones and needle foliage. Most conifers, such as pine and spruce, are evergreen, and larches are certainly coni-fers. But larches belong in the small group of deciduous conifers. Their needles turn yellow in fall before drop-ping for winter, leaving the tree's bare frame and cones showing. Larches are large trees (often reaching more than 15 m [50']), with slightly drooping branches. They are typically and effectively used as specimens.

Growing

Larches grow best in **full sun**. The soil should be of **average fertility, moist** and **well drained.** Though they tolerate most conditions, larch trees generally require good drainage. *L. laricina* is an exception; it tolerates wet soils because it naturally grows in bogs. Pruning is rarely required.

Tips

Larches make interesting specimen trees. They also look good when planted in groups, especially when mixed with evergreen conifers where the brilliant golden fall colour really stands out.

Be prepared to reassure your neighbours that your larch is not dying when it loses its needles in fall.

Recommended

L. decidua (European larch) is a large, narrow, pyramidal tree. It grows 12–18 m (40–60') tall and spreads 3.75–7.5 m (12–25'). **'Pendula'** has a weeping habit and is usually grafted to a standard. Specimens vary greatly from the bizarre to the elegant. (Zones 3–6)

L. kaempferi (Japanese larch) grows 9–18 m (30–60') tall and spreads 3.75–9 m (12–30'). It has pendulous branchlets, but its growth is less formal than that of *L. decidua*. The summer colour of the needles is bluer than that of *L. decidua*. Fall colour is excellent. **'Diane'** (contorted larch) has contorted, twisted branches and twisted, bright, light green foliage. It is an interesting selection, especially in winter, when its misshapen form stands out. (Zones 4–7)

L. laricina (tamarack) is an open, pyramidal tree with drooping branchlets. It grows 9–18 m (30–60') tall and spreads 4.5–7.5 m (15–25'). This species is native to Alberta and much of boreal North America. (Zones 1–6)

L. sibirica (Siberian larch) is an open, broadly pyramidal tree with elegant, up-curved branches, drooping branchlets and yellow young bark. It grows 12–18 m (40–60') tall and spreads 4.5–9 m (15–30'). It has bright to medium green foliage and bright yellow fall colour. (Zones 1–6)

Larches are good trees for attracting birds to the garden.

L. laricina

Problems & Pests

Aphids, case bearers, caterpillars, sawflies, needle blight and rust can all be problematic. Canker can be a problem for *L. decidua*.

L. sibirica

Lilac

Syringa

Features: mid-spring to early-summer flowers, habit **Habit:** rounded or suckering deciduous shrub or small tree **Height:** 90 cm–6 m (3–20') **Spread:** 90 cm–6 m (3–20') **Planting:** B & B, container; late winter or early spring **Zones:** 2–8

WE LOVE OUR LILACS. I CAN CLOSE MY EYES AND SMELL LILACS right now. We are blessed that this large group of long-lived shrubs and small trees love cold climates. Lilacs perform far better here than in warmer climes. The nursery industry has devoted millions of dollars to the development of new varieties, and they seem to come up with spectacular new specimens each year. So take your time while choosing, and take care to plant lilacs where existing trees won't shade them in the decades to come.

Growing

Lilacs grow best in **full sun**. The soil should be **fertile, humus rich** and **well drained**. These plants tolerate open, windy locations, and the improved air circulation helps keep powdery mildew at bay.

Lilacs benefit from renewal pruning. On established plants of *S.* x *chinensis, S.* x *hyacinthiflora, S.* x *josiflexa, S. laciniata, S.* x *prestoniae* and *S. vulgaris,* remove one-third of the oldest growth each year after the bloom to make way for vigorous new growth and to prevent the plants from becoming leggy and overgrown. *S. meyeri, S. microphylla, S. patula, S. pekinensis* and *S. reticulata* need only minimal pruning each year after the bloom to remove dead, damaged, diseased and wayward growth. Except for *S. reticulata* and *S. pekinensis* plants being grown as single-trunk trees, all lilacs listed here respond well to hard pruning during dormancy. This pruning can be done all at once but is best spread over two years. On mature plants, remove the thickest stalks at the base after the plants become dormant for the season—borers tend to tunnel into these woody havens, and they can kill the entire bush.

Deadhead lilacs as much as possible to keep the plants neat. Remove the flower clusters as soon as they are spent to give the plant plenty of time to produce next season's flowers.

S. vulgaris 'Sensation'

Lilacs are frost-loving shrubs that bloom poorly or not at all in warm climates. Some cultivars have been developed that bloom well with minimal winter cooling.

S. meyeri 'Palibin'

S. vulgaris 'Charles Joly'

S. x hyacinthiflora 'Maiden's Blush'

Tips

Include lilacs in shrub or mixed borders or use them to create informal hedges. *S. reticulata* can be used as a specimen or small shade tree.

Recommended

S. x *chinensis* (Chinese lilac, Rouen lilac) is a graceful shrub, 1.75–3 m (6–10') tall and wide, with many slender, spreading to slightly arching branches. In mid- to late spring it produces long, nodding clusters of lilac-purple flowers. (Zones 3–7)

S. x *hyacinthiflora* (early-flowering lilac, hyacinth-flowered lilac) is an upright hybrid that spreads as it matures. Plants usually grow 2.5–3.75 m (8–12') tall and wide. Clusters of fragrant flowers appear in mid- to late spring. The following cultivars are among those resistant to powdery mildew and bacterial blight. **'Maiden's Blush'** bears pale pink flowers. It is a vigorous grower and may need more regular pruning than other cultivars of this species. **'Mt. Baker'** bears large clusters of white flowers that completely cover the plant. **'Pocahontas'** grows 3–3.75 m (10–12') tall and wide, producing fragrant reddish purple flowers. (Zones 3–7)

S. x *josiflexa* is an upright to rounded shrub 2.5–3.75 m (8–12') tall and wide. This late bloomer bears pendent clusters of flowers in a range of pink, purple, red and white. (Zones 4–7)

S. *laciniata* (cutleaf lilac) is a dense, rounded shrub 1.75 m (6') tall and 1.75–3 m (6–10') wide. The blue-green foliage is deeply cut, with each leaf having three to nine lobes. In mid- to late spring, the small, open clusters of fragrant, light mauve flowers are borne from deep purple buds where the leaves meet the stem. This species tolerates heat and resists mildew. (Zones 4–8)

S. meyeri (dwarf Korean lilac, Meyer lilac) is a compact, rounded shrub that grows 90 cm–2.5 m (3–8') tall and spreads 90 cm–3.75 m (3–12'); it does not sucker profusely. It bears fragrant pink or lavender flowers in late spring and early summer and sometimes again in fall. The **Fairy Tale Series** is a new group of hybrids that grow 1.5–1.75 m (5–6') tall and wide. FAIRY DUST™ ('Baildust') bears fragrant, dusty pink flowers. TINKER-BELLE® ('Bailbelle') bears fragrant, bright pink flowers that open from dark pink buds. Both hybrids may bloom sporadically over summer. **'Palibin'** bears clusters of fragrant mauve pink flowers. (Zones 3–7)

S. microphylla (littleleaf lilac) is an upright, broad-spreading shrub that grows 1.75 m (6') tall and spreads 2.75–3.75 m (9–12'). It offers small, tidy leaves and attractive, airy clusters of fragrant, lilac pink flowers in early summer and sometimes again in fall. (Zones 4–7)

S. patula (Manchurian lilac) grows 1.5–3 m (5–10') tall, spreads 90 cm–2.5 m (3–8') and bears small clusters of fragrant, lilac-coloured flowers. This species produces few suckers. **'Miss Kim'** is similar to the species in shape and size but is denser in habit. The dark green leaves turn burgundy in fall. (Zones 3–8)

S. pekinensis (Pekin lilac) forms a small, multi-stemmed tree.

S. meyeri TINKERBELLE®

It grows 4.5–6 m (15–20') tall, with an equal spread. It bears nodding clusters of creamy white flowers in early summer. Although similar to *S. reticulata*, it has a more delicate appearance. (Zones 3–7)

S. x prestoniae (Preston hybrid lilacs) are a group of upright hybrids that bear nodding clusters of flowers in early summer, 2–3 weeks after the French lilacs. They generally grow 2.5–3.75 m (8–12') tall and 2.5–3 m (8–10') wide but can grow much larger. These typically nonsuckering hybrids can be trained into small trees. **'Coral'** produces pink, single flowers on a slightly more compact plant. **'Donald Wyman'** bears deep rose-purple flowers. **'Minuet'** is a small, compact, dense plant that produces abundant, single, light purple flowers. It grows only 1.75–2.5 m

S. x prestoniae 'Miss Canada'

S. vulgaris

(6–8') tall. **'Miss Canada'** is a vigorous plant with abundant bright pink flowers arising from deep rosy pink to bright red buds. **'Royalty'** is another vigorous selection that bears deep red-purple flowers. (Zones 2–7)

S. reticulata (Japanese tree lilac) is a rounded large shrub or small tree that grows 4.5–6 m (15–20') tall and 3.75–4.75 m (12–16') wide. It does not produce many suckers, and it bears fragrant, cream-coloured flowers in early summer. This species and its cultivars are resistant to powdery mildew, scale insects and borers. **'Golden Eclipse'** grows 3–4.5 m (10–15') tall and wide. New foliage emerges dark green with light green margins. The margins fade to gold as the leaves mature. **'Ivory Silk'** has a narrower habit and glossy, dark green foliage, and it blooms abundantly. It grows 3–6 m (10–20') tall and spreads 1.75–3 m (6–10'). (Zones 3–7)

S. villosa (late lilac) is one of the parents of the Preston lilacs. It is a large, coarse, rounded to oval, non-suckering shrub with dense, dark green foliage that turns yellow in fall. Small clusters of light pink flowers that fade to whitish are produced in early to midsummer, about 2 weeks after common lilac. Late lilac is drought resistant when established and can handle exposed locations. It grows 3–3.75 m (10–12') tall and 2.5–3.75 m (8–12') wide. (Zones 3–7)

S. vulgaris (common lilac, French lilac) grows 2.5–3.75 m (8–12') tall, spreads 1.75–3.75 m (6–12') and

bears fragrant, lilac-coloured flowers
in late spring and early summer. This
suckering, spreading shrub has an
irregular habit, but consistent maintenance pruning keeps it neat and in
good condition. Many cultivars are
available. '**Agincourt Beauty**' has
large, sweetly fragrant, deep violet-
purple flowers. '**Beauty of Moscow**'
('Krasavitsa Moskvy,' 'Pride of Moscow') bears white flowers that open
from pink buds. '**Belle de Nancy**' has
pink double flowers. '**Charles Joly**'
has magenta, double flowers. '**Fiala
Remembrance**' has fragrant, fully
double white flowers that come from
creamy yellow buds. '**Katherine
Havemeyer**' is a vigorous, mildew-
resistant plant with purple flower
buds and fragrant, lavender-blue,
double flowers. '**Lavender Lady**' has
abundant, fragrant, single lavender
flowers. '**Ludwig Spaeth**' has long-
lasting, fragrant, single dark reddish
purple flowers. '**Mme. Lemoine**' has
large, white, double flowers. '**President Grevy**' bears large clusters of
cobalt blue flowers that open from
reddish purple buds. '**President Lin-
coln**' has fragrant, blue single flowers.
'**Sensation**' bears white-margined,
purple flowers. '**Wedgewood Blue**' is
a compact selection that grows 1.25–
1.75 m (4–6') tall and wide. Large,
arching clusters of fragrant, single,
true blue flowers open from lilac pink
flower buds. (Zones 3–8)

Problems & Pests
Powdery mildew, leaf spot, bacterial
blight, stem blight, borers, caterpillars, scale insects and root-knot nematodes are all possible troublemakers
for lilacs.

S. reticulata (above & below)

Linden

Tilia

Features: habit, foliage **Habit:** dense, pyramidal to rounded deciduous tree
Height: 4.5–18 m (15–60') **Spread:** 4.5–12 m (15–40')
Planting: B & B, bare-root, container; spring or fall **Zones:** 2–7

IF YOU ARE LOOKING FOR A WELL-PROPORTIONED, TROUBLE-free lawn tree, look no further than lindens. They are some of the fastest growing of all large, deciduous shade trees. They tolerate a wide range of soil types and do well in clay soils. The fall leaf colour (yellow) is not spectacular, but the roots are well behaved and will not make your lawn bumpy from exposed roots.

Growing

Lindens grow best in **full sun**. The soil should be **average to fertile, moist** and **well drained**. These trees adapt to most pH levels but prefer an **alkaline** soil. *T. cordata* tolerates pollution and urban conditions better than the other lindens listed here.

Little pruning is required. Remove dead, damaged, diseased or awkward growth as needed. On multi-stemmed specimens, all but the strongest stems should be pruned out.

Tips

Lindens are useful and attractive street, shade and specimen trees. Their tolerance of pollution and moderate size make lindens ideal for city gardens.

The flower clusters of all lindens are attached to long, lance-shaped bracts. The flowers exude a dripping honeydew that will coat any underlying surface or object, so don't plant lindens near a driveway or patio.

T. cordata (above), *T. americana* (below)

T. cordata

Picturesque shape, moderately fast growth and wide adaptability make lindens desirable shade and street trees.

T. cordata

Recommended

T. americana (American linden, basswood) grows 13.5–18 m (45–60') tall and 7.5–12 m (25–40') wide. Fragrant flowers appear in early to midsummer. The species is hardy to Zone 2; its cultivars are less hardy.

T. cordata (littleleaf linden) is a dense, pyramidal tree that may become rounded with age. It grows 10.5–13.5 m (35–45') tall, spreads 7.5–10.5 m (25–35') and bears small summer flowers with narrow, yellow-green bracts. GREENSPIRE ('PNI 6025') has a narrow, oval crown and grows 12–15 m (40–50') tall and 6–7.5 m (20–25') in spread. (Zones 3–7)

T. x flavescens (*T.* 'Flavescens') is a hybrid of *T. americana* and *T. cordata*. It grows 10.5–15 m (35–50') tall and 6–9 m (20–30') wide, with a straight trunk and a pyramidal to rounded crown. Drooping clusters of fragrant, pale yellow flowers are produced in summer. This hybrid is resistant to linden mite. **'Dropmore'** is a vigorous, hardy tree with a dense,

pyramidal form. '**Wascana**' forms a dense, broad pyramid with strong branches. (Zones 3–7)

T. mongolica (Mongolian linden) is a small, elegant tree with a rounded crown. It grows 4.5–9 m (15–30') tall and wide. Fragrant, yellow-white flowers appear in early summer. The deeply cut, shiny, dark green foliage develops a bright yellow fall colour. This species is resistant to aphids, sunscald and leaf spot, but it is susceptible to storm, ice and snow damage. '**Harvest Gold**' is a hybrid of *T. cordata* and *T. mongolica*. This narrow, upright tree, which grows 9–12 m (30–40') tall and 7.5–9 m (25–30') wide and has an oval crown, is not as prone to damage as *T. mongolica*. It produces flowers in abundance and has bark that exfoliates as the tree ages. The deeply serrated, mid-green foliage becomes a golden yellow in fall. (Zones 3–6)

T. platyphyllos (bigleaf linden) is a large, broadly pyramidal to columnar tree that grows 10.5–15 m (35–50') tall and 6–10.5 m (20–35') wide and tolerates wind, salt and air pollution. It has large, glossy, dark green leaves; in spite of the plant's common name, the leaves are not nearly as large as those of *T. americana*. In fall, they turn an undistinguished yellow. The fragrant, creamy yellow-white flowers appear in early summer. (Zones 3–6)

Problems & Pest

Occasional problems can occur with aphids, borers, caterpillars, Japanese beetles, leaf miners, mites, anthracnose, canker, leaf spot or powdery mildew.

T. mongolica 'Harvest Gold'

Given enough space, lindens naturally branch all the way to the ground.

Maackia
Amur Maackia
Maackia

Features: foliage, form, bark, flowers **Habit:** small deciduous tree with a rounded crown **Height:** 4.5–7.5 m (15–25') **Spread:** 4.5–7.5 m (15–25') **Planting:** B & B, container; spring **Zones:** 3–7

AMUR MAACKIA IS AN EXCELLENT BUT UNDERUSED TREE. IT IS a good choice for urban lots and city streetscapes. Its loose, rounded crown forms early and is maintained throughout the life of the tree. Spring foliage emerges a soft, powdery grey before darkening to a lustrous green. Spires of soft, white flowers form in midsummer. The bark is yet another great asset. Shiny and dark brown, it flakes and peels as the tree matures, adding strong winter interest.

The genus name, Maackia, *honours Richard Karlovich Maack (1825–86), the Russian explorer and naturalist who discovered the tree growing in the Amur River region near the border between Russia and China. The species name,* amurensis, *reflects the location of the discovery.*

Growing

This maackia grows well in **full sun** in **average to poor**, **slightly alkaline** to **acidic**, **well-drained** soil. It adapts to many different soils and is drought tolerant. A member of the pea family, it can fix nitrogen in the soil.

Amur maackia needs little to no pruning. Any formative pruning should be done when the plant is young, in late winter to early spring, while the tree is still dormant. A mature tree resents being pruned, and the pruning wounds close slowly.

M. amurensis (above & below)

Tips

Amur maackia is a great tree for use as a specimen, as a street tree and in parks. It is also useful for planting in containers.

Amur maackia flowers have a fragrance like that of a freshly mown lawn.

Recommended

M. amurensis is a slow-growing, small tree with a rounded crown and upright, slightly arching branches. In gardens, it grows 4.5–7.5 m (15–25') tall and wide, but it can grow a fair bit larger in ideal conditions. The compound leaves, initially silvery grey-green, mature to a dark green and produce no appreciable fall colour. Erect clusters of fragrant, dull white flowers that appear in early to midsummer are followed by flattened, pea-like pods. The mature bark, which exfoliates, is orange-brown to copper in colour.

Problems & Pests

Maackia suffers from no serious pests or diseases.

Maple
Acer

Features: foliage, bark, fruit, fall colour, habit, flowers **Habit:** small to large, single or multi-stemmed deciduous tree or large shrub **Height:** 1.5–19.5 m (5–65') **Spread:** 1.5–15 m (5–50') **Planting:** B & B, container; preferably spring **Zones:** 2–8

THE MAPLES FORM A LARGE GROUP OF TREES, AFFORDING extraordinary opportunity for use in the landscape. Maple varieties such as Manitoba maple, Norway maple, red maple and silver maple are tall, wide shade trees and are glorious in large yards, but don't overlook the smaller ornamental varieties discussed below. You don't need to grow huge maples to enjoy their wonderful foliage, stellar form and fiery fall colour.

Growing

Maples do well in **full sun** or **light shade,** but their preference varies from species to species. The soil should be **fertile, moist,** high in **organic matter** and **well drained**. The roots can cause bumpiness in lawns, so try to keep the area underneath maples mulched to the dripline.

If maples are allowed to grow naturally, you simply need to remove dead, damaged or diseased branches whenever necessary. For maples to be grown as hedges or bonsai, begin pruning when the plants are young. All shaping pruning should take place when maples are fully leafed out, in early to midsummer.

Tips

Maples can be used as specimen trees or as large elements in shrub or mixed borders. Some species work well as hedges, some are useful as understorey plants bordering wooded areas, and others can be grown in containers on patios or terraces. Few Japanese gardens are without some attractive small maples. Almost all maples can be used to create bonsai specimens.

Recommended

A. ginnala (Amur maple) can withstand temperatures as low as -45° C (-50° F); in cold climates it is often used in place of *A. palmatum* or *A. japonicum* for Japanese-style gardens. It adapts to many soil types and a wide pH range. Growing 3.75–6 m (12–20') tall, with an equal or greater spread, it can be

A. platanoides samaras

A. palmatum 'Emperor 1'

A. *platanoides* in fall colour

A. *ginnala* samaras

grown as a large, multi-stemmed shrub or pruned to form a small tree. It grows well in light shade, but the fall foliage, often a brilliant crimson, develops best in full sun. Placed in a large planter, it is a popular choice for patios and terraces. **'Bailey's Compact'** ('Bailey Compact,' 'Compactum') is a vigorous shrub with shiny, dark green foliage. It grows 3–3.75 m (10–12') tall and 4.5–6 m (15–20') wide. It has lovely red-purple fall colour. **'Emerald Elf'** is a compact shrub, 1.5–1.75 m (5–6') tall and wide, with shiny, dark green foliage that turns scarlet to purple in fall. **'Flame'** is a densely branched, seed-grown selection. It grows 4.5–6 m (15–20') tall and wide, bears red fruit and has reliable, fiery red fall colour.

A. negundo (boxelder, Manitoba maple) is a fast-growing, upright to spreading, single or often multi-stemmed, suckering tree that grows 9–15 m (30–50') tall and wide. Migrating birds and squirrels consume the seeds with gusto. Its suckering habit, abundance of viable seeds and ability to handle tough conditions better than most maples has given it the reputation of being a weed in many parts of the US and Canada. The cultivars are better choices. **'Baron'** is a seedless male clone that is more upright than the species. **'Sensation'** is slower growing than the species and has better form. This nonsuckering, rounded tree grows 9–12 m (30–40') tall and 7.5–9 m (25–30') wide. The fall colour is orange to red.

A. platanoides 'Crimson King'

A. platanoides

A. rubrum

A. palmatum (Japanese maple) is considered to be one of the most beautiful and versatile trees available. However, because it leafs out early in spring, this tree can be badly damaged or killed by a late-spring frost. **'Emperor 1'** is an upright plant 3–4.5 m (10–15') tall, with an equal or slightly lesser spread. It leafs out later than other Japanese maples and often avoids frost damage. The burgundy purple foliage holds well through summer, turning red in fall. (Zones 5–8)

A. pensylvanicum (moosewood, striped maple) is a small, upright tree with a broad crown. It usually grows 6 m (20') tall and 4.5 m (15') wide, but it can easily reach 12 m (40') tall and 9 m (30') wide in ideal conditions. The large, bright green leaves are often tinged pink when young and turn bright yellow in fall. This tree's most striking feature is the green-and-white-striped bark. (Zones 3–7)

A. platanoides (Norway maple) is a rounded or oval tree 7.5–10.5 m (25–35') tall or taller, with an equal or slightly lesser spread. It has dense growth, so grass may not grow well beneath it. Its yellow fall colour can be good unless an early frost hits before the colour develops. This maple can be a tough city tree, but don't use it near natural wooded areas; the prolific seedlings can out-compete many native plants. **'Crimson Sentry'** is a narrow, upright selection with dark red to red-purple foliage that turns yellowish in fall. It grows 7.5 m (25') tall and spreads about 4.5 m (15') wide. **'Prairie Splendor'** is a hardy selection that bears burgundy red from spring to fall. The yellow leaves are somewhat showy. (Zones 4–8)

A. pseudosieboldianum (Korean maple, purplebloom maple) is a small tree with a rounded crown. It grows 3.75–5 m (12–17') tall and wide and has red-orange fall colour. An unusual feature is the purple flowers—most maples have yellow-green flowers. This species makes a wonderful *A. palmatum* substitute, but it could use a sheltered location. (Zones 3–8)

A. rubrum (red maple, swamp maple) is pyramidal when young, becoming more rounded with age. Single- and multi-stemmed specimens are available. It grows 9–18 m

A. ginnala 'Bailey's Compact' (above & below)

(30–60') tall, with a variable spread of 6–18 m (20–60'), and its cold tolerance depends on where the plant has been grown. Locally bred trees adapt best to the local climate. Fall colour varies from tree to tree, with some developing no fall colour and others turning bright yellow, orange or red. Named cultivars have the best fall colour. **'Autumn Spire'** is an upright tree, 12–15 m (40–50') tall and 6–7.5 m (20–25') wide, with a narrow, oval crown. The red flowers appear before the foliage in spring. Hardy to Zone 3, it is one of the earliest *A. rubrum* cultivars to show bright red fall colour. (Zones 4–8)

A. saccharinum (silver maple) is a fast-growing, large, rounded tree with drooping branches. It grows 15–19.5 m (50–65') tall and spreads 9–12 m (30–40'). Because it has weak

A. negundo 'Baron' (above & below)

wood and tends to drop a lot of debris, this species is a poor choice close to buildings and on small properties. It can also lift sidewalks and damage water and sewer lines. On a rural or large property this fast-growing native can be quite impressive, particularly when a light breeze stirs the leaves and reveals their silvery undersides. **'Kenora'** is a hardier selection than the species. SILVER CLOUD is a hardy, male selection. It has a symmetrical, upright, oval habit, and tends to keep its central leader. It is narrower than the wide-branching species. (Zones 3–8)

A. tataricum (Tatarian maple) is a large shrub or small tree. It can be multi-stemmed or trained to a single trunk, and it grows 4.5–6 m (15–20') tall and wide. The shiny, mid- to dark green foliage yields yellow to red fall colour. The ripening fruit stays red and showy for an extended period. (Zones 3–8)

A. VENTURA ('Durone') is a small, vigorous, upright, spreading, multi-stemmed tree with a low crown that grows 4.5–6 m (15–20') tall and 3.75–4.5 m (12–15') wide. It is an *A. ginnala* x *A. tataricum* hybrid with glossy green foliage that turns orange-red in fall. (Zones 2b–8)

A. saccharinum

Problems & Pests

Aphids, borers, caterpillars, leafhoppers, scale insects, anthracnose, canker, leaf spot or *Verticillium* wilt can affect maples. Nutrient deficiency in alkaline soils can cause chlorosis (leaf yellowing). Prevent leaf scorch by watering young trees during hot, dry spells.

Maple fruits (samaras) have wings that act like miniature helicopter rotors and help in seed dispersal.

Mock Orange
Philadelphus

Features: flowers **Habit:** oval to rounded, multi-stemmed deciduous shrub
Height: 45 cm–1.75 m (18"–6') **Spread:** 45 cm–1.75 m (18"–6')
Planting: B & B, container; spring, fall **Zones:** 2b–8

MOCK ORANGES ARE INDEED A ONE-FEATURE PLANT, BUT SO ARE
many plants we grow as ornamentals. A well-designed landscape can have
something in bloom all the time, and mock oranges can serve as background
plants when not in bloom. Two of the best mock oranges are Alberta natives.
'Blizzard' was discovered in Beaverlodge, and 'Waterton' was found in
Waterton National Park.

Growing

Mock oranges grow well in **full sun** but are tolerant of partial shade and light shade. The soil should be of **average fertility, humus rich, moist** and **well drained**. They are somewhat drought tolerant when established.

On established plants, each year after the bloom, remove one-third of the old wood. Rejuvenate over-grown shrubs by cutting them back to within 15 cm (6") of the ground. 'Galahad' needs only minimal prun-ing to keep its form. Established mock oranges transplant read-ily, though they have a huge mass of woody roots in relation to the amount of top growth.

Tips

Include mock oranges in shrub or mixed borders or in woodland gar-dens. Use them in groups to create barriers and screens.

Recommended

P. x **'Galahad'** is a small, multi-stemmed, oval to rounded shrub that grows 1.25–1.5 m (4–5') tall and wide and has medium to dark green foli-age. It bears a plethora of fragrant, large white flowers in early summer. (Zones 3–8)

P. lewisii 'Blizzard' is a hardy, upright, oval to rounded shrub that bears abundant, fragrant white flowers. It grows 1.5–1.75 m (5–6') tall and 90 cm–1.75 m (3–6') wide, and is hardy to Zone 2b. **'Waterton'** is an upright, rounded selection that grows 1.25–1.75 m (4–6') tall and wide and has somewhat arching branches. It bears white flowers in profusion. Both

Philadelphus 'Minnesota Snowflake' (above & below)

cultivars bloom in late spring to early summer. (Zones 3–8)

P. **'Snowbelle'** is a low-grow-ing shrub with graceful, arch-ing branches. It grows 45–90 cm (18–36") tall with an equal to slightly lesser spread. Fragrant white flowers completely cover the plant in sum-mer. (Zones 4–8)

P. x *virginalis* **'Minnesota Snow-flake'** is a hardy, dense, upright shrub 1.5–1.75 cm (5–6') tall and 1.25–1.75 m (4–6') in spread. It bears fragrant, white, double flowers in midsummer. (Zones 3–7)

Problems & Pests

Mock oranges may be affected by fungal leaf spot, grey mold, powdery mildew, rust and scale insects, but these problems are rarely serious.

Mountain Ash
Sorbus

Features: form, flowers, foliage, fruit **Habit:** rounded to broadly pyramidal, single or multi-stemmed deciduous tree **Height:** 4.5–10.5 m (15–35') **Spread:** 3–9 m (10–30') **Planting:** B & B, container; spring, fall **Zones:** 3–8

MOUNTAIN ASH *(SORBUS)* AND ASH *(FRAXINUS)* ARE NOT related; the only thing they have in common is that they are both deciduous trees. Mountain ashes are in the rose family, along with roses, cherries, apples, hawthorns and many other ornamental plants. Mountain ashes have wonderful flowers; the showy fruits rarely despoil the yard and are enjoyed greatly by birds. These trees quickly develop extremely handsome, rounded-to-oval form and varied bark colour; mountain ashes are very attractive in winter. They are, however, susceptible to borer infestations and fire blight, but proper care when planting, ample water in the first three years and proper fertility help minimize these occurrences.

Growing

Mountain ashes grow well in **full sun**, **partial shade** or **light shade** in **humus-rich, average to fertile, moist, well-drained** soil. They prefer **neutral to slightly acidic** soil but tolerate a slightly alkaline situation. *S. aucuparia* tolerates pollution and urban conditions.

These plants need little pruning. Remove damaged, diseased and awkward growth as needed.

Mountain ashes are susceptible to fire blight. If a plant contracts the disease, it will eventually die, so you might need to replace it after 12 to 15 years. Most people with mountain ashes agree that having them is worth the risk.

S. aucuparia

S. americana

Most mountain ashes, such as S. aucuparia, *have compound leaves with many leaflets per leaf. Two exceptions are* S. hybrida, *which has deeply lobed leaves, and* S. alnifolia, *which has simple leaves.*

S. aucuparia

Mountain ash berries, especially of
S. aucuparia, *are a favourite food
of birds, which often strip them
from the trees before winter arrives.*

S. americana

Tips

Use mountain ashes as specimen
trees in small gardens, or plant them
in woodland and natural gardens.
They can attract a variety of wildlife,
and many birds enjoy the fruit.

Recommended

S. americana (American mountain
ash) is an oval to rounded tree or
large shrub that grows 4.5–7.5 m
(15–25') tall and 3–4.5 m (10–15')
wide. It has light green foliage that
turns yellow to red in fall. In late
spring and early summer, it bears
dense clusters of fragrant, white
flowers, which are followed by spherical, orange to red fruit.

S. aucuparia (European mountain
ash) is a single to multi-stemmed
tree, 6–9 m (20–30') tall and wide,
with a low, rounded crown. It has
mid- to dark green foliage that turns
red to orange in fall. This floriferous
tree produces clusters of white flowers in late spring. Many birds feed
on the orange-red fruit. **'Fastigiata'**

is a narrow, upright selection that grows 4.5–7.5 m (15–25') tall and 1.5–1.75 m (5–6') wide. **'Rossica'** grows 4.5–7.5 m (15–25') tall and 3–3.75 m (10–12') wide and has red fruit. **'Skinner'** has an upright, oval form and is resistant to sunscald. (Zones 3–7)

S. decora (showy mountain ash) is an upright tree or large shrub that grows 4.5–6 m (15–20') in height and spread. The dark blue-green foliage turns a wonderful orange-red in fall. Clusters of white flowers appear in late spring. The spherical fruit is bright red.

S. hybrida (oakleaf mountain ash) is a cross between *S. aucuparia* and *S. aria*. Growing 6–10.5 m (20–35') tall and 4.5–6 m (15–20') wide, it is a vigorous, erect tree. When mature, it becomes broadly pyramidal, with wide, spreading branches. The deeply lobed, oak-like foliage is dark green to blue-green. (Zones 4–8)

Problems & Pests
In addition to fire blight, other potential problems include powdery mildew, anthracnose, rust, borers, sawflies, scale and aphids.

Many parts of mountain ash trees have been used in herbal medicine. The ripe berries are made into a gargle for sore throats and inflamed tonsils. The berries have also been used to combat scurvy.

S. aucuparia 'Fastigiata' with DIABOLO ninebark

Delicious jams and jellies can be made from mountain ash berries, but wait for a few good frosts before harvesting the fruit clusters.

S. decora

Ninebark

Physocarpus

Features: mid-spring or early-summer flowers, fruit, bark, foliage
Habit: upright, sometimes suckering deciduous shrub **Height:** 60 cm–3 m (2–10')
Spread: 60 cm–3.75 m (2–12') **Planting:** container; spring or fall **Zones:** 2–8

NINEBARKS ARE POPULAR SHRUBS, AND FOR GOOD REASON.
They feature attractive foliage, ranging from green to gold to purple-bronze,
and they have eye-popping early-summer flowers. Tough as nails to Zone 2,
they are perfect for use in foundation plantings and mixed shrub borders.
These plants respond well to pruning, and they make a lovely, dense hedge in
full sun. The gold and darker foliaged cultivars look terrific placed to the rear
of the mixed perennial and annual garden.

Ninebark is an easy-growing shrub that adapts to most garden conditions.

Growing

These ninebarks grow well in **full sun** or **partial shade**, but the best leaf colouring develops in a sunny location. The soil should be **fertile, moist** and **well drained**, and these shrubs adapt well to alkaline soil.

Little pruning is required. You can encourage vigorous new growth by removing one-third of the old stems each year after the plants have finished flowering.

Tips

Ninebarks can be included in a shrub or mixed border or in a woodland or naturalistic garden.

Recommended

P. opulifolius (common ninebark) is a suckering shrub that has long, arching branches and exfoliating bark. It grows 1.75–3 m (6–10') tall and spreads 1.75–3.75 m (6–12'). Light pink flowers in early summer give way to fruit that ripens to reddish green. CENTER GLOW ('Center Glow') grows 1.75–2.5 m (6–8') tall and wide. This DIABOLO x 'Darts Gold' cross has bright gold new foliage that is reddish around the margins. The leaves change to a deep burgundy red from the leaf margins inwards, and turn a brighter red in fall. COPPERTINA ('Mindia') is an upright shrub that grows 1.75–2.5 m (6–8') tall and is slightly narrower than tall. The new foliage emerges a coppery orange-red, maturing to dark red. **'Dart's Gold'** grows 1.5 m (5') in height and spread. The bright gold leaves hold their colour well in summer. DIABOLO ('Monlo') has

'Nugget'

attractive purple foliage and grows 1.75–2.5 m (6–8') in height and spread. **'Nanus'** (var. *nanus*; dwarf ninebark) is a bushy shrub that grows about 60 cm (24") (occasionally 1.25 m [4']) tall and 60–90 cm (24–36") wide, with small, dark green leaves. **'Nugget'** is a compact plant that grows 1.75 m (6') tall, with an equal spread. The bright yellow foliage matures to lime green over summer. SUMMER WINE ('Seward') is a neat, compact plant 1.5–1.75 m (5–6') in height and width. It has dark crimson foliage and pinkish white midsummer flowers.

Problems & Pests

Occasional problems with leaf spot, fire blight and powdery mildew may occur.

DIABOLO

Oak

Quercus

Features: summer and fall foliage, bark, habit, acorns **Habit:** rounded, spreading deciduous tree **Height:** 9–15 m (30–50') **Spread:** 6–15 m (20–50')
Planting: B & B, container; spring, fall **Zones:** 2–8

ALL SPECIES AND VARIETIES OF OAKS MATURE INTO TALL, impressive shade trees, but it will take a while here in Alberta. Starting an oak from an acorn is relatively easy, and most oaks are propagated this way. Many acorns need cold stratification before they germinate. Remove the cups from the seeds, then place the seeds and some moist peat moss in a sealable plastic bag and put it in the refrigerator. Check the seeds after one month, then again every couple of weeks until you see the root structure breaking through the seed coat. Ensure the peat moss remains moist, but not wet. Plant the germinated seed into a container or into its permanent spot in the ground in spring when the soil warms.

Growing

Oaks grow well in **full sun** or **partial shade**. The soil should be **fertile, moist** and **well drained**. Most oaks prefer slightly acidic soils. *Q. rubra* needs acidic soil to thrive.

Oaks can be difficult to establish. Most species should be transplanted only when young. Do not disturb the ground around the base of oaks—they are sensitive to changes in grade.

No pruning is needed.

Oaks are important commercial trees. The wood is used for furniture, flooring, veneers, boatbuilding and casks for wine and whiskey.

Q. macrocarpa (above & below)

Q. REGAL PRINCE (above & below)

Tips

Oaks are large trees best suited to be grown as specimens or in groves in parks and large gardens.

Acorns are generally not edible, but some kinds can be eaten after the bitter tannins have been leached out.

Recommended

Q. alba (white oak) is a rounded, spreading tree with peeling bark. It grows 9–15 m (30–50') tall, with an equal spread. The leaves may turn purple-red in fall. (Zones 3–8)

Q. ellipsoidalis (jack oak, northern pin oak, Hill's oak) grows 10.5–15 m (35–50') tall and 9–15 m (30–50') wide, with an irregular, oval to rounded crown and low-hanging branches. The deeply cut foliage turns orange to scarlet in fall. This species likes full sun and is drought tolerant. (Zones 3–6)

Q. macrocarpa (bur oak, mossy-cup oak) is a large, broad tree with furrowed bark. This species grows 10.5–15 m (35–50') tall and 7.5–9 m (25–30') wide. The leaves turn shades of yellow in fall.

Q. mongolica (Mongolian oak) is a large, spreading tree, 9–15 m (30–50') tall and 9–12 m (30–40') wide, that develops an open, irregular crown with age. The wide, dark green leaves have shallow lobes and turn reddish brown in fall. (Zones 3–8)

Q. REGAL PRINCE (*Q*. x *warei* 'Long') grows 12–15 m (40–50') tall and 6–9 m (20–30') wide, forming an upright, oval shape. The mildew-resistant, glossy, dark green leaves with silvery undersides turn rusty red-orange in fall. (Zones 4–8)

Q. rubra (red oak) is a rounded, spreading tree 9–13.5 m (30–45') tall and 7.5–10.5 m (25–35') wide. The fall colour ranges from yellow to red-brown. Be careful not to damage the shallow roots if cultivating close to the tree. (Zones 4–8)

Problems & Pests

"Sudden oak death," caused by a fungus-like organism, was first reported in California in 1995 and has moved into the American Midwest, but it is not yet in Alberta. *Q. rubra* is most susceptible. Other possible problems, rarely serious, are borers, gypsy moth caterpillar, leaf miners, leaf rollers, leaf skeletonizers, scale insects, canker, leaf gall, leaf spot, powdery mildew, rust, twig blight and wilt.

Oaks have been held sacred by many cultures throughout history. The ancient Greeks believed these trees were the first ones created, and the Roman poet Virgil said that they gave birth to the human race.

The stately oaks can deliver adaptability, fast growth and a long life span if chosen carefully.

Pine

Pinus

Features: foliage, bark, cones, habit **Habit:** upright, columnar or spreading, evergreen tree or shrub **Height:** 45 cm–24 m (18"–80') **Spread:** 60 cm–12 m (2–40')
Planting: B & B, container; spring or fall **Zones:** 2–8

WHETHER LARGE OR SMALL, EVERY LANDSCAPE SHOULD HAVE
at least one pine—they are essential to northern gardens. There is a tremendous variety of sizes and growth forms, and pines are also quite variable
within each species. Be prepared for your pine to develop its own unique
character. Most of the cultivars are reproduced asexually, resulting in more
uniformity. For example, the dwarf mugo pine cultivar 'Mops' will stay
dwarf, which is not always the case with the *P. mugo* var. *pumilio* or var. *mugo*.

Growing

Pines grow best in **full sun**. They are not heavy feeders, but soil of **moderate fertility** is recommended. They adapt to most well-drained soils. *P. flexilis* tolerates partial shade and needs moist, well-drained soil.

Little or no pruning is required. Trim hedges in midsummer. Pinch up to one-half the length of the "candles," the fully extended but still soft new growth, to shape the plant or regulate its growth.

Tips

Pines can be used as specimen trees, hedges or windbreaks. Smaller cultivars can be included in shrub or mixed borders to provide texture and interest year-round.

P. ponderosa

Recommended

P. aristata (bristlecone pine) is a slow-growing, irregular conical to shrubby tree that grows 2.5–6 m (8–20') tall and 1.75–4.25 m (6–14') wide. It doesn't tolerate pollution but survives in poor, dry, rocky soil. The needles may dry out if exposed to winter winds. (Zones 4–8)

P. banksiana (jack pine) is rounded to conical when young, becoming irregular with age. It grows 9–15 m (30–50') tall, with a variable but lesser spread. It is often considered too scruffy for areas where more attractive species thrive. **'Schoodic'** is a mat-forming, prostrate plant, 30–45 cm (12–18") tall and 1.75–3 m (6–10') wide, with twisted branches and bright green needles.

Pines are more diverse and widely adapted than any other conifers.

P. aristata

P. flexilis

Pines are easy to distinguish from other needled evergreens. Their needles are borne in bundles of two, three or five, whereas spruce, fir and hemlock needles are borne singly.

P. cembra

P. bungeana (lacebark pine) is a slow-growing bushy, multi-stemmed, pyramidal, columnar or rounded tree. It grows 7.25–12 m (24–40') tall and 4.5–9 m (15–30') wide. The smooth, reddish bark flakes off in scales to reveal creamy or pale green bark beneath. (Zones 4–8)

P. cembra (Swiss stone pine) is dense and columnar, growing slowly to 7.5–12 m (25–40') tall and 3–4.5 m (10–15') wide. It is resistant to white pine blister rust. **'Klein'** (SILVER WHISPERS™) is narrow and upright, bearing dense, dark green needles with silvery white stripes and attractive, violet blue cones. It grows 3–3.75 m (10–12') tall and 1.5–1.75 m (5–6') wide. (Zones 3–7)

P. contorta **var. *latifolia*** (lodgepole pine) has a straight trunk and a narrow, open crown. Growing 18–24 m (60–80') tall and 6–9 m (20–30') wide, it has twisted, yellow-green to bright green needles and persistent cones. **'Taylor's Sunburst'** is broadly pyramidal, growing 3.75–4.5 m (12–15') tall and 2.5–3 m (8–10') wide. The new foliage is bright golden yellow, maturing to light yellow-green. (Zones 3–7)

P. flexilis (limber pine) is a broad, pyramidal tree, 4.5–12 m (15–40') tall and 4.5–9 m (15–30') wide, with flexible, wind-tolerant branches. **'Cesarini Blue'** is broad and upright with light powder-blue needles and grows slowly to 3–6 m (10–20') tall and 1.75–3.75 m (6–12') wide. (Zones 3–7)

P. koraiensis (Korean pine) is an open, columnar to pyramidal tree with long, blue-green needles, large, resinous cones and edible seeds.

P. sylvestris

It usually grows 9–12 m (30–40') tall and 4.5–7.5 m (15–25') wide, but can get much taller in the wild. The crown becomes irregular with age. (Zones 3–7)

Young P. sylvestris *(Scots pine) trees are popular as Christmas trees.*

P. mugo (mugo pine, Swiss mountain pine) is a low, rounded, spreading shrub or tree, 3–6 m (10–20') tall and 4.5–6 m (15–20') wide. **'Big Tuna'** is a dense, upright, multistemmed shrub with dark green needles. It grows 1.75–2.5 m (6–8') tall and 1.25–1.75 m (4–6') wide. **'Mops'** is a dense, tidy shrub with dark green needles. It grows 90 cm (3') tall and wide. **Var. *mugo*** is a dense, slow-growing, moundingvariety, 60 cm–2.5 m (2–8') tall and 60 cm–3 m (2–10') wide. **Var. *pumilio*** is a dense, slow-growing, mounding variety, 60 cm–1.75 m (2–6') tall and 60 cm –2.5 m (2–8') wide. **Var. *rostrata* 'Tannenbaum'** is a single-stemmed, small tree, 2.5–3 m (8–10') tall and 1.25–1.75 m (4–6') wide with an upright, dense, pyramidal form. (Zones 2–7)

P. nigra (Austrian pine) is an upright tree with a broad, flat-topped to

P. ponderosa

P. mugo

rounded crown. It grows 15–18 m (50–60') tall and 9–12 m (30–40') wide in gardens. It tolerates urban conditions, drought, heat and clay or alkaline soils. (Zones 3–7)

P. ponderosa (ponderosa pine, western yellow pine) is a conical, columnar or spreading tree, 15–21 m (50–70') tall and 4.5–6 m (15–20') wide. It has striking orange-brown bark with black fissures. It is extremely heat and drought tolerant. (Zones 3–8)

P. resinosa (red pine) is a conical to rounded tree with long, stiff needles. It grows 15–18 m (50–60') tall and 6–9 m (20–30') wide, and is useful for creating windbreaks. **'Morel'** is a dense, rounded to broadly pyramidal shrub with soft, light green needles. It grows 1.25–1.75 m (4–6') tall and 1.25–2.5 m (4–8') wide. (Zones 3–7)

P. strobus (eastern white pine) is a slender, conical tree, 15–18 m (50–60') tall and 6–9 m (20–30') wide, with soft, plumy needles. It is

sometimes grown as a hedge. Young trees can be killed by white pine blister rust, but mature trees are resistant. **'Blue Shag'** is a rounded, compact shrub 1.75–2.5 m (6–8') tall and 1.25–1.75 m (4–6') wide with blue-green to blue-grey foliage. **'Compacta'** is a dense, rounded, slow-growing cultivar that grows 1.75 m (6') tall and wide. It is wider than tall when young. **'Fastigiata'** is a narrow, columnar form that grows up to 12 m (40') tall and 4.5 m (15') wide. **'Macopin'** is a large, upright shrub growing 2.5–3 m (8–10') tall and wide, with an irregular, rounded crown, blue-green needles and a plethora of cones. **'Nana'** is a compact, rounded to flattened shrub with light green to blue-green foliage. It grows 1.75–2.5 m (6–8') tall and 1.5 m (6') wide. **'Pendula'** has long, ground-sweeping branches. It must be trained to form an upright leader when young to give it some height and shape; otherwise, it can be grown as a groundcover or left to spill over the top of a rock wall or slope. It develops an unusual soft, shaggy, droopy appearance with age. (Zones 3–8)

P. sylvestris (Scots pine) grows 9–18 m (30–60') tall and spreads 6–9 m (20–30'). It is rounded or conical when young and develops an irregular, flat-topped, spreading habit when mature. This species varies in size, habit, needle colour and needle length. **'Glauca Nana'** is a rounded to flattened shrub with dark green to blue-green needles. It grows 1.75–2.5 m (6–8') tall and wide. **'Globosa Viridis'** is a dense, upright shrub, 1.5–1.75 m (5–6') tall and 1.25– 1.5 m (4–5') wide, with bright green foliage borne in tufts at the branch tips. **'Hillside Creeper'** is a dense, prostrate plant that hugs the ground as it spreads. It grows 45–60 cm (18"–2') tall and 1.75–2.5 m (6–8') wide with green to grey-green foliage. (Zones 2–7)

P. uncinata (mountain pine) is sometimes listed as a subspecies of *P. mugo*. It is a single-stemmed, broadly pyramidal tree that has dark green foliage and grows 15–24 m (50–80') tall and spreads 6–12 m (20–40'). (Zones 3–7)

Problems & Pests
Borers, caterpillars, leaf miners, mealybugs, sawflies, scale insects, blight, blister rust, cone rust, pitch canker or tar spot can cause problems. European pine-shoot moths (minor pests) attack pines with needles in clusters of two or three.

Austrian pine (*P. nigra*) is susceptible to diplodia tip blight. Provide good air circulation to help prevent the disease.

P. nigra (above)

P. koraiensis (below)

Poplar and Aspen
Cottonwood
Populus

Features: fast, dense growth **Habit:** rounded, upright or narrow, deciduous trees
Height: 9–30.5 m (30–100') **Spread:** 1.75–22.5 m (6–75')
Planting: bare-root, container; spring, fall **Zones:** 1–8

POPLARS CAN GROW INTO LARGE, IMPRESSIVE TREES,
and a large space is truly needed. Poplars are indispensable as shelterbelt
trees. They are great for quick shade and good
summer windbreaks in large, naturalized
areas where their incessant leaf and twig
drop can be ignored. The narrow
selections are great for
screening in tighter
urban areas.

Poplar species provide food and
habitat for black bears, deer,
beavers, porcupines, elk, moose,
ruffed grouse and many smaller
birds, mice, voles, shrews,
chipmunks and rabbits.

Growing

Poplars and aspens grow best in **full sun** in **deep, fertile, moist, well-drained** soil. They adapt to a wide range of soils, except constantly wet ones, and are quite tolerant of urban pollution.

Aspens and poplars need only minimal pruning to remove awkward and wayward growth and any diseased, damaged or dead wood. Pruning can be done in late summer to early fall to reduce bleeding.

Tips

Poplars and aspens are large, fast-growing trees useful for naturalizing, in shelterbelts and on large, open properties. *P. tremuloides* is excellent for reclamation of disturbed sites; it looks best when planted in clumps. *P.* x *canescens* 'Tower,' *P.* x 'Griffin,' *P.* x 'Prairie Sky' and *P. tremula* 'Erecta' are used in tight spots and as screens.

These trees tend to drop their twigs and foliage, and the female plants often shed copious amounts of fluffy seed. Plant them well back from water pipes, drains and building foundations, which can be damaged by the aggressive and often-invasive roots.

Recommended

P. x ***acuminata*** (lanceleaf poplar) is a dense, upright tree with a pyramidal to rounded crown that grows 12–18 m (40–60') tall and 6–10.5 m (20–35') wide. The shiny, dark green leaves, which have very pointed tips and lighter undersides, turn yellow in fall. (Zones 3–8)

P. tremula 'Erecta'

The flat leaf petioles of P. tremuloides *are easily moved by the wind. The leaves appear to tremble in the slightest breeze, hence the common names.*

P. tremula 'Erecta'

P. angustifolia (narrowleaf poplar) is an upright, sucker-producing tree, 12–16.5 m (40–55') tall and 7.5–10.5 m (25–35') wide, with a pyramidal crown and ascending branches. The narrow, dark green foliage does not produce appreciable fall colour. (Zones 3–8)

P. 'Assiniboine' is an attractive, upright, male tree with a rounded crown that grows 12–18 m (40–60') tall and 7.5–12 m (25–40') wide. The shiny, dark green foliage turns yellow in fall. It is resistant to some diseases and bud gall mite. (Zones 2–8)

P. balsamifera (balsam poplar) grows 18–30.5 m (60–100') tall and 6–9 m (20–30') wide, with a narrow, oval-shaped crown and thick, ascending branches. The shiny, dark green leaves have greenish white undersides. The sticky leaf buds have a balsam fragrance. This species needs lots of moisture to reach its full potential. (Zones 3–8)

P. x 'Brooks #6' is a seedless male tree that grows 15–21 m (50–70') tall and 7.5–13.5 m (25–45') wide, with an oval crown. The shiny, dark green leaves turn golden yellow in fall. It is tolerant of partial shade. (Zones 3–8)

P. x canescens 'Tower' (tower poplar) is a short-lived male plant, 9–15 m

(30–50') tall and 1.75–2.5 m (6–8') wide, with a narrow, columnar form and sharply ascending branches. The shiny, dark green leaves have lighter undersides. (Zones 3–8)

P. deltoides (eastern poplar, cottonwood) is a very large tree, 22.5–30.5 m (75–100') tall and 15–22.5 m (50–75') wide, with a broad, open, irregular crown and massive, spreading branches. The light to bright green foliage sometimes develops bright yellow fall colour. (Zones 2–8)

P. grandidentata (bigtooth aspen) develops an open, irregular crown. It grows 9–15 m (30–50') tall and 4.5–9 m (15–30') wide, and is pyramid-shaped when young. The dark green leaves have large-toothed margins and whitish undersides, and turn yellow in fall. SABRE ('Durman') is an upright, male clone that grows 12 m (40') tall and 4.5 m (15') wide, and is hardy to Zone 2. The new foliage emerges purple-red, and fall colour is golden yellow. (Zones 3–8)

P. x 'Griffin' is a narrow, pyramidal, seedless clone, 9–15 m (30–50') tall and 3–4.5 m (10–15') wide, with ascending branches and dark green foliage. It is resistant to galls but susceptible to canker and borers. (Zones 3–8)

P. x 'Hill' is a narrow, upright female clone that grows 12–18 m (40–60') tall and 6–9 m (20–30') wide. It has good disease and bud gall mite resistance. Fall colour is yellow. (Zones 2–8)

P. x *jackii* 'Northwest' (northwest poplar) grows 15–18 m (50–60') tall and wide. This upright seedless

P. tremuloides

selection with a broad, oval to rounded crown has dark green foliage (susceptible to rust) and golden yellow fall colour. (Zones 2–6)

***P.* x 'Prairie Sky'** is a narrow, upright male tree that reaches 12–15 m (40–50') in height and spreads 2.5–3.75 m (8–12') wide and has good disease resistance. (Zones 3–8)

***P. tremula* 'Erecta'** (Swedish columnar aspen, European columnar aspen) is a narrow, densely branched, spire-like, seedless tree that grows 9–12 m (30–40') tall and 1.75–3 m (6–10') wide. The branches

ascend sharply, and the upper ones are twisted. Fall turns the glossy green foliage yellow. (Zones 2–6)

P. tremuloides (trembling aspen, quaking aspen) is a widespread, native, colony-forming tree with an upright form, whitish bark and a dense, oval to rounded crown.

Many parts of the poplar tree, including the bark, buds, new shoots and fallen leaves, are eaten by local wildlife.

Adapting to a wide range of soil conditions, it grows 9–12 m (30–40') tall and 3–6 m (10–20') wide. The glossy, light to bright green foliage turns bright yellow in fall. (Zones 1–6)

Problems & Pests

Poplars and aspens are susceptible to a wide range of insects and diseases, including borers, caterpillars (especially forest tent caterpillar), leaf beetles, leaf miners, leaf hoppers, black spot, bacterial and fungal canker, leaf rust, powdery mildew, root rot, aphid-caused petiole gall, and scale.

Scientists Jeffrey B. Mitton and Michael C. Grant discovered a P. tremuloides *clone colony in Utah's Wasatch Mountains that occupies 6.96 hectares (17.2 acres) and has in excess of 47,000 stems. It is largest single organism in the world and may be one million years old.*

P. x *jackii* 'Northwest'

Potentilla
Shrubby Cinquefoil
Potentilla

Features: flowers, foliage, habit **Habit:** mounding, deciduous shrub
Height: 30 cm–1.25 m (1–4') **Spread:** 60 cm–1.25 m (2–4')
Planting: bare-root, container; spring or fall **Zones:** 2–8

THERE ARE SOME GOOD, SOLID REASONS FOR ADDING POTENTILLAS
to Alberta landscapes. These shrubs are extremely winter hardy, shrug off
all manner of meteorological abuse and bloom for an extended period from
early summer through fall in a rainbow of colours including white, yellow,
pink, orange and red.

Growing

Potentilla prefers **full sun** but tolerates partial or light shade. The soil should be of **poor to average fertility** and **well drained**. This plant tolerates most conditions, including sandy or clay soil and wet conditions, but not drought. Too much fertilizer or too rich a soil encourages weak, floppy, disease-prone growth.

If you wish to shape a potentilla, do so in late winter. For plant rejuvenation, either cut back all of the stems by one-third, or do selective pruning by removing one or two of the oldest stems annually.

Tips

Potentilla is useful in a shrub or mixed border. Small cultivars can be included in rock gardens and on rock walls. On slopes that are steep or awkward to mow, potentilla can prevent soil erosion and reduce the time spent maintaining a lawn. It can even be used to create a low, informal hedge.

'Abbotswood' (above)

'Tangerine' (centre)

In the scientific community, the plant we call "potentilla" is now known as Dasiphora floribunda. *Botanists have changed the scientific name a number of times.*

P. fruticosa

'Tangerine'

A potentilla's flowers may fade in bright sun or hot weather (yellow or white flowers are least affected). The colours should revive in fall as the weather cools. Or try moving the plant to a more sheltered location. A cooler site that still gets lots of sun or a spot with some shade from the hot afternoon sun may be all your plant needs to keep its colour.

Recommended

P. fruticosa is the yellow-flowered parent of many, many cultivars, of which the following are a few popular and interesting examples. **'Abbotswood'** is one of the best white-flowered cultivars. It grows 60–90 cm (24–36") tall and wide or slightly wider. **'Coronation Triumph'** is a dense, mounding shrub that grows 90 cm (36") tall and wide. One of the earliest potentil-las to bloom, it bears a multitude of bright yellow flowers. **'Gold Drop'** ('Farreri') is a bushy dwarf cultivar with small leaves and bright yellow flowers. It grows 45–60 cm (18–24") tall and spreads up to 90 cm (36"). **'Goldfinger'** has large, yellow flowers and a mounding habit. It grows up to 90 cm (36") tall, with an equal spread. **'Gold Star'** ('Goldstar') has very large, golden yellow flowers and a mounding habit. It grows 30–60 cm (12–24") tall and 60–90 cm (24–36") wide. **'Jackmannii'** has good dark green foliage and yellow flowers; it finishes blooming earlier than 'Goldfinger.' It grows 90 cm–1.25 m (3–4') tall and wide. **'Katherine Dykes'** grows 60–90 cm (24–36") tall, with an equal spread. Its arching branches bear yellow flowers. MANGO TANGO® ('UMan') is a compact plant, up to 60 m (24") tall and wide, introduced by the University of Manitoba. Orange-red tinting emanates from the centre of each deep yellow flower. In cool weather, the flowers take on more red colour. **'McKay's White'** bears creamy white flowers but doesn't develop seedheads. It grows 60–90 cm (24–36") tall, with an equal spread. MOONLIGHT ('Maanelys') has pale yellow flowers and dark green to bluish green foliage. It grows 90 cm–1.25 m (3–4') tall with an equal spread, and is hardy to Zone 3. **'Orange Whisper'** has pale orange flowers and a good mounding habit. It grows 90 cm (36") tall and 60–90 cm (24–36") wide. **'Pink Beauty'** bears pink, semi-double flowers that stand up well in the heat and sun of summer. It grows 60–90 cm (24–36") tall and wide. **'Red Ace'** is a small, mounded plant with red flowers that fade to orange. It grows 60 cm (24") tall and 60–90 cm (24–36") wide. **'Snow-bird'** bears large, white, semi-double flowers. This robust, somewhat spreading plant grows 60–90 cm (24–36") tall and 90 cm–1.25 m (3–4') wide. **'Tangerine'** has orange flowers that bleach to yellow in excessive direct sunlight, so place it in partial or light shade. This cultivar grows 30–60 cm (12–24") tall and 60–90 cm (24–36") wide. **'Yellow Gem'** has bright yellow flowers. This low, mounding, spreading plant grows 30–45 cm (12–18") tall and spreads up to 90 cm (36").

Problems & Pests

Although infrequent, problems with spider mites, fungal leaf spot or mildew are possible.

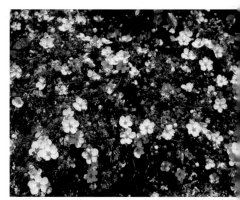

'Abbotswood' (above)

'Pink Beauty' (centre), 'McKay's White' (below)

Rhododendron
Azalea
Rhododendron

Features: late-winter to early-summer flowers, foliage, habit **Habit:** upright, mounding, rounded, evergreen or deciduous shrub **Height:** 90 cm–1.75 m (3–6') **Spread:** 90 cm–1.75 m (3–6') **Planting:** B & B, container; spring or fall **Zones:** 3–8

AMONG THE MOST BEAUTIFUL OF ALL FLOWERING SHRUBS, *Rhododendron* species have wonderful blooms in spring and attractive form and foliage throughout the growing season. They include many varieties that retain their leaves—and charm—through winter. Plants in the azalea group within the *Rhododendron* genus are, with a few exceptions, deciduous and drop their leaves in fall. Key to the value of *Rhododendron* shrubs is that they flourish and bloom in less than full sun. You must also ensure they have the acidic soil they need for the best results.

Growing

Rhododendrons prefer **partial** or **light shade**. Deciduous azaleas typically perform best in **full sun** or **light shade**, whereas evergreen azaleas tend to appreciate **partial shade**. A location **sheltered** from strong winds is best. The soil should be **fertile, humus rich, acidic, moist** and **well drained**. These plants require a soil pH of around 4.5 to 6.0. They are very sensitive to salt. Regular watering is necessary during periods of drought.

R. Northern Lights hybrid (all photos)

Shallow planting with good mulching is essential, as is excellent drainage. In heavy soils, elevate the crown 2.5 cm (1") above the soil level when planting to ensure surface drainage of excess water. Don't dig near rhododendrons and azaleas; they resent having their shallow roots disturbed.

Dead and damaged growth can be removed in mid-spring. Spent flower clusters should be removed, if possible. Grasp the base of the cluster between your thumb and forefinger and twist to remove the entire cluster. Be careful not to damage the new buds that form directly beneath the flower cluster.

Tips

A single placement of rhododendron in the mixed shrub border can be stellar, but these plants grow and look better when planted in groups. Use them in shrub or mixed borders, in woodland gardens or in sheltered rock gardens. Take care to give them a suitable home with protection from the wind and full sun.

In a protected location, they should not need a burlap wall in winter.

Rhododendrons and azaleas are grouped together in the genus *Rhododendron*. In general, rhododendrons are robust, evergreen shrubs with flowers that have 10 stamens. Azaleas tend to be smaller, evergreen or deciduous shrubs with smaller flowers that have five stamens. Hybridizing is tending to blur this distinction, however, and some people use the word rhododendron to mean any *Rhododendron*.

Recommended

R. catawbiense (Catawba rhododendron, mountain rosebay) is a rounded, evergreen rhododendron. It grows 1.25–1.75 m (4–6') tall, with an equal spread. Clusters of reddish purple flowers appear in late spring. **'Nova Zembla'** has purple-hued, red flowers and is heat tolerant. (Zones 4–8)

R. x marjatta (Marjatta Hybrids) were developed at the University of Helsinki in Finland by Marjatta Uosukainen. These rhododendron hybrids have large, dark green, evergreen leaves and large showy flowers. **'Hellikki'** is a dense, spreading shrub that grows 1.5–1.75 m (5–6') tall and wide, with shiny foliage and dark violet-red flowers in midspring. The buds and new growth are covered in yellowish fuzz. **'Helsinki University'** has bright pink mid-spring flowers with orange-red spots. The dense foliage is tinged red when young. This upright shrub reaches 1.5– 1.75 m (5–6') tall and 1.25–1.5 m (4–5') wide. **'Mikkeli'** ('St. Michel') is the hardiest Marjatta hybrid (to Zone 3) and the last to bloom, usually in early to midsummer. It is a rounded shrub growing 1.5–1.75 m (5–6') tall and wide, bearing pink-tinged, white flowers with green spots. **'Pohjola's Daughter'** ('Pohjolan Tytär') is a low, dense, spreading shrub that grows 90 cm (3') tall and 1.25 m (4') wide. The light pink flowers arising from the bright violet-red buds fade to white with green or brown spots. (Zones 4–8)

R. **Northern Lights Hybrids** are broad, rounded, deciduous azaleas developed by the University of Minnesota Landscape Arboretum. They grow about 1.5 m (5') tall and spread about 90 cm (3'). They are very cold hardy and are excellent choices for gardens in Alberta. **'Golden Lights'** has fragrant, yellow flowers. **'Lemon Lights'** bears lemon yellow flowers. **'Mandarin Lights'** has bright orange flowers. **'Orchid Lights'** is a bushy, compact plant with light purple flowers. (Zones 3–7)

R. **'PJM'** is a compact, rounded, evergreen rhododendron that grows 90 cm–1.5 m (3–5') tall, with an equal spread. It has lilac flowers that bloom in early to mid-spring. (Zones (3b)4–8)

R. prinophyllum (*R. roseum*; roseshell azalea) is a well-branched, spreading, deciduous azalea with dense trusses of fragrant (clovescented), white to bright rose pink flowers in mid- to late spring. It grows 90 cm–1.75 m (3–6') tall

and 1.75 m (6') wide and tolerates a higher (more alkaline) pH than most other plants in this genus. The bright green foliage is tinted bronze in fall. *R. prinophyllum* is one of the parents of the Northern Lights hybrids. (Zones 3–8)

Problems & Pests

In good conditions with well-drained soil, rhododendrons and azaleas suffer few problems. Stressed plants may be troubled by aphids, black vine weevil, caterpillars, Japanese beetles, lace bugs, leafhoppers, scale insects, leaf gall, petal blight, powdery mildew, root rot or rust.

R. Northern Lights hybrid 'Mandarin Lights'

Roses

Rosa

Features: flowers, fragrance, form, foliage, hardiness, fruit **Habit:** deciduous, compact, rounded to upright, arching shrubs **Height:** 30 cm–3 m (1–10') **Spread:** 30 cm–2.5 m (1–8') **Planting:** bare-root, container; spring, fall **Zones:** 2–8

THERE IS A GREAT SELECTION OF ROSES THAT CAN HANDLE ANY winter weather we are likely to experience. The small sampling of roses listed here are good, easy to grow, tough roses for the Alberta landscape, providing interest all year. They can be compact or quite large and often have prickly stems. The newer varieties bloom continuously and have good pest and disease resistance.

Growing

Roses grow and flower best with a **minimum of six hours of sunlight** per day. If your garden gets intensely hot in summer, some light afternoon shade will help prevent sun damage to the flowers and foliage, especially white flowers. Ideally, the soil should be **fertile, moist, slightly acidic** and **well drained** with **lots of organic matter**. Regular top-dressing with good compost will help keep your roses fed and healthy.

Protect roses from the strongest winds.

To deadhead reblooming roses, remove the spent blooms as quickly as possible after they droop and retain as much foliage as possible. For cluster-flowered roses, remove the entire cluster to just above the first leaf with an outward facing bud or new shoot. Stop deadheading in late summer or early fall 4–6 weeks before the first frost date. This allows some hip production, which signals the plant to prepare for winter dormancy. Do not deadhead once-blooming roses.

Prune roses once a year in late winter or early spring just before the rose breaks winter dormancy, or about 30 days before the last spring frost date. Prune to remove any dead, diseased, damaged, crossing or rubbing canes, to keep the centre open to allow for good air circulation and to keep large roses from

'William Baffin' (above)

'Jens Munk' (centre)

'Morden Ruby' (below)

growing out of bounds. Wear puncture proof leather gauntlet gloves.

Pruning shrub roses involves thinning and shaping. You can remove up to one-quarter of the old, unproductive canes annually on mature plants, and cut remaining main canes back by one-third and lateral branches by two-thirds.

Remove suckers and their latent buds by exposing the sucker where it attaches to the root, and pull it sharply away from the root. This is easiest when the sucker is still small. If the sucker is too large to pull off without damaging the root then prune off the root, if possible. Standard roses tend to sucker along the stem. These suckers can be removed by hand as they sprout or sharply pulled off when a little larger.

Tips

Roses can be grown in formal or informal beds, mixed and shrub beds and as foundation plants (ensuring

'Prairie Joy' (above & below)

adequate water). They make good informal hedges. Trailing roses make the best groundcovers and look good draping over retaining walls and on steep slopes. Very prickly roses make a great security barrier, stopping animals and people from going where you do not want them to go. Planting a large rose in front of or under a window will deter access. Climbing roses can be used to cover or mask structures such as fences, arbors and posts. Climbers will need to be tied to a supporting structure solid enough to handle their weight. Roses make beautiful accents and features, and they adapt well to growing in decorative containers.

Recommended

Rugosa Roses

This group contains a large number of varieties and hybrids of *Rosa rugosa*, a widespread, very hardy rose with attractive, disease-resistant, wrinkled foliage. These roses bloom in spring and fall; they have attractive foliage, and the large orange-red hips provide colour through late fall and winter. They respond well

'Champlain'

'Winnipeg Parks'

'Morden Sunrise' (above & below)

to heavy pruning but should not be sprayed with any type of chemical—the foliage is easily burned. Because they tolerate salt, rugosas can be used near roads, sidewalks, pathways and driveways.

R. **'Blanc Double de Coubert,'** a moderately dense shrub with arching branches, bears double white flowers with a strong, sweet scent in early summer and again in fall. It grows 1.25–2.5 m (4–8') tall and wide. (Zones 3–8)

R. **'Hansa'** is a durable, long-lived, reblooming shrub with very prickly, arching canes. It grows 1.25–1.5 m (4–5') tall and 1.5–1.75 m (5–6') wide. The double, mauve purple flowers have a strong clove aroma. It may suffer in alkaline soils. (Zones 3–8)

R. **'Thérèse Bugnet'** is a repeat blooming selection with grey-green, rather smooth leaves and canes with very few prickles. It grows 1.5–1.75 m (5–6') tall and wide, bearing clove-scented, ruffled, double, lilac pink flowers in summer and sporadically to fall. Fall colour is bronzy green, which goes nicely with the red canes and orange hips.

Explorer Roses

The roses in this group are some of the toughest on the planet. Bred in L'Assomption, Quebec, and Ottawa, Ontario, by Agriculture Canada, these roses thrive from year to year with little to no care or winter protection. They are moderately to highly disease resistant. Most Explorer series roses are repeat blooming. These roses are available in a range of colours and sizes, including climbers, and are most often found growing on their own roots.

R. 'Alexander Mackenzie' is extremely hardy, vigorous and highly resistant to powdery mildew and blackspot. It bears clusters of double, deep red blooms with hot pink tinges, and a mild, raspberry scent. Plants grow 1.5–2.5 m (5–8') tall and wide. (Zones 3–8)

R. 'Champlain' is compact, bushy and upright, growing 90 cm–1.25 m (3–4') tall and wide. It bears abundant clusters of semi-double, dark velvety red flowers from summer to fall. (Zones 2b–8)

R. 'Henry Hudson' is a dwarf, repeat blooming, rounded rose that bears semi-double, intensely clove-scented, white flowers. It grows 60–90 cm (24–36") tall and 60 cm–1.25 m (2–4') wide.

R. 'Jens Munk,' a rounded, dense shrub with large, abundant prickles, grows 1.5–2.5 m (5–8') tall and 1.25–1.5 m (4–5') wide. It bears clusters of semi-double, mildly sweet and spicy, pink to purple flowers from summer to fall, followed by bright red hips. (Zones 3–8)

R. 'John Cabot' is a climbing rose that reaches 2.5–3 m (8–10') tall and 1.5–1.75 m (5–6') wide. It produces clusters of semi-double, deep, vivid magenta pink blooms with a strong, sweet aroma in midsummer and sporadically to fall. (Zones 3–8)

R. 'John Franklin' is compact and bushy, and it blooms continuously from summer to fall, bearing large clusters of sweet-scented, semi-double, medium red flowers.

'Hansa' (above), 'Alexander MacKenzie' (below)

'Hope for Humanity'

It grows 1.25–1.5 m (4–5') tall and 1.25 m (4') wide. (Zones 3–8)

R. **'William Baffin'** is a repeat blooming rose that grows 2.5–3 m (8–10') tall and 1.5–1.75 m (5–6') wide, and bears large clusters of semi-double, deep pink flowers from summer to fall. It can be trained as a climber or pillar rose, or left in its natural, slightly arching form. (Zones 2–8)

Parkland Roses

Parkland roses were bred specifically for the prairies at Agriculture Canada's Morden Research Station in Manitoba. The result was a mix of tough, hardy roses in beautiful colours, shapes and sizes. Most roses in this series bloom repeatedly after the large flush of blooms in early summer and continue blooming until a hard fall frost. They bloom primarily on new wood and are grown on their own roots.

R. **'Hope for Humanity'** is a small, open, compact rose that grows 60 cm (24") tall and wide. It bears clusters of blood red, double flowers with a light, sweet scent continuously from midsummer to fall. (Zones 3–8)

R. **'Morden Blush'** is a repeat blooming rose that bears clusters of fully double, pale pink flowers with a light tea scent from late spring to fall. Plants grow 60–90 cm (2–3') tall and wide. (Zones 2b–8)

R. **'Morden Fireglow'** is an everblooming rose that has an upright, hybrid tea-like form and grows 60 cm–1.25 m (2–4') tall and 60–90 cm (24–36") wide. Sprays of mild scented, double, deep scarlet red with orange flowers bloom from early summer to fall. (Zones 2b–8)

R. **'Morden Ruby'** bears clusters of mild scented, double flowers that are a unique, mottled light and dark pink blend continuously from spring to fall. This vigorous and somewhat lanky shrub grows 90 cm–1.25 m (3–4') tall and 1.25 (4') wide.

R. **'Morden Snowbeauty'** is a variable, low-spreading, repeat blooming shrub that grows 30–90 cm (12–36") tall and 45 cm–1.25 m (18"–4') wide. It bears clusters of large, semi-double, white flowers robustly in early summer and sporadically to fall. (Zones 2b–8)

R. **'Morden Sunrise'** is a repeat blooming, compact, erect, dense rose that produces semi-double, mild scented, apricot yellow flowers from summer to fall. It grows 60–75 cm (24–30") tall and wide. (Zones 3–8)

R. 'Prairie Joy' is an upright, arching shrub that grows 90 cm–1.5 m (3–5') tall and wide. It bears profuse clusters of fully double, old-fashioned looking, mild scented, medium pink flowers in summer, with a sparse repeat. (Zones 2b–8)

R. 'Winnipeg Parks' is a tight, dense, compact, repeat blooming rose that grows 30–60 cm (1–2') tall and wide. It produces clusters of velvety, double, vivid reddish pink, lightly scented blossoms from summer to fall.

Species Roses

Species roses are roses that, when self-fertilized, produce seedlings that are identical to the parents. Species roses are very cold hardy and come in a variety of growth habits from vigorous climbers to compact shrubs. They tend to be more resistant to drought and disease than modern roses. Species roses usually flower once a year and produce attractive hips. Some species roses have excellent fall colour.

R. glauca (*R. rubrifolia*; red-leafed rose) is a vigorous, upright shrub with arching, thorny, purple stems and violet-tinted foliage. It grows 1.5–1.75 m (5–6') tall and wide, and bears clusters of small, single, white-centred, pink flowers in early summer, followed by small, dark red hips.

R. glauca

Problems & Pests

Roses may experience a range of pests including blackspot, powdery mildew, root rot, rust, sooty mould, crown gall, rose mosaic, aphids, beetles, cane borers, caterpillars, leaf cutter bees, leafhoppers, scale, spider mites, thrips and whiteflies. Leaf cutter bees are an aesthetic concern only.

Standard roses, often referred to as tree roses, have two grafts and an elongated main stem. The lower graft is between the rootstock and the stem. The other graft is between the stem and the variety at the top. Standard roses are used as accent and feature plantings, and may require winter protection.

Russian Cypress
Russian Arborvitae, Siberian Cypress
Microbiota

Features: winter foliage, form **Habit:** wide-spreading, prostrate, evergreen shrub
Height: 30–45 cm (12–18") **Spread:** 1.75–3 m (6–10')
Planting: container; spring **Zones:** 2–8

RUSSIAN CYPRESS IS AN EXQUISITE, EXTREMELY COLD-HARDY, low-growing evergreen shrub that deserves our attention. When it comes to evergreen options for shady areas, there are extremely few choices. If what you need is a beautifully textured, low-growing evergreen in light to partial shade, give Russian cypress strong consideration. And don't freak out in fall when the entire plant turns plum-coloured. That's just a nice late-season bonus.

Russian cypress is easily propagated by semi-hardwood stem cuttings and has few disease or pest problems.

Growing

Russian cypress grows best in **partial to nearly full shade** because it prefers life on the cool side, but it struggles in dense shade. If mulched and watered regularly, it does well in full sun. The soil should be of **moderate fertility** and must be **well drained**, or the plant can die from root rot. Mulching around the base of the plant and regular watering help keep the soil cool. Russian cypress tolerates windy sites and can adapt to poor, dry soil if the drainage is good.

Russian cypress needs little to no pruning. Remove any wayward growth.

Tips

Russian cypress makes an excellent groundcover. It can be used for erosion control on slopes, and it cascades gracefully down walls and raised planters. It can be used in shrub beds and rock gardens, but some people might find it too large for that purpose. Russian cypress is a good substitute for prostrate junipers.

Recommended

M. decussata is an extremely cold hardy, slow-growing evergreen shrub that has wide-spreading, prostrate branches with pendent branch tips that radiate out from the crown of the plant. The flattened splays of bright green foliage gradually darken over summer and become an attractive reddish brown to bronze-purple in winter. In spring, the green colour returns very quickly. This shrub can grow a little taller and definitely much wider than it is reputed to.

M. decussata (above & below)

'**Northern Pride**' is a named selection available in nurseries. Despite its fancy name, it has no apparent distinguishing features.

Russian Olive
Wolf Willow
Elaeagnus

Features: fragrant summer flowers, summer foliage, fruit **Habit:** rounded, spreading, deciduous tree or shrub **Height:** 1.75–6 m (6–20') **Spread:** 1.75–6 m (6–20') **Planting:** B & B, container; spring or fall **Zones:** 2–8

RUSSIAN OLIVE AND WOLF WILLOW ARE TOUGH PLANTS THAT thrive in adverse conditions, such as bitingly cold winters and oppressively hot summers. This toughness makes them ideal plants for Alberta landscapes. The silver-grey leaves make a terrific backdrop and contrast plant for evergreen trees and shrubs, and for plants with purple or reddish foliage. Russian olive makes a great specimen tree, but watch out for its long, very sharp spines.

E. angustifolia (all photos)

Growing

Russian olive and wolf willow grow best in **full sun** and **well-drained, sandy loam** of **average to high fertility**. Wolf willow will be more aggressive in overly fertile soil. These plants adapt to poor soil because they can fix nitrogen from the air. They also tolerate salty and dry conditions.

In midsummer after it has finished flowering, Russian olive can be pruned to remove wayward and crossing branches. It tolerates hard pruning and can be grown as a single-stemmed tree. For wolf willow, remove wayward growth and unwanted suckers after blooming is complete.

Tips

Russian olives are used in shrub or mixed borders, as hedges and screens and as specimen plants. Wolf willow is great for use in shelterbelts and for naturalized and wilder areas. It can be used as a specimen in a large container for silvery accents. The fruits of both species are edible but are dry and mealy.

Recommended

E. angustifolia (Russian olive) is a rounded, spreading large shrub or small tree with a low crown, somewhat arching branches and narrow, silver-grey leaves. It grows 3.75–6 m (12–20') tall and wide. The fragrant, yellow summer flowers are often obscured by the foliage, as is the silvery fruit.

E. commutata (wolf willow) is an upright, suckering shrub with bright silvery foliage. Individual shoots are sparsely branched, but thickets can appear dense. The new twigs are an attractive silvery orange. The yellow, late-spring to early-summer flowers have an intensely sweet fragrance. Silvery fruit follows. This shrub grows 1.75–3 m (6–10') tall and 60 cm–1.25 m (2–4') wide, but thickets can spread much wider. (Zones 2–6)

Problems & Pests

In stressful conditions these plants are susceptible to canker, dieback, fungal leaf spot, nematodes, root rot and rust. Plants may suffer chlorosis in shallow, alkaline soils.

Salt Bush
Salt Tree
Halimodendron

Features: flowers, foliage, drought tolerance **Habit:** spreading, deciduous shrub **Height:** 1.5–2.5 m (5–8') **Spread:** 90 cm–1.75 m (3–6') **Planting:** container, bare-root; spring or fall **Zones:** 3–8

SALT BUSH, A NITROGEN-FIXING PLANT, IS A MEMBER OF THE PEA family. It is a tough, low-maintenance, drought-tolerant shrub from the salty plains of central Asia. It is uncommon but worth trying, especially for those in southern Alberta and other areas where saline soils limit what will thrive in their gardens.

Trust the British gardeners to overcome difficulties. They graft salt bush onto the roots of Caragana *and* Laburnum *(golden chain tree, which is not hardy here) to keep the plant from suffering from excess moisture.*

Growing

Salt bush prefers a **sunny, hot** location and **extremely well-drained, neutral to alkaline** soil of **poor fertility.** It thrives on sunny slopes where excess moisture is not a problem. It will grow in very alkaline and saline soils, making it a good choice for roadside planting. Avoid disturbing the roots because they tend to sucker from root damage.

H. halodendron (all photos)

Salt bush needs only minimal pruning to remove wayward and crossing branches. Prune in late winter to early spring while the plant is dormant.

Tips

This spring bloomer makes a nice addition to shrub borders and dry-garden plantings. Salt bush is useful as an informal hedge, as a windbreak and as screening. The spines make it a reasonable security barrier. It can also be trained into a small tree.

Recommended

H. halodendron is a medium-sized, open shrub with downy, grey foliage and spiny stems. The compound foliage also terminates with a spine, and it turns yellow in fall. Pale lilac, lightly scented flowers bloom in early spring. The fruit is a long seedpod.

Problems & Pests

Salt bush rarely suffers from any pests or diseases. Excess winter moisture may cause problems.

This shrub is perfect for gardens with poor soil or gardeners with little time.

Saskatoon
Serviceberry, Juneberry
Amelanchier

Features: spring or early-summer flowers, edible fruit, fall colour, habit, bark
Habit: single- or multi-stemmed, deciduous shrub or small tree
Height: 1.75–7.5 m (6–25') **Spread:** 1.25–6 m (4–20')
Planting: B & B, container; spring or fall **Zones:** 3–8

THESE TOUGH, EASY-TO-GROW SHRUBS ARE SPLENDID IN
informal mass plantings and are well suited for naturalized areas. They are
equally at home in a shrub border or as a specimen. Clusters of attractive
white flowers in spring, edible fruit and attractive fall colour make choosing
saskatoons for your landscape an easy choice.

With a similar but generally sweeter flavour, saskatoon fruit can be used in place of blueberries in any recipe.

Growing

Saskatoons grow best in **full sun**. 'Autumn Brilliance' prefers partial shade. The soil should be **fertile, humus rich, moist** and **well drained**.

Dead, damaged, diseased and awkward branches can be removed as needed. To encourage healthy growth and an attractive habit, you can prune young plants, particularly multi-stemmed ones, after flowering has finished. Keep only the strongest, healthiest stems.

Tips

Saskatoons make beautiful specimen plants or even shade trees in small gardens. They can be grown along the edges of a woodland garden or in a border, and can make beautiful pondside or streamside plants.

Recommended

A. alnifolia (saskatoon) is a large, rounded, suckering shrub 2.75–4.5 m (9–15') tall and 1.5–1.75 m (5–6') wide. This native plant bears clusters of white flowers in late spring and edible, dark purple fruit in summer. Shades of yellow, orange and red colour the fall foliage. **'Honeywood'** is a minimally suckering shrub that grows 2.5–3 m (8–10') tall. It blooms a little later than some of the other cultivars and bears large clusters of large, juicy, very flavourful fruit. **'Northline'** is a suckering, spreading selection that grows 1.75–2.5 m (6–8') tall. It bears its large, juicy, sweet fruit in abundance at a younger age than the other cultivars. **'Pembina'** grows 2.5–3 m (8–10') tall and has few suckers.

It bears large, sweet-tasting fruit. **'Smoky'** is a suckering, spreading plant that grows 1.75–2.5 m (6–8') tall and produces large, sweet fruit in abundance. The fruit has the highest sugar/acid ratio of all the cultivars listed here. **'Thiessen'** is a tall, narrow, suckering shrub that grows 3–3.75 m (10–12') tall and 1.25–1.5 m (4–5') wide. It produces a plethora of very large, sweet, mild fruit.

A. x *grandiflora* **'Autumn Brilliance'** is a fast-growing, spreading, often multi-stemmed tree that prefers partial shade. It grows 4.5–7.5 m (15–25') tall and 3–6 m (10–20') wide. The new foliage is often a bronze colour, turning green in summer and brilliant red in fall. White flowers in spring give way to edible, purple summer fruit.

Problems & Pests

Problems with borers, leaf miners, fire blight, leaf spot, canker, powdery mildew or rust can occur but are generally not serious.

A. alnifolia cultivar

Sea Buckthorn

Hippophae

Features: foliage, fruit, habit, toughness **Habit:** deciduous, upright, spreading shrub **Height:** 2.5–4.5 m (8–15') **Spread:** 2.5–3.75 m (8–12')
Planting: container, bare-root; spring or fall **Zones:** 3–8

SEA BUCKTHORN HAS EXCELLENT FORM AND CAN DEVELOP some very interesting character. The fruits are incredibly nutritious. They can be eaten fresh or made into jams, jellies and wine, and they taste best before frost. The fruit can mildly ferment on the branches, and birds can get a little drunk if they consume enough. Don't drink and fly! Like its kin in the genus *Elaeagnus*, sea-buckthorn has silvery scales and is also a nitrogen fixer.

Hippophae is Latin for "shining horse." The name arises from the ancient practice of using the leaves as horse feed, which improved the horse's health and gave it a shiny coat.

Growing

Sea buckthorn needs **full sun** for the best growth. It can grow in a range of soil conditions, including saline soils, but it prefers **neutral to alkaline, moist, well-drained, sandy** soil. Sea buckthorn is tolerant of drought and extreme weather.

Sea buckthorn needs minimal to no pruning. Dead, wayward and crossing branches, overly dense growth and suckers can be removed in summer. Excess pruning can stimulate sucker growth.

Tips

Sea buckthorn can be used in shrub or mixed borders, in dry-garden plantings, as hedges and as specimen plants. Its salt tolerance makes it good for street plantings. The extensive root system makes this plant good for erosion control and soil stabilization. It is great for use in shelterbelts and in prairie orchards.

Recommended

H. rhamnoides is an upright, spreading, leggy, large shrub with silvery, narrow, grey-green foliage and spiny branches. It grows 2.5– 4.5 m (8–15') tall and 2.5–3.75 m (8–12') wide, and produces suckers from the roots, especially when the roots are damaged. Inconspicuous yellow flowers bloom on the second-year growth before the leaves emerge in spring. The ovoid fruit is most often orange but can be yellow to red, and it persists on the branches all winter. Male and female plants are both required for fruit production. Pollination is by wind.

Problems & Pests

Sea buckthorn rarely suffers from any pests or diseases.

Sea buckthorn fruit is somewhat difficult to harvest because it holds tightly to the branches, and there are the sharp spines.

Smokebush
Smoketree
Cotinus

Features: early-summer flowers, summer and fall foliage **Habit:** bushy, rounded, spreading, deciduous tree or shrub **Height:** 1.5–9 m (5–30') **Spread:** 1.5–9 m (5–30') **Planting:** container; spring or fall **Zones:** 4–8

I'M TRYING TO RECALL IF I'VE EVER DESIGNED A RESIDENTIAL landscape in full sun where I didn't include a smokebush. Nope, I don't think I've missed an opportunity to place another *Cotinus* in the ground. I find little use for the varieties with green foliage, though. *C. obovatus*, which gets gangly and rather weedy-looking, is best used for naturalizing or in a corner of the back 40, but still visible enough so you can enjoy the fall colour. The great joy is in growing the varieties with mesmerizing purple leaves. My favourite purple variety is *C. coggygria* 'Royal Purple.' It tends to die back in most Zone 4 winters, keeping the shrub at around 1.5 m (5') tall, with new annual foliage to maintain a rich colour. 'Royal Purple' makes a magnificent addition to the formal and informal perennial garden. If the space calls for a taller, wider shrub, try 'Velvet Cloak.'

Growing

Smokebushes grow well in **full sun** or **partial shade,** but strongly purple foliage develops only in full sun. They prefer soil of **average fertility** that is **moist** and **well drained.** Established plants can adapt to dry conditions in sandy soils. Smokebushes are very tolerant of alkaline, gravelly soil.

Long, lanky growth develops from pruning cuts. Plants grown for their foliage are often pruned to the ground each spring, encouraging lush, colourful growth. Alternatively, to avoid lanky growth, shear or prune lightly when the plants are young, then leave them to develop and mature more naturally.

Tips

Smokebushes can be used in a shrub or mixed border, as single specimens or in groups. They are good choices for rocky hillsides.

Recommended

C. coggygria (Eurasian smokebush) grows 3–4.5 m (10–15') tall and wide. It develops large, puffy plumes of flowers that start out green and gradually turn pinky grey in summer. The green foliage turns red, orange and yellow in fall. **'Grace'** is a hybrid of 'Velvet Cloak' and *C. obovatus.* Featuring large, pink flower panicles and purple-red foliage that fades to blue-green with age, it is the hardiest of the purple-leaved cultivars. **'Nordine'** ('Nordine Red') has pink flowers, showy red fruit and plum purple foliage that turns yellow-orange in fall. **'Royal Purple'** (purple smokebush) has purplish red flowers and dark purple foliage that turns reddish purple in fall. In Zone 4 it rarely grows taller than 1.5 m (5'). **'Velvet Cloak,'** which grows 3–3.75 m (10–12') tall and wide, also has deep purple foliage with a reddish purple fall colour. Its flowers are purple.

C. obovatus (American smoketree, chittamwood) is a small tree or large, multi-stemmed shrub. It grows 6–9 m (20–30') tall and wide, forming an oval to rounded crown. The blue-green to dark green foliage turns shades of yellow, orange, red and purple in fall. The grey-brown bark flakes with age and is quite attractive. In late spring and early summer it produces large clusters of insignificant yellow-green flowers that turn smoke-pink to purple-pink over summer.

Problems & Pests

Verticillium wilt is a serious problem that excellent drainage helps prevent. Powdery mildew is also possible, especially on the purple-leaved forms.

C. coggygria 'Royal Purple'

Snowberry
Symphoricarpos

Features: foliage, fall and winter fruit, habit **Habit:** rounded or spreading deciduous shrub **Height:** 60 cm–1.5 m (2–5') **Spread:** 90 cm–3.75 m (3–12')
Planting: container, bare-root; spring or fall **Zones:** 2–7

SNOWBERRIES ARE GREAT, LOW-MAINTENANCE, TOUGH SHRUBS
that can handle some rough conditions. They can be somewhat scruffy looking and may not be appropriate for show areas. However, they are great for mixing in a shrub border and are a must for naturalizing any area.

Symphoricarpos *translates as "together to bear fruit," referring to the clustered berries.*

These low-maintenance shrubs spread readily and are good for filling in gaps in shady areas.

Growing

Snowberries prefer **partial to light shade** but tolerate full sun. These plants adapt to any soil that is **fertile** and **well drained**, and they can handle pollution, drought and exposure to the elements.

Little pruning is required, but it helps keep the shrub tidy. On established plants, one-third of the old growth can be removed each year in early spring.

Tips

Snowberries can be used in shrub and mixed borders, in woodland gardens or as screens or informal hedges.

The berries are not edible and should be left for the birds.

Recommended

S. albus (common snowberry) is a rounded, suckering, native shrub with arching branches. It grows 90 cm–1.5 m (3–5') tall and wide. The small, delicate, pinkish white summer flowers are rather inconspicuous but still attractive. The clusters of white berries that follow persist through fall and winter. (Zones 3–7)

S. x doorenbosii 'Kordes' (amethyst snowberry) is a vigorous, thicket-forming hybrid that grows 90 cm–1.5 m (3–5') tall and wide, and spreads by suckers. It bears pink-tinged, greenish white flowers and an interesting pastel, mauve to white fruit. (Zones 3b–7)

S. occidentalis (coralberry, western snowberry) is a dense, well-branched, upright to arching native shrub with thick, dark green leaves. It grows 60 cm–1.5 m (2–5') tall and wide, bearing pink-tinged, yellowish white flowers and small, bright red-pink to darker red-purple fruit. (Zones 2–6)

Problems & Pests

Snowberries are occasionally inflicted with powdery mildew and anthracnose.

S. albus (all photos)

Spirea
Spiraea

Features: summer flowers, habit **Habit:** round, bushy deciduous shrub
Height: 30 cm–2.5 m (1–8') **Spread:** 60 cm–2.5 m (2–8')
Planting: bare-root, container; spring or fall **Zones:** 3–8

IF YOU ARE LOOKING FOR DURABLE, EASY-TO-GROW, PROFUSELY
blooming small shrubs to use in formal or semi-formal foundation plantings, look no further than spirea. Depending on the variety, blooming times
range from spring to midsummer. All spireas sport clean, striking foliage,
including yellow-, bronze- and lime-coloured varieties. Many have a naturally rounded form that can be maintained by shearing immediately after
blooming. Left to the their own devices, these plants often develop an
outward-arching habit that fits well into the mixed shrub border.

Growing

Spireas prefer **full sun** but tolerate light shade. The soil should be **fertile, moist** and **well drained**.

Pruning is necessary to keep spireas tidy and graceful. The tight, shrubby types require less pruning than the larger, more open forms, which may require heavy renewal pruning in spring.

The correct pruning method varies with the species and depends on the flowering time. Plants that bloom in spring and early summer usually form their flower buds the previous year and should be pruned immediately after flowering is complete. Cut out one-third of the old stems to encourage new growth.

Plants that flower later in summer or in fall usually form their flower buds during the current year. Cut these plants to within 30 cm (12") of the ground in early spring, as the buds begin to swell, to encourage plenty of new growth and flowers later in the season.

S. japonica 'Shirobori'

Adapting to a variety of situations and requiring only minimal care once established, spireas have become popular as ornamental shrubs.

S. japonica 'Little Princess'

S. japonica 'Goldmound'

Spireas come in sizes, forms, flower colours and leaf colours (summer and fall) to suit almost any sunny area.

S. x vanhouttei

Tips

Spireas are used in shrub or mixed borders, in rock gardens and as informal screens and hedges.

Recommended

S. x *arguta* (*S.* 'Arguta'; garland spirea) is a dense, rounded shrub with arching stems and bright green foliage. It grows 1.5–2.5 m (5–8') tall and wide and bears dense clusters of snow white flowers at the branch tips in mid- to late spring. **'Compacta'** (dwarf garland spirea) grows 90 cm–1.25 m (3–4') tall and spreads up to 90 cm (36"). (Zones 4–7)

S. *betulifolia* (birchleaf spirea) is a dense, mound-forming shrub that grows 60 cm–1.25 m (2–4') tall, with an equal spread. It bears clusters of small, white flowers in early to mid-summer. The foliage turns golden yellow and bronze in fall and provides a long-lasting, colourful display. **'Tor'** has purple fall foliage.

S. x *cinerea* is covered with white blooms before the foliage emerges in early spring. It grows in a rounded form that is 1.25–1.5 m (4–5') tall and wide. **'Grefsheim'** has a mounding habit. (Zones 4–7)

S. **'Dart's Red'** is a dense, compact, mounded shrub that grows 60–90 cm (24–36") tall and 90 cm–1.25 m (3–4') wide and has dark red flowers that fade to rosy pink with age. The green to blue-green foliage is tinted red in spring, and fall colour is red-purple.

S. japonica (Japanese spirea) forms a clump of erect stems. It grows 1.25–1.75 m (4–6') tall and spreads up to 1.5 m (5'). Pink or white flowers are borne in mid- and late summer. Many cultivars and hybrids are available—check your local nursery. **'Anthony Waterer'** grows 90 cm–1.25 m (3–4') tall and spreads 90 cm–1.5 m (3–5'). The foliage, reddish when new, turns blue-green over summer and then red again in fall. **'Froebelii'** grows 90 cm–1.25 m (3–4') tall and wide; it has purple-tinged, green foliage in spring and may develop good burgundy fall colour. It bears red-pink flowers. **'Goldflame'** grows 60–90 cm (24–36") tall and 60 cm–1.25 m (2–4') wide. The new foliage emerges red and matures to yellow-green, with red, orange and yellow fall colours. **'Goldmound'** has bright yellow foliage and bears pink flowers in late spring and early summer. **'Little Princess'** forms a dense mound 45 cm (18") tall and 90 cm–1.75 m (3–6') wide. The flowers are rose pink. **'Magic Carpet'** grows 30–45 cm (12–18") tall and wide. Its red new

S. *nipponica* (above)

S. *japonica* 'Anthony Waterer' (below)

S. *betufolia* 'Tor' (above)
S. *japonica* 'Little Princess' (below)

growth stands out above the gold and lime green of its older foliage. The flowers are dark pink. **'Neon Flash'** bears vivid pink flowers. It grows to 90 cm (36") tall and wide. **'Shirobori'** ('Shibori,' 'Shirobana') grows 60 cm (24") tall and wide. Pink and white flowers both appear on the same plant.

S. nipponica (Nippon spirea) is an upright shrub with arching branches. It grows 90 cm–2.5 m (3–8') tall, with an equal spread. White flowers appear in midsummer. **'Halward's Silver'** is a compact, hardy shrub that grows 60–90 cm (24–36") tall and 60 cm–1.25 m (2–4') wide. **'Snowmound'** (snowmound Nippon spirea) has spreading, arching branches that are covered with flowers in early summer. Grown more commonly than the species, this cultivar grows 90 cm–1.5 m (3–5') tall, with an equal spread. (Zones 4–8)

S. prunifolia (bridalwreath spirea) is an upright shrub, 1.5–2.5 m (5–8') tall and wide, with arching branches and shiny, dark green foliage. In late spring to early summer, it produces a plethora of button-like, white, double flowers. The fall foliage colour ranges from yellow-orange to red or purple. (Zones 4–8)

S. trilobata (dwarf bridal wreath spirea, dwarf Vanhoutte spirea) is a dense, bushy shrub with arching branches. It grows 1.25–1.5 m (4–5') tall and wide. White flowers are borne in clusters in early summer. **'Swan Lake'** is a smaller plant with arching branches. It grows 90 cm–1.25 m (3–4') tall and wide or slightly wider and bears abundant white flowers along its branches.

S. x 'Snow White' is a dense, upright shrub with arching branches and dark green foliage. It grows 1.25–1.5 m (4–5') tall and 90 cm–1.25 m (3–4') wide and bears large, white flowers in clusters in late spring to early summer.

S. x *vanhouttei* (bridal wreath spirea, Vanhoutte spirea) is a dense, bushy shrub with arching branches. It grows 1.5–2.5 m (5–8') tall and wide. White flowers are borne in clusters in late spring to early summer. **'Renaissance'** has disease-resistant foliage.

Problems & Pests

Aphids, dieback, fire blight, leaf spot or powdery mildew can cause occasional problems.

S. nipponica (above), *S. japonica* 'Little Princess' (centre)

S. japonica 'Neon Flash'

S. japonica 'Magic Carpet' (below)

Spruce
Picea

Features: foliage, cones, habit **Habit:** conical, columnar or globe-like evergreen tree or shrub **Height:** 30 cm–27.5 m (1–90') **Spread:** 45 cm–7.5 m (18"–25') **Planting:** B & B, container; spring or fall **Zones:** 2–8

PICEA IS A LARGE, INVALUABLE GENUS OF TREES THAT INCLUDES some of the most popular, hardy evergreens for Alberta gardeners. From tall, narrow spires that are great for smaller lots, or broad, dense evergreens that protect your home from chilling northwest winds, to the wonderful dwarf varieties including *P. abies* 'Nidiformis' and *P. pungens* 'Globosa' that make spectacular foundation plantings, you will not go wrong by choosing a spruce.

Because spruces can maintain their lower branches right to the ground as they mature, they make excellent screens and windbreaks or graceful specimens.

Growing

Spruces grow best in **full sun**. *P. glauca* 'Conica' and its branch sports prefer **light shade** and a **sheltered** location. Spruces prefer **neutral to acidic, deep, well-drained** soil, but they tolerate alkaline soil. *P. mariana* grows in boggy and wet areas and tolerates poor soil.

Spruces are best grown from young stock because they dislike being transplanted when larger or more mature. Pruning is rarely needed.

Tips

Spruce trees are used as specimens and windscreens. The dwarf and slow-growing cultivars also work well in shrub or mixed borders and in containers. *P. mariana* is best used for reclamation or naturalization.

Oil-based pesticides such as dormant oil can take the blue out of your blue-needled spruce.

P. abies (both photos)

Antonio Stradivari used spruce to make his renowned violins. The resonant, lightweight but tough wood is still preferred for violins, guitars, harps and the sounding boards of pianos.

P. pungens var. *glauca* 'Globosa'

Recommended

P. abies (Norway spruce) is a fast-growing, pyramidal tree with dark green needles. This wind-tolerant species grows 12–18 m (40–60') tall and spreads about 6 m (20'). **'Little Gem'** (miniature bird's nest spruce) is a dense, slow-growing, rounded to flat-topped shrub with small, dark green needles that are light green when young. It grows 30–60 cm (12–24") tall and 60–90 cm (24–36") wide. **'Nidiformis'** (bird's nest spruce) is a slow-growing, compact, low, mounding cultivar. It grows about 90 cm–1.25 m (3–4') tall and spreads 90 cm–1.5 m (3–5'). **'Pendula'** can be staked to a desired height to create a weeping form, or it can be left to sprawl along the ground. It spreads 3–4.5 m (10–15'). **'Pumila'** is a flattened globe, 90 cm –1.25 m (3–4') tall and 1.25–1.75 m (4–6') wide, with dense branching and short, dark green needles.

P. engelmannii (Engelmann's spruce) is a tall, narrow, conical tree that can reach 21–27.5 m (70–90') tall and 3–4.5 m (10–15') wide. It has blue-green to dark green needles that are odiferous when crushed. It is similar in appearance to white spruce. (Zones 2–6)

P. glauca (white spruce) is a conical tree with blue-green needles. It grows 15–24 m (50–80') tall and spreads 3–6 m (10–20'). **'Conica'** (dwarf Alberta spruce) is a dense, conical, bushy shrub that grows

1.75–2.5 m (6–8') tall and spreads 60–90 cm (24–36"). 'Jean's Dilly' and 'North Star' are branch sports of 'Conica.' **'Jean's Dilly'** grows 1.25–1.75 m (4–6') tall and 45–60 cm (18–24") wide, with shorter, thinner needles and twisted branch ends. New growth occurs later than on 'Conica.' **'North Star'** is a dense, compact, upright pyramid with green needles that resist winter windburn. It grows 2.5 m (8') tall and 1.5 m (5') wide. **'Pendula'** is a narrow conical tree that grows 9–12 m (30–40') tall and 2.5–3 m (8–10') wide. It has pendulous branches and greyish green needles that point downward. (Zones 2–6)

P. mariana (black spruce, bog spruce) is a narrow, spire-like, conical tree that typically grows 9–12 m (30–40') tall and 1.75–3 m (6–10') wide. It has dull, blue-green to blue-grey foliage and small, purple cones that mature to brown. **'Ericoides'** (blue nest spruce) is a flat-topped mound that grows 30–45 cm (12–18") tall and 75–90 cm (30–36") wide. It has short, blue-grey foliage and heath-like stems. (Zones 2–5)

P. omorika (Serbian spruce) is a slow-growing, spire-like tree with upward-arching branches and drooping branchlets. Two white stripes run the length of each needle. It grows 9–15 m (30–50') tall and spreads 3–4.5 m (10–15'). It is best planted in spring. **'Pendula'** grows 75 cm (30') tall and 3–4.5 m (10–15') wide, with pendent, slightly twisted branches that ascend at the tips. **'Pendula Bruns'** has more pronounced weeping branches

P. glauca 'Conica' (above)

P. abies 'Nidiformis' (centre)

P. glauca (below)

P. pungens 'Mission Blue' (above)

P. abies 'Pendula' (below)

than 'Pendula.' **'Pimoko'** is a dense, low-growing, irregular shrub that is globe-shaped when young. It grows 60 cm–1.25 m (2–4') tall and wide. (Zones 4–8)

P. pungens (Colourado spruce) is a conical or columnar tree with stiff, blue-green needles and dense growth. This drought-tolerant tree grows 15–24 m (50–80') tall and 3–6 m (10–20') wide. **Var. *glauca*** (Colourado blue spruce) is similar to the species but has blue-grey needles. The following cultivars arise from this variety. **'Fat Albert'** is a dense, cone-shaped tree with

ascending branches and steel blue
needles. It typically grows 3–4.5 m
(10–15') tall and 1.75–3 m (6–10')
wide but can grow 12 m (40') tall
and 4.5 m (15') wide in perfect
conditions. **'Globosa'** forms a flattened globe, 90 cm–1.5 m (3–5')
tall and 1.25–1.75 m (4–6') wide,
with blue foliage. It is often grown
as a standard. **'Hoopsii'** is a dense,
pyramidal tree, 18 m (60') tall and
6 m (20') wide, with foliage that is
more blue-white than on var. *glauca*.
'Mission Blue' is a dense form
up to 12 m (40') tall and 6–7.5 m
(20–25') wide, with bold blue foliage. **'Montgomery'** has silvery blue-
grey foliage. It grows 90 cm–1.5 m
(3–5') tall and wide and is rounded
when young, becoming broadly
pyramidal with age. **'Pendula'** has
graceful, weeping branches and
silver-blue foliage. Stake the plant
when young to develop a small,
weeping tree, or leave it alone for a
prostrate groundcover.

*Spruce trees frequently produce branch
mutations (witches' brooms). They can
be propagated to form new cultivars
of various sizes, shapes and colours.
'Nidiformis' originates from a witches'
broom. 'Little Gem' came from a
witches' broom on 'Nidiformis.'*

Problems & Pests
Aphids, caterpillars, gall insects,
nematodes, scale insects, sawflies,
spider mites, needle cast, rust or
wood rot can all be problematic.

P. pungens 'Hoopsii'

*Try using a slow-growing dwarf
cultivar, such as dwarf Alberta
spruce, for plant sculpture and
bonsai.*

Sumac

Rhus

Features: summer and fall foliage, summer flowers, late-summer to fall fruit, habit
Habit: bushy, suckering, colony-forming deciduous shrub **Height:** 60 cm–3.75 m
(2–12') **Spread:** 90 cm–3.75 m (3–12') or more; often exceeds height
Planting: container; spring or fall **Zones:** 2–8

MUCH NURSERY RESEARCH AND EXPERIMENTATION HAVE BEEN
invested in this native genus, and the resulting plants are excellent additions
to the landscape. They are long-lived, often spreading and always easy to
grow. The season-long foliage displays outstanding form and colour, with
many varieties putting forth a stellar fall show of brilliant yellows, oranges
and reds. Sumacs bear male and female flowers on different plants, and both
produce interesting, greenish yellow, catkin-like flowers. If pollinated from
a nearby male plant, the female flowers develop into dense, pyramidal clusters of small, red fruits that attract birds. *R. aromatica* 'Gro-Low' is a great
groundcover for hills and banks near water. An exciting new compact variety
to look for is the yellow-leaved *R. typhina* 'Bailtiger.'

Growing

Sumacs develop the best fall colour in **full sun** but tolerate partial shade. The soil should be of **average fertility, moist** and **well drained**. Once established, sumacs are drought tolerant.

These plants can become invasive. Remove suckers that come up where you don't want them; a lawnmower works well for suckers in lawns. Cut out some of the oldest growth each year and allow some replacement suckers to grow in.

Tips

Sumacs can be used to form a specimen group in a shrub or mixed border, in a woodland garden or on a sloping bank. Both male and female plants are needed for fruit to form.

When pulling up suckers, be sure to wear gloves to avoid getting the unusual, onion-like odour all over your hands.

R. typhina

The fruit of the recommended sumac species is edible. For a refreshing beverage that tastes like pink lemonade, soak the ripe fruit in cold water overnight and then strain and sweeten to taste. The species R. coriaria, also edible, is the source of the important Middle Eastern spice sumac.

R. glabra

R. typhina

Recommended

R. aromatica (fragrant sumac) forms a low mound of suckering stems 60 cm–1.75 m (2–6') tall and 1.5–3 m (5–10') wide. Clusters of inconspicuous yellow flowers appear in spring, followed in late summer by fuzzy fruit that ripens to red. The aromatic foliage turns red or purple in fall. This species tolerates hot, dry, exposed conditions. It can be used to prevent erosion on hills too steep for mowing. **'Gro-Low'** is a ground-cover growing about 60 cm (24") tall and spreading up to 2.5 m (8'). (Zones 3–8)

R. glabra (smooth sumac) grows 2.5–3.75 m (8–12') tall, with an equal or greater spread, and forms a bushy, suckering colony. Green summer flower spikes are followed, on female plants, by fuzzy, red fruit. The foliage can turn brilliant shades of orange, red and purple in fall. (Zones 2–8)

R. trilobata (lemonade sumac, skunkbush sumac) is an upright, vase-like shrub that forms colonies by suckering. It grows 90 cm–1.5 m (3–5') tall and wide, producing yellow-green flowers in late spring to early summer, followed by spherical, red fruit. Foul smelling when bruised, the dark green foliage turns

R. aromatica 'Gro-Low'

shades of yellow to red in fall. This plant is closely related to *R. aromatica* but has smaller leaves, flowers and fruit. (Zones 3–8)

R. typhina (*R. hirta;* staghorn sumac) is a suckering, colony-forming shrub whose branches are covered with velvety fuzz. This species grows 2.5–3 m (8–10') tall and spreads 3–3.75 m (10–12') or more. Fuzzy, yellow early-summer blooms give way to hairy, red fruit. The leaves turn stunning shades of yellow, orange and red in fall. **'Bailtiger'** (TIGER EYES™) has finely cut, burn-resistant, golden yellow foliage that is bright yellow-green when new and turns bright red in fall. This open, low-branched shrub grows 1.75–3 m (6–10') tall and 3–3.75 m (10–12') wide. **'Laciniata'** (cutleaf staghorn sumac) has finely cut, lace-like leaves and lace-like bracts that give the plant a graceful appearance. (Zones 3–8)

Problems & Pests

Caterpillars, scale insects, canker, dieback, leaf spot, powdery mildew, wood rot or *Verticillium* wilt can afflict sumacs.

*The sap of poison-sumac (*Toxicodendron vernix, *formerly* R. vernix) *may cause severe skin reactions. When its white to yellowish fruit is absent, it can be difficult to distinguish from other sumacs. Carefully crush a fresh leaf on a piece of white paper; poison-sumac juice stains turn black over about 24 hours.*

R. glabra (above)

R. typhina 'Laciniata' (centre & below)

Summersweet Clethra
Sweet Pepperbush, Sweetspire
Clethra

Features: fragrant summer flowers, habit, fall foliage **Habit:** rounded, suckering deciduous shrub **Height:** 60 cm–2.5 m (2–8') **Spread:** 90 cm–2.5 m (3–8') **Planting:** B & B, container; spring **Zones:** 3–8

SUMMERSWEET CLETHRA IS A relatively small, charming shrub that blooms well in shady spots and has a wide variety of uses. Its midsummer bloom features long spires of white, pink or reddish pink flowers. The foliage is a clean, rich green. Plant summersweet clethra as single specimens, placing one here and there wherever a compact shrub is needed, be it in the foundation planting, in front of the mixed shrub border or for extra structure in the perennial garden. Summersweet clethra doesn't like dry conditions, so give it a little extra water.

Summersweet clethra's late-season flowers are much appreciated in damp, shaded gardens.

Growing

Summersweet clethra grows best in **light shade** or **partial shade**. The soil should be **fertile, humus rich, acidic** and **moist**; this plant tolerates poor drainage in organic soils.

Deadheading keeps the shrub looking neat. Summersweet clethra does best with minimal pruning; dwarf cultivars typically require little, if any. One to three of the oldest unproductive stems can be removed every second or third year if the growth seems congested.

Tips

This shrub tends to sucker, though not aggressively, forming a colony of stems. Use it in a border or in a woodland garden. The light shade of a woodland edge is ideal.

Recommended

C. alnifolia is a large, rounded, upright, colony-forming shrub. It grows 90 cm–2.5 m (3–8') tall, spreads 90 cm–1.75 m (3–6') and bears attractive spikes of white, highly fragrant flowers in mid- to late summer. The foliage turns yellow in fall. **'Compacta'** ('Nana') is a compact shrub, 90 cm–1.25 m (3–4') tall and wide, that is hardier than 'Hummingbird.' It has shiny, dark green foliage and abundant clusters of fragrant, creamy white flowers. **'Hummingbird'** is a compact plant that grows 60 cm–1 m (24–40") tall, with a spread of 90 cm–1.75 m (3–6'). The dark green foliage turns yellow in fall. **'Paniculata'** produces large, intensely fragrant flowers. It grows 1.5–2.5 m

C. alnifolia 'Hummingbird' (above), 'Ruby Spice' (below)

(5–8') tall and wide. **'Pink Spires'** ('Rosea') bears pink flowers and grows up to 2.5 m (8') tall and wide. **'Ruby Spice'** bears fade-resistant, deep pink flowers.

Problems & Pests

Although generally trouble free, this plant may suffer some fungal infections, such as root rot.

Viburnum
Viburnum

Features: flowers, summer and fall foliage, fruit, habit **Habit:** bushy or spreading deciduous shrub **Height:** 60 cm–4.5 m (2–15') **Spread:** 60 cm–3 m (2–10') **Planting:** bare-root, B & B, container; spring or fall **Zones:** 2–8

VIBURNUMS ARE SUPERB, SHOWY SHRUBS FOR ALBERTA landscapes, and the many wonderful recently developed varieties available at nurseries keep them as popular as ever. Take your time when deciding which would work best for you. Viburnums feature a wide assortment of attractive foliage choices and ornate, often fragrant flowers. Many produce large clusters of decorative black, blue or red berries in addition to splendid fall colour.

Growing

Viburnums grow well in **full sun, partial shade** or **light shade**. The soil should be of **average fertility, moist** and **well drained**. Viburnums tolerate both alkaline and acidic soils.

Little pruning is needed. Remove awkward, dead, damaged or diseased branches as needed.

Tips

Viburnums can be used in borders and woodland gardens. They are a good choice for plantings near patios, decks and swimming pools.

Viburnum fruit varies in its palatability. The tart fruits of *V. opulus* and *V. trilobum* are popular for making jellies, pies and wine. They can be sweetened somewhat by freezing or by gathering after the first frost or two.

Fruiting is better when more than one plant of a species is present, provided they flower at the same time, to allow for cross-pollination.

V. sargentii 'Onondaga' (above)

V. opulus 'Roseum' (centre), *V. opulus* (below)

V. opulus

Viburnums look lovely in the shade of evergreen trees. Their richly textured foliage complements shrubs and perennials that bloom in late spring.

V. opulus 'Nanum'

Recommended

V. dentatum (arrowwood) is an upright, arching shrub that grows 1.75–4.5 m (6–15') tall, with an equal spread. Clusters of white flowers appear in late spring or early summer, followed by dark blue fruit in fall. This hardy, durable shrub adapts to almost any soil conditions. BLUE MUFFIN® ('Christom') is a compact cultivar that flowers prolifically and bears clusters of bright blue fruit. It grows 1.5–2.5 m (5–8') tall, with an equal spread.

V. dilatatum (linden viburnum) is an open, upright shrub that grows 2.5–3 m (8–10') tall and spreads 1.75–3 m (6–10') but it is only hardy to Zone 5. Late-spring or early-summer clusters of white flowers give way to bright red berries in fall, and the fall foliage is bronze, red or burgundy. CARDINAL CANDY™ ('Henneke') bears plentiful flowers and fruit. It grows 1.5–1.75 m (5–6') tall, with an equal spread, and is hardy to Zone 4. (Zones 4–7)

V. x 'Emerald Triumph,' a compact hybrid, was developed through complex breeding. It grows 1.75–2.5 m (6–8') tall and wide and bears flat-topped clusters of white flowers in late spring and early summer. The following bright red fruit ripens to black. The shiny, dark green foliage is disease resistant. (Zones 4–7)

V. lantana (wayfaring tree) is a large, rounded, multi-stemmed shrub that grows 1.5–3 m (5–10') tall and wide. Clusters of white flowers are borne in late spring and early summer, followed by green fruit that ripens to orange and red before finally turning black in fall. **'Mohican'** has fruit that stays red longer than that of the species. (Zones 3–8)

V. lentago (nannyberry, sheepberry) is an upright, deciduous, suckering large shrub or small tree with arching branches. It grows 3–4.5 m (10–15') tall and 1.75–3 m (6–10') wide, with shiny, dark green leaves that turn purple-red in fall. It produces flattened clusters of fragrant, cream white flowers in spring. The pinkish red fruit ripens to blue-black.

V. opulus (V. opulus var. opulus; European cranberrybush, guelder-rose) is a rounded, spreading shrub that grows 1.75–3 m (6–10') tall and wide. The white flower clusters consist of an outer ring of showy sterile flowers surrounding the inner fertile flowers, giving the plant a lacy look when in bloom in late spring. The fall

V. lantana (above)

V. trilobum 'Bailey Compact' (centre)

V. lantana 'Mohican' (below)

V. dentatum BLUE MUFFIN® ('Christom')

foliage and bitter, inedible fruit are red. **'Nanum'** ('Compactum') is dense and slow growing, reaching 60 cm–1.5 m (2–5') in height and spread. **'Roseum'** ('Sterilis,' European snowball bush) bears large clusters of white flowers but does not form fruit. **'Xanthocarpum'** bears bright golden yellow fruit. (Zones 3–8)

V. sargentii (Sargent viburnum) is a large, bushy shrub that grows 3–4.5 m (10–15') tall, with an equal spread. The white early-spring blossoms consist of clusters of inconspicuous fertile flowers surrounded by showy sterile flowers. Red fruit follows in summer and early fall. In fall, the foliage is yellow, orange and red. **'Onondaga'** has purple stems and red to pink fertile flowers ringed with showy, pinkish white, sterile flowers. The purple-green foliage turns red in fall. (Zones 3–7)

V. trilobum (*V. opulus* var. *americanum;* American cranberrybush, highbush cranberry) is a dense, rounded shrub that is native to much of central North America. It grows 2.5–4.5 m (8–15') tall, with a spread of 2.5–3.75 m (8–12'). White clusters of showy sterile and inconspicuous fertile flowers appear in early summer, followed by edible red fruit. The fall colour is red. This species is resistant to aphids. **'Alfredo'** has green to dark green foliage and

burgundy to red fall colour. It grows
1.5–1.75 m (5–6') tall and wide.
'Bailey Compact' is a compact plant,
1.5–1.75 m (5–6') tall and wide, with
bright red fall foliage. **'Compactum'**
is a non-flowering upright shrub,
60–90 cm (24–36") tall and wide,
that has straight, non-branching,
yellow stems and good fall colour.
(Zones 2–7)

Problems & Pests

Aphids, borers, mealybugs, scale
insects, treehoppers, weevils, dieback,
downy mildew, grey mould, leaf spot,
powdery mildew, *Verticillium* wilt or
wood rot can affect viburnums.

V. opulus 'Xanthocarpum' (above)

V. dilatatum CARDINAL CANDY™ 'Henneke' (centre)

V. sargentii 'Onondaga' (below)

V. lentago

Virginia Creeper
Parthenocissus

Features: summer and fall foliage, habit **Habit:** clinging, woody deciduous climber **Height:** 9–15 m (30–50') **Spread:** 9–15 m (30–50') **Planting:** container; spring or fall **Zones:** 3–8

THIS EASY-GROWING VINE IS PERFECT FOR softening hard edges in the landscape. The wonderful foliage is a nice rich green, turning bright red and burgundy in fall. Virginia creeper looks great when allowed to ramble over a rock pile or scale a tree. Keep your pruners handy to keep it from covering windows or other things you want free and clear.

Growing

These vines grow well in any light from **full sun to full shade**. The soil should preferably be **fertile** and **well drained**, but the plants adapt to clay or sandy soils.

Trim back these vigorous growers frequently to keep them where you want them.

Tips

Given enough time, these vines can cover an entire building, wall, fence or arbour. With clinging rootlets that can adhere to just about any surface—even smooth wood, vinyl, glass or metal—they need no support; however, the little marks left where a vine is pulled off can be hard to remove or even paint over. As groundcovers, these plants spread 15 m (50') but grow only up to 30 cm (12") tall.

The fruit is poisonous.

Recommended

P. quinquefolia (Virginia creeper, woodbine) is a clinging, woody climber that can grow 9–15 m (30–50') tall. The dark green foliage turns flame red in fall. **'Engelmanii'** (var. *engelmanii*) clings better and spreads less rapidly than the species. The rich, deep green leaves turn crimson in fall. Birds relish the bluish black berries.

Problems & Pests

Aphids, grape-leaf beetle, leafhoppers, leaf skeletonizers, scale insects, bacterial leaf scorch, canker, dieback, downy mildew, leaf spot, powdery mildew or scab can cause trouble.

P. quinquefolia (above & centre)

Virginia creeper can cover the sides of buildings, helping keep them cool in summer. Cut the plants back to keep windows and doors accessible.

P. quinquefolia

Weigela
Weigela

Features: flowers, foliage, habit **Habit:** upright or low, spreading deciduous shrub
Height: 45 cm–1.75 m (18"–6') **Spread:** 45 cm–1.75 m (18"–6')
Planting: bare-root, container; spring or fall **Zones:** 3–8

A HOT SPOT IN FULL SUN IS A GREAT PLACE FOR WEIGELA.
The early-summer bloom is a dazzling display but is noticeably reduced in
partial shade (plant *Clethra* instead). The listed varieties vary greatly in size,
from rounded, compact cultivars such as 'Minuet' to the broad, upright 'Red
Prince.' WINE & ROSES® is a fine mid-sized variety, with intensely rose pink
flowers that contrast magically with the plant's dark burgundy foliage. Weigela is unsurpassed in sunny foundation plantings or when grouped to form
a mid-sized informal hedge.

Growing

Weigela prefers **full sun** but tolerates partial shade. For the best leaf colour, grow purple-leaved plants in full sun and yellow-leaved plants in partial shade. The soil should be both **fertile** and **well drained**, but these shrubs adapt to most well-drained soils.

Once flowering has finished, cut the flowering shoots back to strong buds or branch junctions. Up to one-third of the old growth can be cut back to the ground at the same time.

Tips

Weigela can be used in a shrub or mixed border, in an open woodland garden or as an informal barrier planting.

Recommended

W. florida is a spreading shrub with arching branches. Dark pink flower clusters appear in late spring and early summer. The species is rarely grown; its many wonderful cultivars

W. florida 'Polka'

Plant breeders have given us weigela cultivars with yellow, purple or variegated foliage and pink, red, purple or white flowers.

W. florida MIDNIGHT WINE ('Elvera')

W. florida WINE & ROSES ('Alexandra')

are preferred. **'Centennial'** bears dark pink to red flowers in early summer with sporadic reblooming. It has purple-tinged dark green leaves and grows 1.25–1.75 m (4–6') tall and wide. MIDNIGHT WINE ('Elvera') is a dwarf plant that grows up to 45 cm (18") tall and spreads 45–60 cm (18–24"). The foliage is purple, and the flowers are pink. **'Minuet'** is a compact, spreading shrub 60–90 cm (24–36") tall and 90 cm–1.25 m (3–4') wide. The dark

W. florida cultivar

pink flowers have yellow throats. The purplish green foliage matures to dark green over summer. **'Pink Poppet'** is a small shrub that grows 60 cm (24") tall and wide and has shell pink flowers. **'Red Prince'** is an upright shrub. It grows 1.5–1.75 m (5–6') tall and spreads about 1.5 m (5'). Bright red flowers appear in early summer, with a second flush in late summer. **'Tango'** is a hardy selection that grows 60–75 cm (24–30") tall and wide. Its dark purple-green foliage has some bronze tinges. The deep red flowers have yellow throats. MY MONET ('Veriweig') is a compact, mounded plant that grows 30–45 cm (12–18") tall and 45–60 cm (18–24") wide. The flowers are pink, and the variegated leaves change colour

The name weigela honours German botanist Christian Ehrenfried von Weigel (1748–1831).

depending on how much light they
receive. The leaves have creamy
white margins in shadier locations
and pink margins in full sun. WINE
& ROSES ('Alexandra') has dark purple foliage and vivid pink flowers.
It grows 1.25–1.5 m (4–5') tall and
90 cm–1.5 m (3–5') wide.

Problems & Pests

Foliar nematodes, scale insects, twig
dieback and *Verticillium* wilt are
possible problems but are not usually serious.

W. florida 'Red Prince'

W. florida WINE & ROSES

Willow

Salix

Features: form, foliage, catkins, young stem colour **Habit:** small to large, oval to rounded deciduous shrub, or small tree with oval to rounded crown
Height: 30 cm–19.5 m (1–65') **Spread:** 60 cm–18 m (1–60')
Planting: B & B, container; spring or fall **Zones:** 2–8

INTEREST IN WILLOWS HAS BEEN RISING STEADILY IN RECENT years as more gardeners are becoming familiar with the splendid varieties only recently made available in the north. These plants are star performers in moist areas and are ideal for naturalizing in low, marshy areas. Most varieties have curling branches that add sculptural interest in winter.

Growing

Willows generally grow best in **full sun** in **deep, moist, well-drained** soil. *S.* 'Flame' and *S. integra* 'Hakuro Nishiki' grow well in light shade. *S. discolour*, *S. exigua* and *S. purpurea* are suitable for wet areas. The large *Salix* species and cultivars should not be planted near water supply and drainage lines because the roots may invade the pipes and cause expensive blockages.

Prune in early spring before new growth begins. For all willows, remove dead, diseased and damaged branches and any branches that spoil the form. For grafted standards, remove all suckers below the graft union.

Young growth has the best stem colour. Shrubs grown for this feature need regular rejuvenation pruning. *S.* 'Flame' and *S. integra* 'Hakuro Nishiki' look best when cut to within 15 cm (6") of the ground every few years. *S. purpurea* can be pruned lightly, if needed. For rejuvenation, *S. purpurea* can also be cut back hard to within two to three buds above the ground. *S. alba* var. *vitellina* can be cut back yearly to produce an abundance of the golden stems.

Tips

Willows make excellent specimen plants. The small species look great when used in shrub and mixed borders, and some species make wonderful hedges. Many willows are effective next to water features.

Willow bark contains salicin, the original source of aspirin (acetylsalicylic acid).

S. exigua cultivar

S. integra 'Hakuro Nishiki'

Recommended

S. acutifolia (narrow-leaf willow) is an upright, spreading, multi-stemmed tree that grows 7.5–15 m (25–50') tall and 5.5–9 m (18–30') wide. The narrow, pointed, glossy, dark green foliage retains its colour into fall. (Zones 2–7)

S. alba (white willow) is a large, rounded tree with a low crown and silvery green foliage. It grows 13.5–19.5 m (45–65') tall and 12–18 m (40–60') wide. **'Sericea'** (Siberian white willow) has bright silvery foliage and grows 9.75–12 m (32–40') tall and wide. **Var. vitellina** (golden willow) grows 7.5–10.5 m (25–35') tall and 6–9 m (20–30') wide. The younger stems have excellent golden yellow to orange stem colour. (Zones 3–8)

S. babylonica **'Lace'** (weeping willow) is a small, rounded tree with strongly weeping branches. It has long, narrow foliage that turns yellow in fall. It grows quickly to 3–4.5 m (10–15') tall and 2.5–3 m (8–10') wide. Growth then slows somewhat, and the tree may reach 6–7.5 m (20–25') tall at maturity. (Zones 4–8)

S. brachycarpa **'Blue Fox'** is an upright, rounded shrub that grows 90 cm–1.5 m (3–5') tall and 90 cm–1.75 m (3–6') wide. It has blue-grey foliage that can provide excellent contrast in shrub and mixed beds. 'Blue Fox' does not tolerate alkaline soils. (Zones 2–7)

S. discolour (common pussy willow) is a small, upright tree or large shrub that grows 3.75–4.75 m (12–16') tall and 1.75–3.75 m (6–12') wide. The wonderfully soft, fuzzy, grey catkins are produced in mid- to late spring. (Zones 2–7)

S. exigua (coyote willow) is a delicate, wispy, suckering shrub that has narrow, silvery green foliage and grows 3.75–4.75 m (12–16') tall and 60–90 cm (24–36") wide. It forms thickets, so give it some room to spread. It is a bamboo substitute for containers here in Alberta.

S. **'Flame'** is a large, densely branched shrub, 4.5–6 m (15–20') tall and 4.5 m (15') wide, with an oval crown. The young stems are bright orange-red, and the fall colour is golden yellow.

S. integra **'Hakuro Nishiki'** (dappled willow) is a somewhat weeping shrub that grows 90 cm–1.5 m (3–5') tall and wide. Its stems and flower buds are tinged orange-pink, and its light green foliage is mottled with white and pink. This shrub is often grafted onto a stem to create a standard form. (Zones 4–8)

S. pentandra (laurel-leaf willow) is large, broad tree, 7.5–15 m (25–50') tall and wide, with a low, oval to rounded crown and large, glossy, dark green foliage. (Zones 2–7)

S. purpurea (basket willow, purple osier willow, purple willow) is a large, spreading shrub or small, upright tree with arching branches. It grows 3–4.5 m (10–15') tall and wide. The foliage is dark green to blue-green, and the young stems are purple. The silvery green catkins appear before the foliage. **'Gracilis'** is a mounding shrub, 1.25–1.75 m (4–6') tall and 1.25–2.5 m (4–8') wide, with thin, upright, unbranched stems arising from a central crown. The fine foliage is blue-green to grey-green.

S. purpurea weeping cultivar

Since ancient times, S. purpurea *has been cultivated as a source of flexible withes for basketry.*

S. purpurea 'Nana'

S. exigua 'Silvar' (above & below)

*Most willows grow easily from
cuttings, an attribute that has
allowed plants with desirable
features to be cloned thousands
of times over many years.*

'**Nana**' is a compact shrub, 90 cm–
1.5 m (3–5') tall and wide, with
blue-green to grey-green foliage.
(Zones 4–7)

S. repens **var.** *argentea* (silver creeping willow) is a small, prostrate
shrub that grows 30–60 cm (12–24")
tall and spreads 1.25–1.75 m (4–6')
and has fuzzy grey-green foliage
with a silvery sheen. The reddish
branches are upright when young,
eventually arching over. The yellow
catkin blooms in spring. (Zones 3–7)

S. salicola '**Polar Bear**' is a tough,
urban-tolerant, multi-stemmed
upright shrub that grows 3–4.5 m
(10–15') tall and 1.75–3 m (6–10')
wide. The stems and oval leaves are
silvery blue to silvery grey-green,
fuzzy and soft. (Zones 2–7)

Problems & Pests

Possible problems include aphids, borers, caterpillars, leaf beetles, leaf and crown galls, scale insects, canker, heart and root rot, powdery mildew and rust. When willows are grown in appropriate conditions, serious problems are unlikely.

Many willows readily hybridize, creating headaches for scientists who must classify the plants in this large and complex group.

Willows are fast-growing shrubs or trees that come in a wide range of growth habits and sizes, and some have colourful stems and foliage.

S. purpurea 'Nana'

S. babylonica 'Lace'

Yew

Taxus

Features: foliage, habit, red seed cups **Habit:** conical or columnar evergreen tree, or bushy or spreading shrub **Height:** 45 cm–16.5 m (18"–50')
Spread: 60 cm–9 m (2–30') **Planting:** B & B, container; spring or fall
Zones: 2–7

YEWS ARE NOT GROWN A LOT IN ALBERTA BECAUSE THEY PREFER a much moister climate. However, that does not mean that the moist micro-climate in your garden would not be suitable, and indeed there are some wonderful specimens growing in our province.

Growing

Most yews grow well in any light conditions from **full sun to full shade**. The soil should be **fertile, moist** and **well drained**. They generally tolerate soils of any acidity, most urban pollution and windy or dry conditions. Avoid very wet soil, such as near downspouts, and areas contaminated with road salt. *T. canadensis* prefers a cool site in **partial to full shade**, with **shelter** from strong winds.

Because new growth sprouts from old wood, yews can be cut back hard to reduce their size or for rejuvenation. Hedges and topiary can be trimmed back in summer and fall.

All parts of yews are poisonous, except the pleasant-tasting, fleshy red cup that surrounds the hard seed.

T. cuspidata 'Monloo'

Tips

Use yews in borders or as specimens, hedges, topiary or groundcovers. Male plants must be present for most females to bear the attractive red arils (seed cups).

Recommended

T. canadensis (American yew, Canadian yew, ground-hemlock) is a low-growing, spreading, native shrub with prostrate branches that root at the nodes. It usually grows 30–90 cm (12–36") tall and spreads 1.75–2.5 m (6–8') wide but can sometimes reach 1.75 m (6') tall and 3.75 m (12') wide. Mostly self-fertile, it produces light red to orange-red fruits. The dense, shiny, dark green foliage is tinged red in winter. (Zones 2–6)

T. cuspidata (Japanese yew) '**Monloo**' (EMERALD SPREADER®) is a low-growing, flat-topped shrub, 45–75 cm (18–30") tall and 2.5–3 m (8–10') wide, with shiny, emerald to dark green foliage that holds its colour through winter. (Zones 4–7)

T. x *media* (English Japanese yew, Anglo-Japanese yew) forms a rounded, upright tree or shrub of variable height and spread. '**Morden**' is globe shaped and about 60 cm (24") in height and spread. It has blue-green foliage and bears small red berries. '**Tauntonii**' is a spreading cultivar 90 cm–1.25 m (3–4') tall and up to 1.75 m (6') wide. It suffers little foliage browning in either heat or cold. (Zones 4–7)

Problems & Pests

Black vine weevils, mealybugs, mites, scale insects, dieback, needle blight or root rot are possible problems, but not serious ones. Deer browsing can be a concern in some areas.

Yucca

Yucca

Features: foliage, habit, flowers **Habit:** clump-forming evergreen shrub
Height: 25–75 cm (10–30") **Spread:** 60 cm–1.5 m (2–5')
Planting: container; spring **Zones:** 3–8

YUCCAS ARE PERFECT PLANTS TO USE IN A LOW-maintenance landscape that requires little water. Soapweed (*Y. glauca*) is native to the southeastern tip of our province. It prefers drier climates, so look for a dry, sunny spot to plant it. Adam's needle (*Y. filamentosa*) is a good choice for providing contrast in mixed and perennial beds.

Yucca fruits are rarely seen in cultivation. The yucca moth, which pollinates the flowers, is uncommon outside the plant's natural range.

Growing

Yucca grows best in **full sun** in any **well-drained** soil. It is drought toler-ant and thrives in arid locations.

Pruning is not needed, but the flower spikes can be removed when blooming has finished, and dead leaves can be removed as needed.

Tips

Yucca is used as a specimen, usu-ally in groups or in planters, to give a garden a southern appearance. In pots, planters and urns, this plant also makes a strong architectural statement.

Recommended

Y. filamentosa (Adam's needle) has long, stiff, finely serrated, pointed leaves with threads that peel back from the edges. It is frost-hardy but may suffer dieback in the colder parts of the province. It grows 50–75 cm (20–30") tall and 1–1.5 m (40–60") wide. **'Bright Edge'** has leaves with yellow margins. **'Golden**

Y. filamentosa 'Bright Edge'

Sword' has leaves with yellow centres and green margins. (Zones 4–8)

Y. glauca (soapweed) forms a clump of sword-like, blue-green, serrated foliage that grows 25–50 cm (10–20") tall and 60–90 cm (24–36") wide. Creamy white flowers are produced in late spring to early summer on stalks 60 cm–1 m (24–40") in height.

Problems & Pests

Cane borers, fungal leaf spot and scale insects can cause problems.

Y. filamentosa 'Golden Sword'

OTHER TREES & SHRUBS TO CONSIDER

CHERRY PRINSEPIA
Prinsepia

A number of plants we grow in Alberta have their origins in northern China. Cherry prinsepia is an attractive Manchurian native, but it is underused. The fruit is tasty and somewhat tart, but not so tart that your lips purse and your cheeks pucker. Try highbush cranberry (*Viburnum trilobum*) for that reaction.

The dense growth habit and sharp spines make cherry prinsepia an excellent plant for forming a barrier, either as a hedge or planted in the foundation below a window. It is a good shrub for providing contrast in a shrub border, and it does well at the edge of a woodland. *P. sinensis* is a dense, rounded to spreading shrub with erect to arching, spiny branches. It grows 2 m (6') tall and 2–3 m (6–10') wide. The bark of the older stems is brown and peels off in long strips. Bright green leaves emerge early in spring, and they may turn yellow-green in fall. (Zones 3–7)

Cherry prinsepia grows best in full sun and well-drained, fertile soil. It tolerates partial shade and is adaptable to a range of soil types but prefers moist soil, especially when it is forming fruit. Cherry prinsepia requires little pruning and responds well to rejuvenation pruning. Prune in late winter to early spring for form.

CHINESE CATALPA
Catalpa

Chinese catalpa is an attractive, coarse-textured tree that makes an excellent contrast specimen in the landscape. It blends well with other deciduous trees in larger plantings. The tall clusters of bell-shaped flowers bloom in mid-summer, when many of our flowering trees have passed their blooming time. Chinese catalpa can be messy throughout the year with twig and branch fall (because of the tree's somewhat brittle nature) and when the leaves and fruits drop in fall.

Chinese catalpa is best used as a specimen tree sited where the leaf, fruit and potential branch drop will not damage vehicles or your home. *C. ovata* is a vigorous, rounded, spreading tree with an open irregular canopy. It grows 7.5–9 m (25–30') tall and wide. This plant bears large, lightly fragrant, heart-shaped, pale green foliage and produces showy, upright clusters of large, yellowish white flowers marked with orange and purple in mid-summer. (Zones 3–8)

Chinese catalpa prefers full sun in well-drained, fertile, moist soil, but it is quite adaptable to many soil conditions. This plant needs a site that is sheltered from strong winds because the wood is somewhat brittle. Chinese catalpa is tolerant of heat, humidity, short periods of drought and some urban pollution. Minimal pruning is needed other than for form. Leave the crown as low as possible. Prune in late winter to early spring when the tree is still dormant and the threat of severe cold has passed.

OTHER TREES & SHRUBS TO CONSIDER   317

Cliff Green
Mountain Lover
Paxistima

Cliff green is an underused shrub that has wonderful evergreen foliage that makes an excellent groundcover. It is quite hardy and has few maintenance requirements once it is established. A dense planting will easily compete with weeds.

Cliff green is a great plant for underplanting trees and tall shrubs. It can be used as an evergreen groundcover and is at home in a rock garden. It can also be used as a low hedge. *P. canbyi* is a low-growing, dense, evergreen shrub with decumbent branches that root where the branch nodes touch the ground. It grows 15–30 cm (6–12") tall and spreads 60–90 cm (24–36") wide or wider, and will continue spreading slowly. The tiny green to red flowers bloom in spring and are inconspicuous. (Zones 3–7)

Cliff green grows well in full sun, partial shade or light shade in moist, well-drained soil that has a fair to middling amount of organic matter mixed in. Cliff green is tolerant of high pH soils. Provide protection from the early spring sun. Deep snow cover is ideal.

Corktree
Amur Corktree
Phellodendron

Corktree is a good four-season tree, with an interesting winter silhouette, great foliage and really interesting mature bark. It is usually not available in abundance, but it is out there and well worth the effort to track down.

Corktree is best used as a specimen tree or a shade tree in an open space or large yard. It is not recommended for restricted root areas, such as parking lots or medians. *P. amurense* is a rounded to spreading, irregular tree with a short trunk and stout branches that tend to droop with age. The tree grows 9–13.5 m (30–45') tall and wide, and is often wider than tall. It has large, dark green, compound foliage that is aromatic when crushed and turns yellow in fall. (Zones 3–7)

Corktree prefers to grow in full sun in deep, fertile, well-drained soil but is tolerant of partial shade and a wide range of soil types and conditions. It is drought tolerant once established and is somewhat urban tolerant, especially when the roots have plenty of space to grow. Corktree roots need a lot of space; they can lift pavement and affect mowing if space is restricted. It is a good idea to prune this tree when it is young to establish a good framework of branches and a central leader. Minimal pruning is needed after the initial framework is developed. Prune while the tree is dormant in late winter to early spring.

European Beech
Fagus sylvatica

European beech is a magnificent tree, particularly when allowed to grow its densely foliated branches nearly to the ground. Beech has attractive foliage and great growth form, and it retains the very smooth and elastic bark long into maturity. European beech is used as a shade tree and makes an excellent specimen. This tree needs a lot of space, but *F. sylvatica*'s adaptability to pruning makes it a reasonable choice in a small garden. The nuts are edible when roasted.

European beech is a large, oval, deciduous tree that can grow 12–18 m (40–60') tall and wide or even larger. 'Fastigiata' ('Dawyck') is a narrow, upright tree that spreads only about 3 m (10'). Yellow- or purple-leaved forms are available. 'Pendula' (weeping beech) has pendulous branches that sweep the ground. It varies from a wide-spreading, cascading form to a more upright form with branches drooping from the central trunk. 'Purpurea' (copper beech) is a purple-leaved form with the same habit as the species. Purple-leaved weeping forms are also available. (Zones 4–8)

European beech grows equally well in full sun or partial shade. The soil should be of average fertility, loamy and well drained, though almost all well-drained soils are tolerated. Very little pruning is required. Remove dead or damaged branches in spring or at any time after the damage occurs. This tree responds well to severe pruning. Too massive for most settings, it is often used as a hedge in smaller gardens.

Fringe Tree
Chionanthus virginicus

Small and tolerant of pollution, fringe trees are good choices for city gardens. The smooth, slender leaves are attractive all summer and turn yellow in fall, then drop to reveal an irregular form that adds winter interest to the landscape. The brief, early-summer blooming period (two weeks in ideal conditions) graces the landscape with a tropical elegance unequalled by other shrubs. Flowering is noticeably diminished for fringe trees grown in partial shade. Fringe trees begin flowering at a very early age, and work well as specimen plants, in borders or beside water features. In the wild, they are often found growing alongside streams and in rock crevices near water.

Fringe tree is a deciduous, spreading small tree or large shrub that can be found in both single-trunk and clump forms. It grows 3–6 m (10–20') tall, with an equal or greater spread. In early summer it bears fragrant, drooping, white flowers. Only occasionally does the dark blue fruit follow. Male flowers, which are sometimes on the same tree as the female flowers, must be present to produce fruit. (Zones 4–8)

Fringe trees prefer full sun and fertile, moist, well-drained soil, but adapt to most soil conditions, including salt. Fringe trees appreciate regular watering and fertilizing, particularly while young, and benefit greatly from winter mulching. Mature fringe trees require little pruning. To encourage an attractive habit, thin out the stems of young plants. Young plants that aren't yet flowering can be pruned in spring, but older plants should not be pruned until they have finished flowering.

HORNBEAM
Carpinus

Hornbeam is easy to care for and tolerates great variance in soil moisture, fertility and pH. European hornbeam matures into a well-proportioned, medium-sized tree. American hornbeam is the smaller cousin. Both trees have attractive, smooth, steely grey bark. These trees can be used as specimens or shade trees in small gardens. The narrow, upright cultivars are often used to create barriers and windbreaks.

European hornbeam (*C. betulus*) is a pyramidal to rounded, deciduous tree, 6–12 m (20–40') tall and 4.5–9 m (15–30') wide, with bright yellow or orange fall foliage. 'Columnaris' is a narrow, slow-growing cultivar. 'Fastigiata' is an upright cultivar that is narrow when young, and broadens as it matures. 'Globosa' is a densely branched, rounded to globe-shaped tree with no central trunk and abundant foliage near the branch tips. It grows 3–6 m (10–20') tall and wide. (Zones 4–8) American hornbeam (*C. caroliniana*) is a small, slow-growing tree 3–6 m (10–20') tall, with an equal spread. It tolerates shade and city conditions. The fall foliage is yellow to red or purple. (Zones 3–8)

Hornbeam prefers full sun or partial shade and does well in average to fertile, well-drained soil. *C. caroliniana* grows well near ponds and streams and does best if the soil is also evenly moist and acidic. Although hornbeam is very tolerant of heavy pruning, pruning is rarely required. Remove damaged, diseased and awkward branches as needed. Do any formative pruning in late summer to early winter to reduce bleeding. Trim hedge varieties in late summer.

KATSURA-TREE
Cercidiphyllum japonicum

Katsura-tree is a true standout among shade trees. Its foliage is purplish when it emerges in spring, maturing to a bluish green in summer and changing to mostly yellows in fall, with some apricot hues in more acidic soils. Katsura-tree is drought sensitive, so watering is recommended during dry periods, especially when the trees are young. This plant is useful as a specimen or shade tree. The species can sizable and is best used in large landscapes. The cultivars can be wide spreading but are more appropriate than the species for smaller gardens. Katsura-tree is native to eastern Asia, and the delicate foliage blends well into Japanese-style gardens.

Katsura-tree is a slow-growing, rounded or spreading, often multi-stemmed, deciduous tree that takes a long time to reach 12 m (40'). The heart-shaped, blue-green leaves turn yellow and orange in fall and develop a spicy scent. 'Pendula' is one of the most elegant weeping trees available. It is usually grafted to a standard and grows 3–7.5 m (10–25') tall, with an equal or greater spread. Mounding, cascading branches sweep the ground, giving the entire tree the appearance of a waterfall tumbling over rocks. (Zones 4–8)

Katsura-tree grows equally well in full sun or partial shade. The soil should be fertile, humus rich, neutral to acidic, moist and well drained. This tree will become established more quickly if watered regularly during dry spells for the first year or two. Pruning is unnecessary. Damaged branches can be removed as needed.

TREE HEIGHT LEGEND: Short: < 6 m (20') • Medium: 6–12 m (20–40') • Tall: > 12 m (40')

SPECIES by Common Name	FORM						FOLIAGE							
	Tall Tree	Med. Tree	Short Tree	Shrub	Groundcover	Climber	Evergreen	Deciduous	Variegated	Blue/White	Purple/Red	Yellow/Gold	Dark Green	Light Green
Ash	•	•	•					•						•
Barberry				•				•			•	•	•	
Bearberry				•	•		•						•	
Beauty Bush				•				•				•		•
Birch	•	•	•					•					•	
Bittersweet					•	•		•					•	
Black Locust	•	•	•					•				•		•
Blueberry				•				•					•	•
Bog Rosemary				•			•			•				
Boxwood				•			•						•	
Buffaloberry				•				•		•			•	
Bush Honeysuckle				•				•					•	
Caragana				•				•					•	
Cedar		•	•	•			•		•			•	•	•
Cherry		•	•	•				•			•		•	
Chokeberry				•				•					•	
Cotoneaster				•	•			•					•	
Crabapple		•	•					•			•		•	
Currant				•				•					•	•
Daphne				•			•	•	•				•	
Dogwood		•	•					•	•				•	•
Douglas-fir	•						•			•			•	
Elderberry				•				•			•	•	•	•
Elm	•	•						•					•	
Euonymus		•	•	•	•	•	•	•	•			•	•	•
False Cypress		•	•	•			•					•	•	•
False Spirea				•				•						•
Fir	•	•	•	•			•				•		•	

	FEATURES								BLOOMING					SPECIES by Common Name
Form	Flowers	Foliage	Bark	Fruit/Cones	Scent	Spines	Fall Colour	Winter Interest	Spring	Summer	Fall	Zones	Page Number	
		•					•		•			2–8	78	Ash
	•	•		•		•	•		•			4–8	82	Barberry
	•	•		•				•	•			2–7	86	Bearberry
	•	•							•			4–8	88	Beauty Bush
•	•	•	•				•	•	•			2–8	90	Birch
		•		•			•		•			2–8	94	Bittersweet
	•	•			•					•		3–8	96	Black Locust
	•	•		•			•		•	•		3–7	98	Blueberry
	•	•							•	•		2–6	100	Bog Rosemary
•		•						•				4–8	102	Boxwood
		•	•	•					•			3–9	104	Buffaloberry
•	•	•								•		3–8	106	Bush Honeysuckle
•	•	•							•			2–8	108	Caragana
•		•	•		•			•				2–8	112	Cedar
	•	•	•		•		•		•	•		2–8	116	Cherry
	•			•			•		•	•		3–8	122	Chokeberry
•	•	•		•			•		•	•		2–8	124	Cotoneaster
•	•	•	•	•			•		•			2–8	128	Crabapple
	•	•		•					•			2–7	134	Currant
	•	•			•				•			4–7	136	Daphne
		•	•				•	•	•	•		2–8	138	Dogwood
•		•	•						•			3–8	144	Douglas-fir
		•		•						•		3–8	146	Elderberry
•			•				•		•			2–8	150	Elm
•		•	•	•			•		•			3–8	152	Euonymus
•		•						•				3–8	156	False Cypress
	•	•								•		2–7	158	False Spirea
•		•		•				•				3–7	160	Fir

TREE HEIGHT LEGEND: Short: < 6 m (20') • Medium: 6–12 m (20–40') • Tall: > 12 m (40')

SPECIES by Common Name	FORM						FOLIAGE							
	Tall Tree	Med. Tree	Short Tree	Shrub	Groundcover	Climber	Evergreen	Deciduous	Variegated	Blue/White	Purple/Red	Yellow/Gold	Dark Green	Light Green
Forsythia				•				•						•
Genista				•				•						•
Ginkgo	•	•						•						•
Hawthorn			•					•					•	
Hazelnut			•	•				•			•			
Hemlock		•	•	•			•						•	
Holly				•			•			•			•	
Honeysuckle				•				•			•		•	
Horsechestnut		•	•					•					•	
Hydrangea				•				•					•	
Juniper		•	•	•			•						•	•
Kiwi						•		•					•	
Larch	•	•						•		•				•
Lilac			•	•				•					•	•
Linden	•	•	•					•					•	
Maackia		•	•					•					•	
Maple	•	•	•	•				•			•		•	•
Mock Orange				•				•					•	
Mountain Ash		•	•					•					•	•
Ninebark				•				•			•	•		•
Oak	•	•						•						
Pine	•	•	•	•			•						•	•
Poplar and Aspen	•	•						•					•	•
Potentilla				•				•					•	
Rhododendron				•			•	•					•	•
Roses				•				•					•	•
Russian Cypress				•			•						•	•
Russian Olive			•					•		•				

| | FEATURES | | | | | | | | BLOOMING | | | | | SPECIES by Common Name |
Form	Flowers	Foliage	Bark	Fruit/Cones	Scent	Spines	Fall Colour	Winter Interest	Spring	Summer	Fall	Zones	Page Number	
	•								•			3–8	164	Forsythia
•	•								•	•		3–8	166	Genista
•		•	•				•		•			3–8	168	Ginkgo
	•	•		•	•		•		•	•		3–7	170	Hawthorn
•	•	•		•			•		•			3–8	172	Hazelnut
•		•		•				•				3–8	176	Hemlock
•		•		•				•	•			4–8	178	Holly
•	•			•					•	•		2–8	180	Honeysuckle
•		•		•					•	•		3–8	184	Horsechestnut
•	•									•	•	3–8	188	Hydrangea
•		•		•				•				2–8	192	Juniper
•	•	•		•	•					•		3–8	198	Kiwi
•		•		•				•				1–7	200	Larch
•	•				•	•			•	•		2–8	202	Lilac
•		•			•					•		2–7	208	Linden
•	•	•	•		•					•		3–7	212	Maackia
•	•	•	•				•		•			2–8	214	Maple
	•				•				•	•		2b–8	222	Mock Orange
•	•	•		•		•	•		•	•		3–8	224	Mountain Ash
	•	•		•					•	•		2–8	228	Ninebark
•		•	•	•			•		•			2–8	230	Oak
•		•	•	•				•				2–8	234	Pine
					•			•	•			1–8	240	Poplar and Aspen
•	•	•								•	•	2–8	246	Potentilla
•	•								•	•		3–8	250	Rhododendron
•	•				•	•			•	•	•	2–8	254	Roses
•								•				2–8	262	Russian Cypress
	•				•	•				•		2–8	264	Russian Olive

TREE HEIGHT LEGEND: Short: < 6 m (20') • Medium: 6–12 m (20–40') • Tall: > 12 m (40')

SPECIES
by Common Name

	FORM						FOLIAGE							
	Tall Tree	Med. Tree	Short Tree	Shrub	Groundcover	Climber	Evergreen	Deciduous	Variegated	Blue/White	Purple/Red	Yellow/Gold	Dark Green	Light Green
Salt Bush				•				•						•
Saskatoon			•	•				•						•
Sea Buckthorn				•				•		•				•
Smokebush		•	•	•				•			•	•	•	
Snowberry				•				•					•	
Spirea				•				•			•	•	•	
Spruce	•	•	•	•			•			•				
Sumac				•				•				•	•	•
Summersweet Clethra				•				•					•	
Viburnum				•				•					•	•
Virginia Creeper						•		•					•	
Weigela				•				•			•		•	
Willow	•	•	•	•				•			•		•	•
Yew				•			•				•		•	•
Yucca				•			•		•			•	•	

| | FEATURES | | | | | | | | BLOOMING | | | | | SPECIES by Common Name |
Form	Flowers	Foliage	Bark	Fruit/Cones	Scent	Spines	Fall Colour	Winter Interest	Spring	Summer	Fall	Zones	Page Number	
	•	•							•			3–8	266	Salt Bush
•	•		•	•			•		•	•		3–8	268	Saskatoon
•		•		•					•			3–8	270	Sea Buckthorn
	•	•	•	•			•		•	•			272	Smokebush
•		•		•							•	2–7	274	Snowberry
•	•										•	3–8	276	Spirea
•		•		•				•				2–8	282	Spruce
•	•	•		•			•				•	2–8	288	Sumac
	•				•		•				•	3–8	292	Summersweet Clethra
•	•	•		•			•		•	•		2–8	294	Viburrnum
•		•					•		•	•		3–8	300	Virginia Creeper
•		•									•	3–8	302	Weigela
•	•	•	•						•			2–8	306	Willow
•		•		•				•				2–7	312	Yew
•	•	•						•	•	•		3–8	314	Yucca

Glossary

B & B: abbreviation for balled-and-burlapped stock, i.e., plants that have been dug out of the ground and have had their rootballs wrapped in burlap

Bonsai: the art of training plants into miniature trees and landscapes

Bract: a modified leaf at the base of a flower or flower cluster; bracts can be showy, as in flowering dogwood blossoms

Candles: the new, soft spring growth of needle-leaved evergreens such as pine, spruce and fir

Crown: the part of a plant at or just below the soil where the stems meet the roots; also, the top of a tree, including the branches and leaves

Cultivar: a cultivated plant variety with one or more distinct differences from the species; e.g., *Hedera helix* is a botanical species, of which 'Gold Heart' is a cultivar distinguished by leaf variegation

Deadhead: to remove spent flowers in order to maintain a neat appearance, encourage a longer blooming period and prevent the plant from expending energy on producing fruit

Dieback: death of a branch from the tip inward; usually used to describe winter damage.

Dormancy: an inactive stage, often coinciding with the onset of winter

Double flower: a flower with an unusually large number of petals, often caused by mutation of the stamens into petals

Dripline: the area around the bottom of a tree, directly under the tips of the farthest-extending branches

Dwarf: a plant that is small compared to the normal growth of the species; dwarf growth is often cultivated by plant breeders

Espalier: the training of a tree or shrub to grow in two dimensions

Forma (f.): a naturally occurring variant of a species; below the level of subspecies in biological classification and similar to variety

Gall: an abnormal outgrowth or swelling produced as a reaction to sucking insects, other pests or diseases

Genus: a category of biological classification between the species and family levels; the first word in a scientific name indicates the genus, e.g., *Pinus* in *Pinus mugo*

Girdling: a restricted flow of water and nutrients in a plant caused by something tied tightly around a trunk or branch, or by an encircling cut or root

Habit: the growth form of a plant, comprising its size, shape, texture and orientation

Heartwood: the wood in the centre of a stem or branch consisting of old, dense, nonfunctional conducting tissue

Hybrid: any plant that results from natural or human-induced cross-breeding between varieties, species or genera; hybrids are often sterile but may be more vigorous than either parent and have attributes of both. Hybrids are indicated in scientific names by an x, e.g., *Forsythia* x *intermedia*

Inflorescence: a flower cluster

Leader: the dominant upward growth at the top of a tree; may be erect or drooping

Nodes: the places on the stem from where leaves grow; when cuttings are planted, new roots grow from the nodes under the soil

pH: a measure of acidity or alkalinity (the lower the pH below 7, the greater the acidity; the higher the pH between 7 and 14, the greater the alkalinity); soil pH influences nutrient availability for plants

Pollarding: a severe form of pruning in which all younger branches of a tree are cut back virtually to the trunk to encourage bushy new growth

Procumbent, prostrate: terms used to describe plants that grow along the ground

Rhizome: a modified stem that grows horizontally underground

Rootball: the root mass and surrounding soil of a container-grown or dug-out plant

Semi-evergreen: describes evergreen plants that in cold climates lose some or all of their leaves over winter

Single flower: a flower with a single ring of typically four or five petals

Species: the original plant from which cultivars are derived; the fundamental unit of biological classification, indicated by a two-part scientific name, e.g., *Pinus mugo* (*mugo* is the specific epithet)

Sport: an atypical plant or flower that arises through mutation; some sports are horticulturally desirable and propagated as new cultivars

Standard: a shrub or small tree grown with an erect main stem; accomplished either through pruning and training or by grafting the plant onto a tall, straight stock

Subspecies (subsp.): a naturally occurring, regional form of a species, often geographically isolated from other subspecies but still potentially able to interbreed with them

Sucker: a shoot that comes up from a root, often some distance from the plant; it can be separated to form a new plant once it develops its own roots

Topiary: the training of plants into geometric, animal or other unique shapes

Variegation: describes foliage that has more than one colour, often patched or striped or bearing differently coloured leaf margins

Variety (var.): a naturally occurring variant of a species; below the level of subspecies in biological classification

Lilac

Blueberry

Index of Plant Names

Entries in **bold** type indicate the main plant headings.